Students' Guide to Desktop Publishing

Books in the series

Students' Guide to Desktop Publishing

Ian Sinclair

BUTTERWORTH
HEINEMANN

Newnes
An imprint of Butterworth-Heinemann Ltd
Linacre House, Jordan Hill, Oxford OX2 8DP

PART OF REED INTERNATIONAL BOOKS

OXFORD   LONDON   BOSTON
MUNICH   NEW DELHI   SINGAPORE   SYDNEY
TOKYO   TORONTO   WELLINGTON

First published 1991

British Library Cataloguing in Publication Data

Sinclair, Ian
Students' guide to desktop publishing.
I. Title
686.2

ISBN 0 7506 0074 8

Typeset by BP Integraphics Ltd, Bath, Avon
Printed in Great Britain by Biddles Ltd,
Guildford & Kings Lynn.

Contents

Contents

Contents

Preface

Desktop publishing is by this time well established, and there are many packages and books for both the large-scale user and the occasional dabbler. As it happens, a large percentage of applications for desktop publishing are for minor uses, often a single page or so, consisting of the contribution to the Church Newsletter, the Bob-a-job week leaflets, the menu for the small cafe or the hand-out advertising sheet for the ironmongers. At the other end of the scale, complete books and newspapers are being produced using DTP at a fraction of the cost and, more importantly, with a fraction of the manpower and resources, of comparable material produced by the methods that were used previously. There are very few areas of printing and publishing that have not been affected by the change to DTP, and some aspects that have changed almost beyond recognition.

The purpose of this book is to introduce the student to DTP techniques and the language of DTP, following the excellent syllabus of the City & Guilds 7261/407 course in desktop publishing. So that the text does not become too abstract, illustrations are taken from the use of a typical modern DTP program, showing the capabilities of DTP by using examples which can be applied to a wide range of applications. Since DTP is liable to be used by students whose subjects cover a wide range of disciplines, some care has been taken to avoid using, without explanation, terms that would be familiar to the student of typography. The advent of DTP makes any user to some extent a student of typography, as far as the traditional teachings of typography can be said to have relevance nowadays. An important point that this book makes, however, is that DTP does not reduce typography to a set of rules. A well-trained eye for good print appearance is worth any amount of theory, as it always was.

One of the main problems with desktop publishing is that it tends to present the user with a rich choice of styles and fonts, sizes and facilities, graphics and commands. The result of this can be printed work that confuses the eye and is difficult to read. Though no book can ever teach the art of typography, the emphasis here is on good-looking results, even if this means that many users will never require more than a few of the huge number of facilities that programs such as Aldus PageMaker can offer. In the course of this book, however, the full range of these possibilities is explored.

An important point about learning DTP techniques is that it often requires the student to hear and use terms before being fully aware of definitions. In this book, such terms will be defined several times, once when first encountered, and later in more detail as the requirement arises. This will make it seem that the same ground is being covered several times, but the emphasis and depth will differ. Questions have been included throughout the text, and though most of these are of the conventional multiple-choice type, a few are multiple-answer and others require an answer to be supplied. The activities and assignments that are suggested throughout the text are intended as a basis for practical work and some of them may be omitted so as to allow more time for the C & G assignments which have to be performed. The amount of time that can be allocated to practical work will determine how much can be achieved in this respect, bearing in mind that each student needs access to a fairly complete system, though the printer and hard disk systems may be shared by networking.

Many students who use this book will have had considerable experience with the PC type of computer, but some may not be well versed in the use of MS-DOS and directories. The initial pages are therefore aimed at the newcomer to the use of the computer, introducing the essential hardware of the system and also showing how some auxiliary devices can be used. These pages will be particularly applicable to users of IBM PC compatible machines. Some of the illustrations have been printed on an Epson dot-matrix printer, others on a laser printer in order to illustrate the range of quality that can be expected from these devices. The inevitable losses of resolution during reproduction tend to make the quality advantage of the laser printer look rather less impressive, however, and allowances must be made for this.

I am very grateful to several people and companies without whose help this book could not have been written. The capture of screen images from Aldus PageMaker was possible only with the help of Iolo Davidson and his excellent Pinch and Punch suite of programs, supplied initially by S & S Services. The 16 MHz 286 computer was supplied by Matmos Ltd. and the laser printer was loaned by Texas Instruments Ltd. I am also most grateful to Roger Carter of The Information Technology Unit, of Buckinghamshire College, for help and encouragement in the course of planning and writing this book.

Note: Throughout this book, the computer key which is variously marked as RETURN, ENTER or carrying the ← symbol is referred to as the RETURN key.

Ian Sinclair

1 Desktop publishing principles

Objectives

After reading this chapter you should be able to:
- define what is meant by desktop publishing
- describe the essential hardware of a desktop publishing system
- describe the differences of speed and capacity between storage on disk and in memory
- explain the meaning of the terms WYSIWYG and aspect ratio
- show how characters can be represented by a dot-matrix pattern
- describe the use of image scanners
- describe the essential maintenance of a basic desktop publishing system.

Scenario

You are required in the course of your work to produce documents which can be used as reports, incorporating graphics along with text. You have the use of a PC computer, and you already keep text on a disk produced by a word-processor. What other essential equipment is needed?

The essential hardware

Computer users work with *hardware* and *software*, and it is important to understand the differences between these and the importance of each. The hardware of a computer system is the mechanical and electrical part; all the pieces that will break if they are dropped. The software is the collection of instructions that make the hardware useful, the programs and the data. A useful comparison is to think of a record player as being

1

hardware, and the records as being software. The hardware, though essential, is useless on its own, and it is the software that makes the system useful. One collection of hardware can be used with any set of software, and often the value of all the software will be greater than the value of the hardware. Your record player could be used to play any kind of music – you need only change the record, not the player – and the value of all your records probably exceeds the value of the player.

The distinction between hardware and software means that a good computer system can be used for a huge variety of purposes. Use one program, and the computer will run an accounting system for a business. Load in another program, and the computer is a word-processor, turning out perfect letters from less-than-perfect typing. Load in another program and the computer is able to create technical drawings and print them. The variety of uses is due to the software provided that the computer system is able to make use of the software. The greatest variety of software is written for the IBM PC type of machine (meaning several hundred brands of machines which are described as PC or PC-compatible), which is why these machines are so predominant in business use.

Figure 1.1 shows in diagrammatic form the essential hardware of the DTP system, along with some items that are optional rather than essential. Most DTP programs allow the use of the keyboard for control, but very much better control can be attained using the mouse. If line drawings and photographs are to be embodied into published documents, the use of a scanner is essential, but the digitizing pad and the X–Y plotter are less important in DTP work, though they have applications to some types of graphics work. The heart of the system is the unit shown as the main processor, the computer unit itself.

The main processor is a very fast-working machine which operates on numbers. The simplest of these number units is called a byte, consisting of a set of eight digits each of which can be 1 or 0, but nothing else. The byte is therefore used as the unit for memory storage and all other actions that make use of data. These numbers are codes which represent items such as letters of the alphabet, digits, lines, curves and other shapes, and the processor can move these numbers about, read them from a disk, write them out to a disk and send a copy to a VDU (see later). None of these actions has anything to do with arithmetic, the numbers are simply a convenient way of coding information. Though the first computers in the 1940s were constructed in order to work out calculations rapidly, most small computers nowadays are used for quite different purposes. The main processor unit contains the memory of the computer which is used for

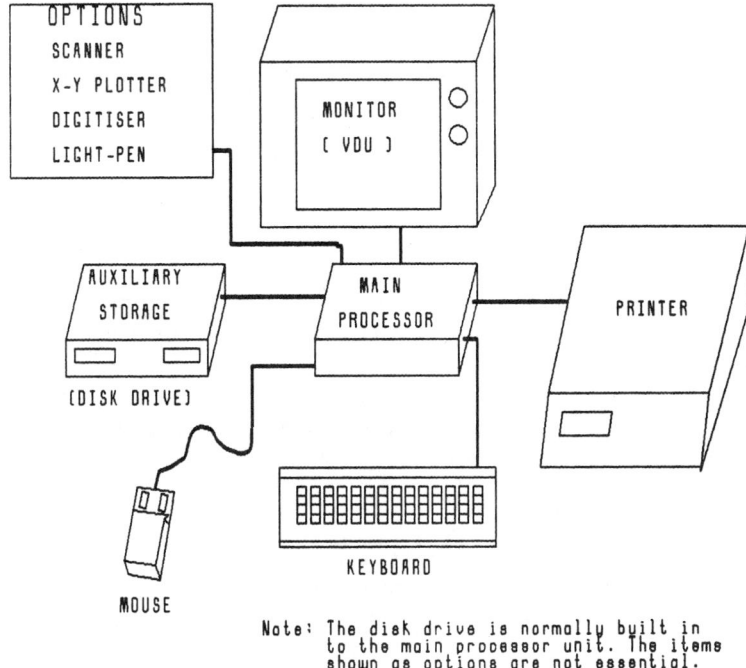

Figure 1.1   A diagram showing the essential hardware of the DTP system along with some optional extras

storing the number codes that it works on. Most modern computers use one casing to hold both the main processor and the disk units (see later). Note that other devices, such as laser printers, VDUs and even keyboards can contain their own processors so that they can work on data for their own purposes. The distinction is that you have no way of programming the processors of these devices for yourself.

The VDU (visual display unit) or monitor is like a TV receiver, but is completely under the control of the main processor. The VDU contains its own electrical circuits, very often a small computer in its own right, that allow signals consisting of number-codes to produce pictures on the screen. When the main processor reads part of its memory and copies the signals to the VDU the result is a picture on the screen, one 'screen page' of information, which can be text or graphics or a mixture of both. The simplest types of signals will create an image in black and white (or black

3

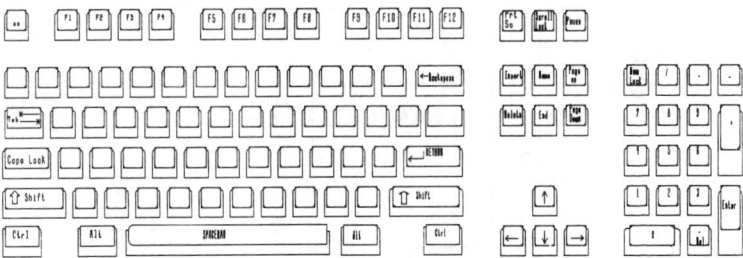

Figure 1.2 A typical 102-key keyboard for a modern computer. There are likely to be minor differences between models, mainly concerning the position of the backslash (\) key

and one single colour); more complicated signals can be used along with a colour VDU to display pictures in colour. The VDU is an output device – it allows signals that exist inside the main processor to be seen by someone on the outside.

The keyboard, Figure 1.2, is the main way in which a user can pass information into the main processor; it is an input device. All keyboards used in the UK, with a few exceptions, are of similar form, with the letter keys arranged like the keyboard of a typewriter. This style of keyboard is often referred to as QWERTY because of the layout of the first six keys on the top row of letters. In addition to these keys, however, the computer keyboard uses a large number of keys which are not used by any type-writer. These include the *function keys*, marked F1 to F10 (or to F12), the Ctrl (Control) key, the Alt (Alternate) key, and the Esc (Escape) key. All of these keys are used for special purposes, and the program that is running will have determined what these special purposes are. There will also be a set of keys that can be used to move a marker, the cursor, around the VDU screen. Some of these cursor keys are marked with arrows that show the direction in which they will move the cursor, others are marked with names such as Home, End, Page Up, Page Down, etc.

In addition, most modern keyboards include a numeric keypad, a set of number keys along with some others which are intended to allow right-handed users to enter numbers easily. The total number of keys on a modern computer keyboard is over 100 (usually 102), and this is what makes the computer keyboard look rather intimidating to anyone who has not used a keyboard before, or who has used only a typewriter.

Information that is fed into the main processor by way of the keyboard will be stored in the memory, but the memory is active only while the whole machine is switched on. Once the main processor is switched off, the memory ceases to work, and all information, which might represent many hours of typing, is lost. This would make a computer unusable if there were not some method of retaining information in some other way, and this is the purpose of auxiliary stores, also known as backing stores. For most computers, this will consist of a disk drive or set of disk drives. The storage capacity of these units is measured in kilobytes (k) equal to 1024 bytes, and Megabytes (Mb) equal to $1024 \times 1024 = 1048576$ bytes.

The disk drives are the record-players of the computer system, allowing information to be recorded (or **written**) and replayed (or **read**). By writing information in its number-coded form from the memory on to a disk the information can be retained on the disk when the computer is switched off. The disk uses a magnetic coating, and retains its information using much the same methods as a cassette recorder. The difference is that the speed of operation of a disk is much higher, and any part of a disk can be read without having to start at the beginning – just as you can put a pickup into any groove of a record (or select any track of a CD) without having to start at the beginning or use any kind of fast-wind control. The disk system is, like the VDU, completely under the control of the main processor.

Disk drives are of two main types, floppy and hard. The floppy drive uses disks which can be inserted and removed and which hold comparatively small amounts of data. These disks, better described as removable disks, exist in two sizes, 5.25″ and 3.5″. The larger disks are enclosed in cardboard holders, but it is possible to touch (and so damage) the surface of the disk if it is carelessly handled. In addition these disks are floppy in the sense that the whole container can easily be bent. The smaller 3.5″ disks are enclosed in rigid plastic containers and are much better protected. The 3.5″ disks were developed later than the 5.25″ type and can hold more information on each disk.

Any computer system that is used for serious purposes, however, will also use a hard disk. This consists of a set of disks which are sealed in an air-tight container and whose drive is built into the computer. These disks spin faster than the floppy type, spin for as long as the computer is in use, and can transfer information much faster, at least ten times faster, than the floppy type. In addition, hard disks can hold very much more information than the floppy type.

The importance of floppy disks is that they can be removed from the machine. This makes it possible to use floppy disks to transfer data from one machine to another; all commercial programs are distributed in this

5

way. In addition, the floppy disk can be used for security and for backup. The security aspect arises because if there is only one copy of a data file and it is on a floppy disk, the disk can be taken out and locked away, preventing the data from becoming available to anyone who uses the computer but does not possess the disk. The backup aspect arises because data on a floppy disk or set of disks is safe for as long as the disks are safely stored, whereas the hard disk which is spinning for as long as the computer is switched on is subject to more wear and tear and will eventually fail catastrophically.

The printer is another output device which translates the codes in the memory of the main processor into marks on paper, *hard copy* as it is called. Printers can be of many types, but the most common types at the time of writing are dot-matrix and laser types. Dot-matrix printers use a set of pins which are controlled by the main processor and the circuits inside the printer, and which can be moved so as to strike an inked ribbon which in turn strikes the paper. As the name implies, the pins are arranged in a line of dots so that by moving this line of dots and activating the correct pins, a character shape can be drawn, Figure 1.3.

The laser printer uses a different method, very much like a photo-copier, and contains a memory so that a complete page can be held and printed at one time. The quality is much higher than can be obtained from most dot-matrix printers, and this type of printer is a standard for desk-top publishing use. No matter what printer is used, however, it will be almost useless if the software does not include a program called a printer driver which is suitable for that type of printer.

The mouse completes the essentials of the DTP setup. The mouse is a small trolley which can be moved on a desktop; by using software which is part of the DTP programs, the movement of the mouse can be used to move a cursor or other marker on the VDU screen. The mouse also has two (sometimes three) buttons, and the DTP software can be arranged so that pressing these buttons produces various effects, such as locking the cursor on to a piece of text or making a choice from a number of options. Many DTP programs can be used without a mouse, but in such a crippled way that the mouse is now counted as an essential rather than an optional part of the system.

All of the hardware needs to obtain its power from the electricity mains, and in common with all electronic devices the power supply needs to be at a steady voltage. The main processor is particularly susceptible to variations in the voltage of the power supply, and it incorporates a unit which will help to stabilize against small fluctuations. There is no built-in

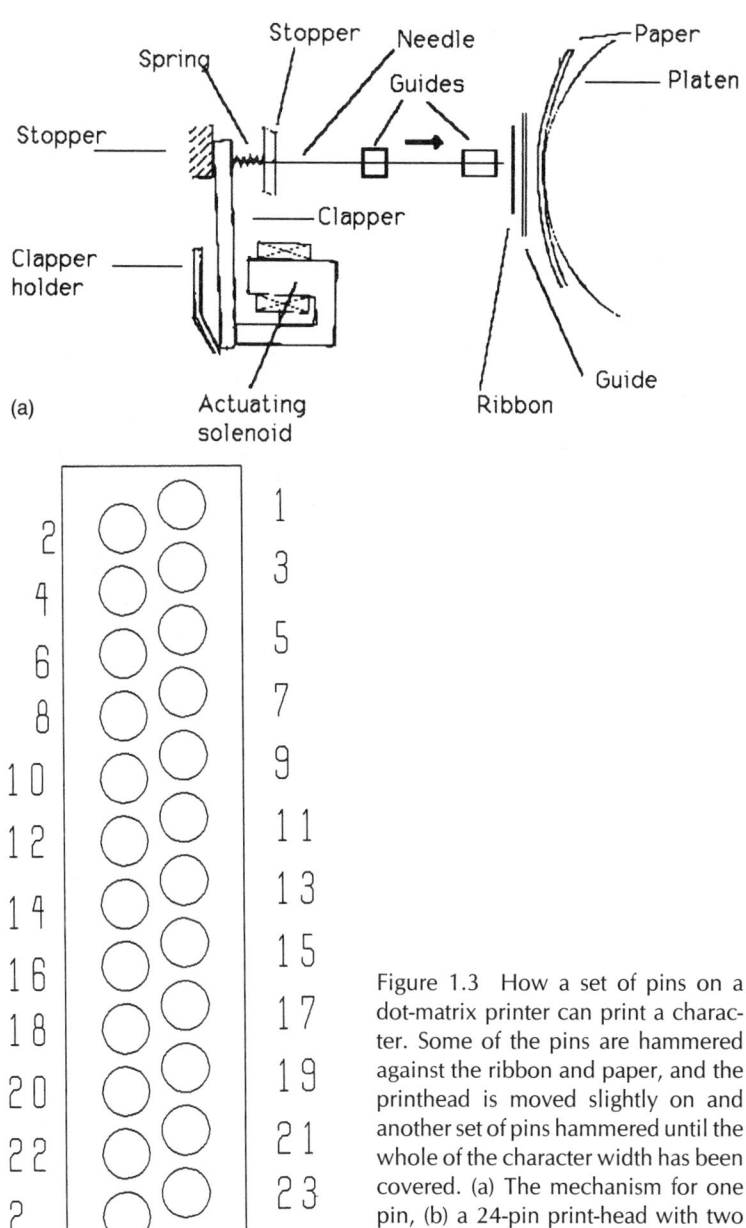

Figure 1.3 How a set of pins on a dot-matrix printer can print a character. Some of the pins are hammered against the ribbon and paper, and the printhead is moved slightly on and another set of pins hammered until the whole of the character width has been covered. (a) The mechanism for one pin, (b) a 24-pin print-head with two staggered lines of 12 pins in vertical line

protection against large fluctuations, however, so that, if lightning hits a power cable several miles away or there is a brief power-cut because of overloads, the effect on the main processor will be disastrous, resulting in the computer re-starting. In a restart, however, the computer clears its memory, so that nothing will remain that was not recorded on disk (hard or floppy). In some buildings, even the action of the lifts can cause bad power-line fluctuations. Where this is a hazard, computers can be supplied from uninterruptable power supplies (UPS). These are units which are plugged in between the computer system and the mains supply. While the mains supply is steady, batteries in the UPS are kept on charge. When the power is interrupted, the batteries are used to generate power for the computer (using a circuit called an inverter) and so maintain the supply. The time for which this can be maintained is limited by the capacity of the batteries, but it will always provide enough time to record data and shut down programs in an orderly way.

Antistatic precautions

Many offices that use computers make use of antistatic mats and carpets. It is desirable to avoid discharges of static electricity in offices, and these mats and carpets can contribute, but the risks are often exaggerated. Even on a day when touching a radiator can result in a decided tingle of static and even a crackling spark, the electronic components of the computer are normally unaffected because they are connected into circuits. The main risk of static occurs when a computer is being repaired and the electronic units, called chips, are being removed from their sockets. The use of antistatic precautions is certainly an aid to comfort, but more for the users than the machines.

Questions

1 Classify the following units as hardware or software:
   (a) disk drive
   (b) text stored on the disk
   (c) keyboard
   (d) program stored in the memory
   (e) printer
   (f) mouse
2 Which of the essential units of the DTP hardware are output devices?

Beginnings and fundamentals

Many of the types of programs that are used on microcomputers have been inherited from the larger mainframe and minicomputers of the 1960s and 1970s, and some database programs still appear as if they had been designed for these older machines. Older mainframe computers used a VDU screen only for fault-finding and diagnostic work, with all of the output taken from the printer, so that the programs that we use which depend heavily on the use of the VDU are nearly all products of the microcomputer age which started in 1978. Desktop publishing programs are one outstanding example, though the first application of a computer to typesetting (printing) was as long ago as 1965, and in Germany rather than in the USA.

Desktop publishing, or DTP, is the name for low-cost publishing, using a computer and its associated printer to prepare material which can be used as a master for further printing work, or to make a limited number of copies of the material directly. Prior to the desktop publishing revolution, anyone who needed material published had the options of duplicating typed material, using ink duplicators (the familiar Roneo and Gestetner machines), photocopiers, or offset-litho machines; or using the services of a local printer to lay out type. At one time, anyone needing printed material of reasonable standard who wanted to take the do-it-yourself approach could do so only by way of a hand-press, such as the excellent Adana range. Many Adana owners learned much about typography in this way, but the time that is needed to assemble type for much more than a visiting card can be prohibitive, and fonts of type are quite costly. In addition, the use of graphical images along with a hand-press is a very difficult and messy operation.

The use of a computer allows typography (the setting of text into type for printing) to be handled in very much the same way as word-processing is handled. This means that the form of the printed material can be seen on the screen and manipulated as much as you like in this form without a single mark being made on paper. Each page of the work can be completed and recorded on disk, and only when the whole set of pages is ready need anything be printed. The page can contain text that uses different forms of type (different **fonts**), in different sizes that allow you to have headlines, sub-headings, main text and notes, along with graphics illustrations that you can prepare for yourself or which you can take ready-made from a selection that comes with the desktop publishing package or on additional disks. The pictures from these sources can be placed into the page, with the words of the text making way for them and arranged around them as you choose. Both text and pictures are then printed together, with no need for the pasting-up processes that will be familiar to anyone who has worked with a mixture of text and graphics, or even with text material that has required insertions.

Hardware and software

The essential equipment for desktop publishing has been described in outline already, but some details of specific equipment are useful. If you were considering buying an expensive computer specially for the purposes of professional-quality desktop publishing, and had no other use for the machine, then it would make sense to buy a machine that featured a very clear and finely-detailed screen display and for which high-quality software exists, such as the Apple Macintosh. In this book, however, we shall assume that the computer you are using is the universal 'business-standard' machine, the IBM PC or one of the many brands which is 100% compatible with the IBM. This machine should use a high-resolution screen, such as the Hercules monochrome or the VGA type, along with a matching monitor, and it should preferably be of the faster AT or PS/2 type, featuring 1 Mb memory or more. Note that the more recent IBM PS/1 machine is not likely to be suitable for DTP work.

This does not mean that DTP is unavailable for the owners of the older XT type of PC computer, or, for that matter, on other machines. The important point is that professional-quality DTP requires the use of a very large program which will not run easily on the smaller machines, either because of memory limitations or speed limitations or both.

Similarly, for professional quality work, the printer needs to be a laser type, preferably one of the high-cost laser printers that features the use of the PostScript (trademark of Adobe Systems Inc.) language for specifying page layout, and which has an independent memory of at least 2 Mb. Once again, this may not be necessary for a smaller scale of work, and the use of a laser printer costing less than £1000, or even a dot-matrix printer of considerably lower cost, can be considered. In this book, most of the illustrations have been printed using a dot-matrix machine to illustrate the differences between this and the laser type. Illustrations of screen appearance (screenshots) have all been printed on a dot-matrix machine.

The laser printer can be used to produce copies directly, or to make a master that can be used to make copies by a process called offset lithography. This uses a master copy to make a printing plate (a flexible metal sheet, usually) which can be used on a rotary press to print several thousands of copies per hour; the process is described in detail in Chapter 8. The other types of printers can be used to make offset-litho masters, but with a lower-quality image, though the difference between the results from a laser printer and an inkjet printer are scarcely discernible.

The preferred print quality of the laser printer is approached only by one type of lower-cost printer, the ink-jet type such as the Hewlett-Packard Ink-jet or the Canon Bubble-jet types. The quality obtained from some dot-matrix printers of the 24-pin type can be reasonable, but only if the DTP software contains a program (a printer driver) for making the best possible use of the printer. The lowest quality is obtained from 9-pin dot matrix printers. The older type of daisywheel printers which are sometimes still used for word-processing, are completely unsuitable for desk top publishing because the characters that they print are determined by the printwheel, a piece of hardware, and cannot be altered by the software of the computer.

Questions

3 State which of the following hardware items are essential for DTP work.
   (a) keyboard
   (b) scanner
   (c) mouse
   (d) plotter
   (e) VDU
4 Which of the following are input devices:
   (a) VDU
   (b) mouse
   (c) printer
   (d) keyboard
5 Arrange in order of decreasing print quality:
   (a) 9-pin dot-matrix (b) laser (c) 24-pin dot-matrix

Disk and memory

When a computer is being used with a word-processing program of the older type, each character (alphabetical letter, digit or punctuation mark) requires one unit of memory, one **byte** of storage. Short documents might require a few hundred bytes, longer ones several thousand, and the terms kilobyte (k) and megabyte (Mb) are used to indicate the amounts of memory required. The kilobyte is not 1000 bytes but 1024, and the megabyte is 1024 kilobytes, 1048576 bytes, because computers carry out counting in a scale of two rather than in tens, and 2^{10} is 1024, the exact power of two that is nearest to 1000. Whatever the storage system or its size, we refer to **writing**, meaning that characters are put into storage, and **reading**, meaning that characters are copied from the store. It is important to note that writing into a store will wipe out what was stored earlier, but reading a store does *not* erase the contents.

The memory of the computer consists of two different types of units referred to as RAM and ROM. RAM is an acronym for random access memory, and the name dates from the time when other types of memory were used that could only be read by starting at the beginning, like a tape as compared to a disk. RAM memory is the volatile type that loses all of its stored information whenever the power supply is switched off; a better name would be read-write memory. Most of the memory of the computer is of this form.

A computer is totally useless without a program, however, and if all of the memory of a computer consisted of this type of RAM the machine could not be used. The use of the keyboard is not possible without a program to guide the actions of the machine, and disks cannot be read or written without a program. This problem is dealt with by using a different type of memory, Read-Only memory (ROM) which retains its information. When the computer is switched on, it is arranged to read from the ROM. This piece of program allows the disk drives to be controlled, so that the remainder of the program that the computer needs to work (the DOS, or disk operating system, see later) is read from a disk.

In addition, many computers use a small piece of RAM memory whose contents need to be altered at intervals, but which are retained by means of a battery, but this memory is for small amounts of data only; data that is used to allow the computer to carry out essential actions when it is switched on again, such as matching the keyboard to the correct symbols for the country of use, keeping the internal clock correct, selecting the correct type of signals for the video display and so on.

Another storage method needs to be used in addition to RAM and ROM memory. The RAM memory of the computer will operate at very high speeds, taking less than a millionth of a second to read or write a unit (the byte), but this memory is **volatile**, meaning that the contents of the memory will be totally and irretrievably lost when the computer is switched off.

Because memory is volatile, essential data, such as the characters of a document, must be stored in a more permanent way. Magnetic disks have replaced the older storage systems that used punched paper tape and, later, magnetic tape. Disks are of two types, 'floppy' (or replaceable) and 'hard'. Each consists of a circular surface coated with a magnetic material, and each byte of the signals from the computer will cause a portion of the disk to be magnetized. Since magnetization is permanent unless the disk is subjected to any other source of magnetism, the signals are retained. All computers must use a program called the disk operating system (DOS) which carries out actions such as selecting positions on the disk, keeping a directory of collections of bytes (files) and controlling reading and writing.

The differences between hard and floppy disks lie in storage space and speed of access. The older type of floppy disk that was 5.25″ in diameter could store 360k of data; later types could store 1.2 Mb. The smaller 3.5″ replaceable disks could store 720k, extended later to 1.44 Mb. Hard disks, however, are obtainable in sizes that range from about 20 Mb to 600 Mb or more, and, because they spin faster than floppy disks, are able to transfer data at up to ten times the speed that can be used with floppy disks. A hard disk is not (usually) inserted or removed, but is permanently connected to the computer so that its stored information is available from the instant that the computer starts working. Floppy disks are removable, and to use a floppy disk you need to find it and insert it into the disk drive of the computer. This takes time, and in addition, the floppy disk does not start to spin until a command is issued to it. By contrast, a hard disk starts spinning when the computer is switched on and continues to spin until the computer is switched off.

Activity

Find out for the computer that you are using:
(a) the total amount of RAM available
(b) the capacity of the floppy disk(s)
(c) the capacity of the hard disk, if fitted
(d) the type of screen display (mono or colour, low or high resolution).

DTP storage requirements

The use of a desktop publishing program requires very much more storage than is needed by a word-processing program. One reason is that the program for desktop publishing will often be considerably longer than that for a word-processor. This will take up more space on the disk and also require more space in the memory. Some programs may require more space than can be provided in memory, so that parts of the program are replaced by others (taken from the disk) as and when required. Such portions are called **overlays**.

The other reason for needing more storage is that for DTP use one character can no longer be represented by one byte. This representation can be used on word-processors by assigning one number code to each letter and other character (see ASCII code, Chapter 3), and this scheme is valid only when the text consists of uniform characters. If the characters are needed in a variety of typefaces, sizes and styles (various *fonts*), this representation is no longer useful, and a much more common method is *bit-mapping*, or dot-matrix representation.

This uses a grid of dots to represent each character, Figure 1.4, so that the shape of the character is plotted as a set of dots whose (foreground) colour is different from that of the background dots. Such a grid requires much more storage space, often two bytes per line of the grid. The memory must be able to hold the bit-maps for all the characters that are being used at the moment, and the disk must hold all the bit-maps for the characters (of other typefaces, styles and sizes) that are not currently in use. Each time a font is changed, one set of bit-maps in memory must be replaced by another. Large fonts require considerably more memory space than the smaller types, and this may make the use of such fonts impossible on machines with restricted memory.

An alternative method of storing character shapes uses descriptions. A description is a set of instructions for drawing a character, and one advantage of this method is that the instructions are the same for all sizes of a character, only the dimensions need to be altered. More storage space is needed for a set of descriptions for a character than for its dot-pattern, however, and drawing a character from its description is a slower process than drawing the dot-pattern.

Ample disk storage is therefore an essential requirement of desktop publishing (DTP), and this can be obtained satisfactorily only by the use of a hard disk of at least 20 Mb capacity and preferably much more. In addition, the memory of the computer needs to be large enough to

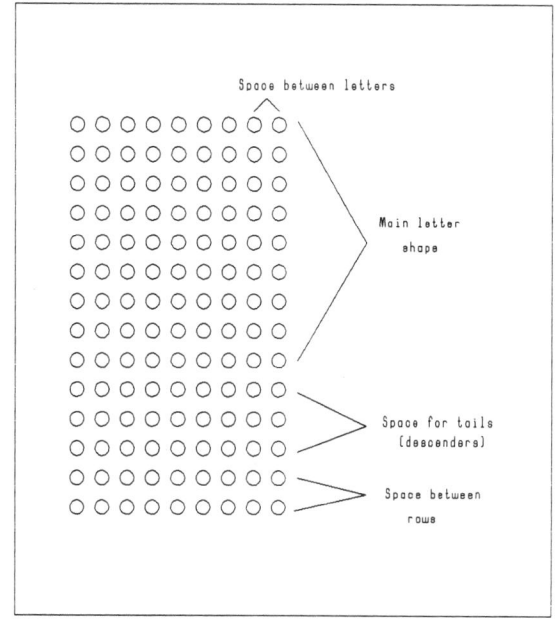

(a)

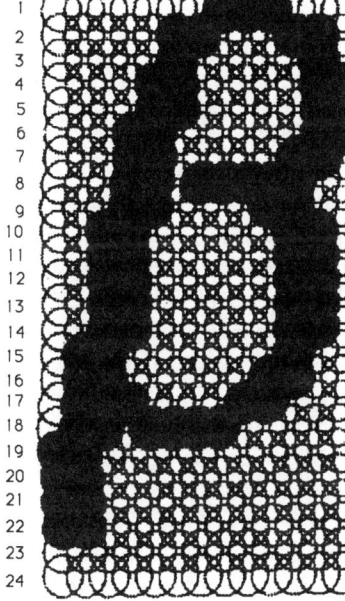

(b)

Figure 1.4 The use of a matrix of dots (a) to represent a character on the screen. Dot-matrix representation is used on screens, printers (other than daisywheel types) and scanners. (b) The character β (Greek Beta) represented on a 24-pin dot-matrix printer

15

contain the program and the set of character descriptions that are being used at any time. The minimum memory that can be satisfactorily used with the PC type of machine is likely to be 640k, which is the **largest** amount of memory that can be used on the older types. Many modern DTP programs demand that the computer should possess at least 1 Mb of RAM memory and preferably more. Small DTP programs can be run on machines that use only 512k of memory and are fitted with floppy disks (though preferably the 3.5″ type or the 1.2 Mb 5.25″ type).

One problem with memory is that the disk operating system takes up some memory, and the amount that is used varies from one version to another. Many kinds of programs can be run using only the basic operating system (the DOS) which takes up about 70k of memory, leaving a reasonable amount of space for the main (applications) program. Most DTP programs, however, make use of elaborate screen displays, and menu selections, all of which require either a larger operating system or a larger program. Of the PC types of machine, only the later types that use the 386 chip will work satisfactorily with really large amounts of memory.

Data security and care of disks

It is normal, when using a DTP program, to create each document or even each page of a document as a disk file. This is because printing is a separate operation which is usually carried out by an **overlay** piece of program; typing and print are not necessarily possible simultaneously and certainly not without first having stored the bytes of the document on the disk. The security of data on a disk is therefore extremely important.

Disk storage is now very reliable, but only when disks are used and stored in suitable conditions. The main enemy of disk storage is magnetism, and, in particular, rapid variations of magnetism. These rapid variations occur near electric motors, loudspeakers and TV screens, so that disks must never be stored near these items. The disk drive in a computer is usually shielded so that it can be used even when the monitor, with its screen, is placed on top of the computer. In some models, however, the monitor may have to be moved in order to obtain reliable use of a hard disk. Colour monitors are much more liable to cause trouble of this kind than monochrome (black and white/green/amber) types.

Stray magnetism of this type causes disk corruption, meaning that the magnetic signals will be changed. If this corruption affects a file of characters for a document it can cause some of the characters to change

16

---

1 Don't bend the disks. They may be called floppy disks but the magnetic coating is liable to be damaged if you bend them.

2 Avoid touching the magnetic surface where it is exposed. The modern 3.5″ disks are very much better protected in this respect than the older 5.25″ types.

3 Store your disks in a box, inside their protective sleeves, in a cool dry place.

4 Keep disks away from dust, smoke, liquids, heat and sunlight.

5 Avoid at all costs magnets or objects that contain magnets. These include electric motors, loudspeakers, TV receivers and computer monitors, tape recorders and tape erasers.

6 Don't write on the labels of 5.25″ disks with a ball-point pen unless the labels are separate from the disks. Use a Berol or similar floppy-disk pen to write on labels that are attached to the disks.

Figure 1.5 A checklist for taking care of floppy disks. Magnetic sources represent the greatest hazard

shape, or, more seriously, some of the bytes that control actions, like taking a new line, to carry out some other action. Corruption of a program is much more serious, because it can cause the program to become unusable, even to the point of corrupting its data disks.

The other enemy of disks is high temperature. Normally, the weak magnetism of the Earth and of magnets that are not close to the disk will have no effect on the magnetic material. This material is said to have **high coercivity**, meaning that only a large change of magnetism will affect the material. As the temperature rises, however, this coercivity becomes lower, so that the disk is more easily affected by magnetism. If the temperature becomes high enough, all magnetism can be lost, but this is unusual and occurs only in fires.

Not all hazards are magnetic. If a disk has been stored in very cold conditions and is suddenly placed into moist warm conditions, condensation of water vapour can make the disk unusable because the magnetic heads that are used for reading and writing will stick to the surface. This should not be a problem for hard disks which are sealed units, but it can cause problems with motors and drive mechanisms. The only remedy is to keep the computer at a fairly even temperature. If a new machine is brought in from a cold place, allow it to reach normal room temperature and do not use it for several hours, giving any moisture time to evaporate.

A more obvious hazard is operator contamination, spilling coffee on a floppy disk or smoking in the room where such disks are handled. Most of the program and other data for a DTP system will be held on the hard disk, but the floppy disks will be used for backup purposes, holding the spare copies which are of such importance. Figure 1.5 is a checklist of disk hazards.

Backup methods

Hard disks have a limited guaranteed life, typically 20,000 hours, and at some stage a hard disk will fail completely, allowing no further access, or very limited access to its data. This requires all data held on hard disk to be duplicated (backed-up) on to floppy disk.

A typical hard disk will contain program files and data files. The program files, perhaps 10 to 100 of them, will all at some stage have been copied on to the hard disk from the floppy disks on which they were supplied. This is not always a straightforward copying process, because it often involves installation, the selection of items from a set of floppy disks, see Appendix E. The original disk, however, should still exist and constitutes one backup. It is advisable also to keep another copy of the files that exist on the hard disk. This constitutes an exact backup which can be used to re-create the program files on a replacement hard disk when the first hard disk fails. A few programs are copy-protected to make this impossible, and the best advice is not to use such programs. The amount of business which could be lost by not having an exact backup makes the use of copy-protected programs very risky, and most manufacturers now realize this.

In addition to the files of programs, however, the hard disk will contain files of data that these programs have created. A DTP program will create many files of documents which are stored directly on to the hard disk and have never existed on floppy disks. It is important to copy these files to floppy disks at the end of each session of use of the files, so that for any file there will be a floppy disk which contains the most recent version of the file. A particularly useful method allows only files that have been altered to be copied, so that time is not wasted in copying files that have remained unchanged for months. Users of PC machines can employ the XCOPY command of the MS-DOS operating system for this purpose.

At one time, disks were not particularly reliable, and users were advised to keep three backups of different ages, using what was called the grand-father–father–son method. Such extensive backing up is not so important now, but at least one backup should exist for each document file, and preferably more than one for really important files that need to be used over and over again.

Questions

6 Place the following devices in ascending order of the speed at which they can be written:
   (a) RAM
   (b) floppy disk
   (c) hard disk
7 Which of the following does not use a dot-matrix system:
   (a) VDU
   (b) plotter
   (c) ink-jet printer
8 Arrange the following list of hazards to floppy disks in ascending order of risk:
   (a) high temperature (b) dust (c) magnets (d) vibration

Formatting floppies

A floppy disk, as bought, cannot immediately be used in the disk drive of the computer, and if you attempt to use such a disk the machine will print an error message on the screen. A disk only becomes usable when it has been 'marked out' magnetically by placing signals on the disk which the computer can use to locate parts of the disk. This process is called 'format-ting' and learning to format a floppy disk is an important part of the use of a computer system.

Formatting is carried out by a program which is available either on the hard disk, or on a special 'master disk' for a machine that uses two floppy drives in place of a hard disk. Formatting floppy disks on a machine that uses a hard disk drive carries a considerable risk that if the procedure is carried out incorrectly the contents of the hard disk can be wiped, and can be recovered only by using special methods. You must, therefore, prac-tise formatting under supervision unless the formatting software that is in use has been modified to prevent it from affecting the hard disk.

The important formatting command is FORMAT A: (or FORMAT B:), and if the command is always used in this form there is no possibility of any problems arising. If, however, due to a mistyping, the command is issued in the form FORMAT C:, it is possible to format the hard disk, with risk to the contents of the hard disk. Always format floppy disks a set at a time, because the FORMAT A: command, once used, allows you to format as many disks as you want. After a format is completed, you will be asked if you want to format another disk of the same type and by answering **Y** you can carry on without the need to start the command all over again. Some users prefer to have no formatting commands on the hard disk, and to carry out formatting only from a floppy disk.

Activity

Discuss the formatting methods for floppy disks with your supervisor – check in particular if any protection method is used to avoid formatting the hard disk. Format a set of floppy disks – you should always have several formatted floppies in hand for backup purposes.

WYSIWYG text and graphics

WYSIWYG is an acronym for what you see is what you get, and it means that in any DTP program, the screen should show an exact representation of the page that is to be printed. This is by no means simple, because it requires a screen of fixed dimensions, typically 10″ wide by 8″ deep, to be able to display a page whose size might range from that of a visiting card to that of a tabloid newspaper page. In addition, print size might range from headlines using letters 1″ or more in height down to footnotes whose characters are little more than one tenth of an inch high. A true WYSIWYG screen would also need to be able to show graphics (pictures and drawings) in full detail, perhaps calling for the reproduction of 300 dots per inch length. A4 size screens are now available on some monitors, and are very much better suited to DTP work than the normal computer monitor. There are also some high-resolution monitors available (from Genoa Systems) which can work with 300 dots per inch.

True WYSIWYG is not always possible or even desirable, and the compromise is that only one set of conditions can be met at one time. If large print is mixed with small, then either the large print is readable and the small print is **greeked**, represented by crosses, or the small print is visible and the large print is not seen on the screen. The expression **greek** originated because many DTP programs represent small text by marks that look like Greek characters. Most DTP programs allow for a full page to be seen on the screen to show layout, even if this means that most or all of the text will be greeked. In order to work with the text, various magnified views can be used, even to the extent of showing parts of a line only.

One important point is that the screen **aspect ratio** of conventional screens is wrong. The aspect ratio is the ratio of width to height/depth, and for a monitor this is usually the conventional TV aspect ratio of 4:3. Most paper printing is on sheets whose width is less than the height – the A series of papers use a width/height ratio of about 7:10. Even if the paper is held sideways (**landscape** orientation as distinct from **portrait** orientation) the aspect ratio is not correct.

This means that the screen can never give a precise representation of a page unless a specialized type of monitor (an A4 monitor) is used. Most DTP programs will show a reduced version of the page shape on the screen occupying the full depth of the screen, and using the space to the side of this page for other images, such as lists of instructions or images (icons) that represent instructions. Some DTP programs such as Aldus PageMaker, featured in this book, can show a double page, such as the pages of a book that normally face each other, in this way. These programs are much easier to work with (and less of a strain on the eyes) if the A4 size and shape of screen is used.

The resolution of the screen also creates problems with graphics. Drawing a circle or a diagonal line reveals that the image consists of a set of steps because of the way that the screen constructs an image in lines. Graphics that are created on the screen and saved as a pattern of bits (a bit-image) will preserve this jagged appearance unless they are printed in a very much smaller size. Only graphics that are created as a set of drawing instructions avoid the effect, but even the 300-dot per inch printer will cause a slightly jagged appearance when the image is examined closely.

The restrictions that the computer system imposes on WYSIWYG mean that most of the time spent with a DTP system is used working with magnified images of portions of a page, using the complete page image only to check that the layout of columns and illustrations is correct. This makes it very important to obtain hands-on experience with a DTP system, because until you see a document on the screen converted into a document on paper you can never be sure that you understand what you are working with.

Activity

Examine a page of a DTP document on screen – learn how to switch between the full-page view and magnified views. Print out the document, and compare the printed version with the screen version. Note how the greeked version on screen shows the layout of the page.

Image scanners

Images are obtained in a document by a variety of methods. DTP programs all contain a limited number of drawing 'tools', meaning that they can be made to produce simple geometrical shapes such as straight lines, circles and boxes. All DTP programs allow for files of images to be imported (copied from other disks), using files that have been created by other programs. Such programs usually include paint programs, which can be used to create illustrations by freehand drawing, or CAD images, produced by the computer equivalent of technical drawing. Another option is the use of clip-art, images which have been produced by artists and which can be supplied as disk files.

The other option is the use of a scanner. A scanner is a device which will convert a drawing or a photograph into a set of bytes which can be stored as a disk file and read into a DTP program. This is possible only if the DTP program and the disk file use the same standards, and there are a bewildering number of possible types. The most common type of file, however, is the tag image format file, abbreviated to TIF. This can be obtained from virtually all scanners and read by virtually all DTP programs (other than very low-cost and simple programs) so that it is not too difficult to find a scanner which is compatible with a DTP program. These files can be identified by the letters TIF following the main name, for example, PATCH.TIF, COMPART.TIF. Do not, however, assume that any file with the extension letters TIF will necessarily be readable by a DTP package that reads TIF files, because there are several varieties of TIF files.

For professional work, a flat-bed or rotary scanner would be used. As

Scanning window

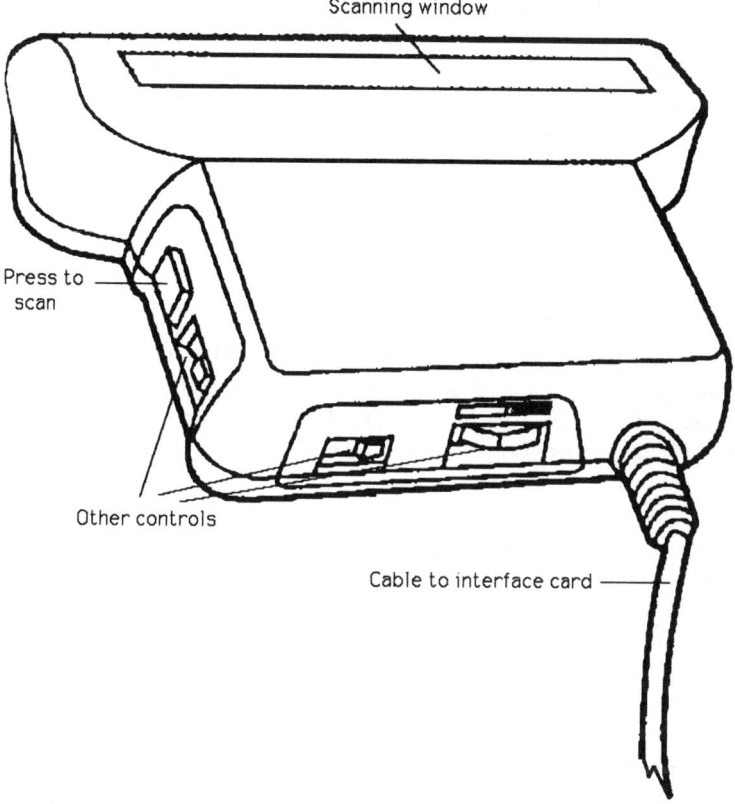

Press to
scan

Other controls

Cable to interface card

Figure 1.6 A typical hand-scanner. Flat-bed scanners resemble fax machines and deal with pages rather than 4″ strips

the name suggests, the flat-bed scanner allows the original illustration, usually a photograph, to be placed on a flat surface, and a scanning head is set to move across and down the image, tracing out a set of parallel lines. The rotary scanner requires the photograph to be clipped to a roller which slowly rotates as the scanning head moves from side to side.

Both flat-bed and rotary scanners can cope with images up to A4 in size, but the files that are created will be very large, several Mb. For many illustration purposes, images of only a few inches across and down are needed, so that smaller files can be used.

Another option is to use a hand-scanner (Figure 1.6). This consists of a device very much like a mouse which is moved at an even speed down the length of an image. The width that can be scanned is limited to about 4″, and because the movement is hand-operated it is difficult to ensure uniformity. For some purposes, however, the images are of usable quality, and if any method can be used of moving the paper image uniformly while holding the scanner still, the quality can be considerably improved. The size limitation is often of little importance, since few documents really need illustrations of more than 4″ width.

Maintenance of the system

Compared to a printing press, maintenance of a DTP system requires very little effort, concentrated mainly on the mechanical parts. The most important maintenance task is that of disk backup, and this should take precedence over all other aspects. Disks of backup files should be stored in a cool, dry place and backups renewed at intervals. Regular checking of the state of the hard disk is also advisable, and this can be done by using diagnostic programs which are often included in 'toolbox' programs. For details of the use of such programs see the book *Disk and RAM Utilities Step by Step*, also published by Heinemann. Always remember to keep an adequate supply of formatted floppy disks for backing up data and to carry out the back-up action at the end of each computing session.

The computer itself needs little maintenance other than keeping the surfaces clean – do not use any spirit-based or abrasive cleaners. A wipe with a clean lint-free duster is all that is called for. The computer should not be kept in a smoky atmosphere. Never close the door clip of a floppy disk when no disk is present, as this could cause the disk heads to grind against each other. Most disk drives are supplied with a cardboard dummy-disk to insert into each drive in order to prevent such damage to the heads.

The keyboard should be kept covered when not in use, because dust settles between the keys and becomes difficult to remove. Most keyboards arrive with a suitable plastic cover, and such covers can be bought separately if needed. If a keyboard becomes dirty, unplug it from the computer, with the machine switched off, and clean the keyboard using soft brushes, dusters and, if necessary, a small low-powered vacuum cleaner such as the type sold for cleaning car upholstery.

The laser printer needs more maintenance and cleaning. Because of the use of electric charges, laser printers attract dust, and the surfaces should be dusted at the end of each working day. The machine should be covered when not in use, and when toner has been added, care should be taken to remove any spilled material. The toner is the powdered ink that the machine uses, and the powder is very fine and easily spread.

Paper also needs to be kept with care, enclosed in its wrapping paper and kept in a cupboard. Packs of paper for laser printers should be dust-free, unlike conventional paper, and the direction of the grain on the paper is important. Do not be tempted to substitute for the recommended type of paper unless you are certain that the substitute is of a quality suitable for laser printers (see later, Chapter 4 and Chapter 8). Toners and other replaceable packs for the laser printer should be kept separately from paper stocks.

Questions

9 Why do circles and diagonal lines look jagged on the screen?
10 Why does a disk need to be formatted?
11 Why is true WYSIWYG impossible for DTP?

Assignment 1

List the minimum requirements of hardware for DTP work. For each item, find the current cost of a suitable make and model so as to arrive at the total cost for a system. Compare this with the cost of the packaged systems that are offered by several suppliers. In addition, find out if computers that contain 1 Mb or more of memory can actually use this extra memory in a useful way, allowing larger programs or longer documents to be used.

Recap

● The basic hardware of a DTP system consists of the main processor and disk unit (usually in one cabinet), the VDU, keyboard, mouse and printer.
● The input units are the keyboard and mouse; the output units are the VDU and printer.

- The disk system is the backing store and can use either a hard disk or floppy disk drives; sometimes a mixture of both.
- Characters as seen on the screen are made up of bright or coloured dots in a rectangular frame or matrix. Dot-matrix printers (including ink-jet types) also use a similar system, and laser printers also create characters out of a dot pattern.
- The highest quality of print is obtained using a laser or ink-jet type of printer, of which the laser type is more common.
- The ideal for DTP is WYSIWYG, meaning that a page could be displayed on screen exactly as it would be printed on paper. This is generally impossible.
- Image scanners are used to convert line drawings or photographs into computer number-codes; they **digitise** the images. By adding OCR software, text characters can be converted into ASCII codes and used in this form.

Answers to questions

1 Hardware: a, c, e, f Software b,d.
2 VDU and printer.
3 Keyboard, mouse and VDU.
4 Mouse and keyboard.
5 Laser, 24-pin dot-matrix, 9-pin dot matrix.
6 Floppy disk, hard disk, RAM.
7 b.
8 d, b, a, c.
9 Because the screen consists of a line structure and a smooth line cannot be drawn by using small pieces of adjacent lines.
10 So that the computer can identify each part of the disk to use for reading or writing.
11 The size and shape of the screen is inadequate to display a page without greeking the smaller characters.

2 Facilities and methods

Objectives

After reading this chapter you should be able to:
- list and explain the types of files involved in DTP work
- describe the essential facilities of a DTP program
- explain the differences between command-driven, menu-driven and WIMP software
- explain the terms font, typeface, style, kerning, case, pitch, point size
- describe the types of graphics images used in DTP
- outline the methods that are used for incorporating graphics into DTP work.

Scenario

You are asked to justify the expense of adding DTP facilities to a computer system that possesses word-processing software. How can you explain without going into details of technical terms?

Software and file types

Software is the most important part of the whole computer system, because the quality of the software determines totally what the hardware can do. All PC machines can provide suitable hardware, though they may differ in operating speed and in the use of memory, so that the main differences that you will encounter will be due to differences in software.

The software that is used can be divided into four classes, and for many types of programs all four will be present in the memory of the computer at the same time. These classes are:

- System software, the operating system of the machine.
- Applications software, such as the DTP program.
- Utility software such as printer drivers, mouse drivers, and screen drivers.
- Data files which are produced by the applications software or imported into the applications software.

The system software is essential in order to be able to use the hardware *at all*, since it controls the use of the essential components of the computer, notably the keyboard and disk drives, and it must remain in the memory of the computer for as long as it is being used. The simpler type of system software such as MS-DOS takes up some of the memory, but not an excessive amount, and allows a large range of commands to be carried out, such as copying files, deleting files, running programs, etc. More elaborate operating systems for the PC type of machine do not replace MS-DOS but add to it the use of windows, the mouse and other facilities to be described in detail later. These programs can be described as system software, but they take up a very much larger amount of the memory, so that a program has to be run by swapping files between the memory and the disk since the memory cannot hold all of the files at one time.

The applications software, unlike the system software, will be changed each time you want to run a different type of program. This allows the hardware of the computer system to be used for all kinds of applications, word-processing, accounts, calculations, DTP, drawing and so on. Most of the total value of a computer system will be due to the applications software; this is often worth many times as much as the hardware of the system.

The utility software consists of small programs each of which carries out some task that has not been included in the main system software, or which is a useful extra. The printer driver is usually provided among the applications software, but it has to be chosen from a large set, one driver for each type of printer, and it must remain in the memory for as long as the printer is being used. The mouse driver, which is likely to be needed all the time DTP software is being used (except while printing), and other short programs of this kind are likely to be placed in the memory. Some DTP programs are so demanding of memory that all but the most essential drivers have to be removed from the memory. As another example of this type of program, many of the illustrations in this book have been produced by using a screendump program which creates a disk file of the screen appearance when the Shift and Print Scrn keys are pressed simultaneously.

Finally, the data files are the result of using the applications program or are fed into the applications program for processing. These are the files that are the most precious in the sense that they represent many hours of work by the user of the applications program, and they must be saved on disk and also backed up on another disk. You can buy a new operating system, new applications software, new drivers, but you cannot buy a file of the book chapter that you wrote last year – it is unique to you.

DTP software

As you will have gathered, the software of desktop publishing is all-important. Unless this software is good, the amount of effort that will be needed to create the effect that you want will be prohibitive, discouraging you from experimenting. The most important features are that the screen should show, as far as possible, what your page will look like, and that it should be possible to print the page in a reasonably short time. As it is, one discouragement to the user of a dot-matrix printer is the time that is needed to print one page in reasonable quality. If you simply want to see what your copy looks like on paper, you can opt for a rough draft which will be printed much more rapidly. The only easy answer to this is the use of a laser printer, and even a laser printer can be quite slow when an elaborate page is to be printed using PostScript methods. Even if you have a ten-page magazine to prepare, however, this time is not really prohibitive compared to the older methods of typing and pasting-up.

All desktop publishing packages are complicated in the sense that there is a lot to learn before you can make really effective use of them. Programs such as First Publisher and Timeworks are good in the sense that you can obtain relatively simple layouts with ease, and still have little trouble in producing more ambitious work. The ease with which the software can be used encourages you to experiment and so learn from experience. The main problems arise from incompatibility between file-types (for graphics, mainly) and from differences between what appears on the screen and what is printed on the paper.

The choice of DTP programs for a machine such as the IBM PC or its 'clones' (such as Compaq, Amstrad, Matmos and many others) is very large and with a corresponding range of prices, typically £50 to £800. The lower-priced programs are intended for less-demanding applications such as the production of advertising hand-outs (called *flyers*), small magazines for restricted circulation, internal reports in small firms, etc. The highest-priced programs are intended for work which can be used directly for single-page leaflets, reports which will be bound and circulated widely, magazines for mass circulation and in setting type for books. An important feature, once possessed only by the most costly software, is that a document can be stored as a file using a special type of code called PostScript (trademark of Adobe Corp.) which consists of lines of descriptive commands in English. A file stored in PostScript form is easily edited and can be used by printing machines which are much more capable than a laser printer of providing large numbers of copies of excellent quality.

Though all desktop publishing programs operate in roughly similar ways, descriptions of actions look much too vague unless they are made applicable to a specific package. In this book, all descriptions of use of a DTP program apply to the Aldus PageMaker program, one of the most widely sold and used packages available at the top end of the market for the PC type of machine. Among the lower-cost packages, both First Publisher and Timeworks attract a considerable following, and both are used for a wide range of purposes, in some cases by book publishers for creating master copies.

When professional output is needed, however, the two leading programs are Aldus PageMaker and Ventura Publisher. The factor that has swayed the choice as far as this book is concerned is that Aldus PageMaker uses a system of managing the computer, called Microsoft Windows. In its latest form, Windows-3, this is a very important step forward in the use of the PC-AT type of machine. The rival, Ventura Publisher, uses an older system, Gem, which does not make such good use of the features of the later types of PC machine. In particular, Windows-3 allows the most powerful types of PC machines (the 386 and 486 machines) to be used in multi-tasking mode, behaving as if they were running several programs at once. This allows data to be transferred easily from one program to another, a useful feature for DTP where text may be taken from a word-processor and graphics from a painting package such as PC Paint II. At the time of writing, Ventura has just announced a new version of Ventura Publisher which uses the latest version of Windows-3, so that the choice between PageMaker and Ventura is now one of personal preference.

Each DTP program consists of a set of program files which contain the essential main program and overlays that are needed during the use of the main program. In addition, there are several other file types such as drivers and font files that are associated with the program, and there are also data files which hold the documents that have been created by the program. The PC type of machine allows sets of files to be held in separate

directories making it easier to identify files because they are kept in related groups.

The driver files are used to allow the DTP program to control the video screen and the printer(s), and have to be selected during the installation of the program. The PC type of computer in particular can make use of detachable hardware cards to control the video image section of the computer, and several types of these graphics cards exist, identified by abbreviated names such as CGA, EGA and VGA, along with the name of one manufacturer, Hercules. If the correct video driver is not available, it is possible that the program could not produce a screen image or that the image would be distorted. One of the great advantages of using a standard type of PC machine is that it is possible to upgrade the video display (and many other features) by adding or replacing one of these cards (it might also be necessary to use an upgraded monitor) rather than having to replace the complete machine.

The printer driver files are also essential because printers differ considerably and the computer must be able to print each and every part of a screen image on to the paper. This is more complicated than it seems, because the shape of a dot on some screens is rectangular, and on some screen types the depth is considerably greater than the width. For the image to look correct on paper, the shapes of the dots must be corrected by the printer driver software, and failure to use the correct printer driver can result in paper prints of very poor quality.

The font files are used to translate the code for a character (usually a single byte) into the pattern of dots that has to appear on the screen for a character of the correct shape and of the font that has been selected. When a font is selected, a font file will be read from the disk and transferred into the memory so that the program can make use of it. This process takes time, and it is the cause of the slight delay between pressing a key and seeing the first character of a new font appear – there should be no delay on subsequent characters of the same font because by that time all of the font has been read into the memory.

Questions

1 A DTP program can be classed as:
   (a) DOS
   (b) text file
   (c) applications software (d) bit-image file

OUR NEW PIZZAS

1. Quattro Stagione. This is the famous Pizza with all four seasons of vegetables incorporated into the delicious deep-pan crust. Ours contains tomatoes, artichoke, mushrooms, olives, cheese ham and bacon to provide that four-season flavour - a dash of Vivaldi in cooking, and at a very special price for you on Mondays, too.

2. Margherita. The classic Pizza that was named for the first Queen of Italy, this colourful Pizza displays the Italian national flag in the colours of the vegetables. Another deep-pan speciality, it uses tomatoes, cheese and basil - delicious.

3. Napoletana. The classic Pizza, using anchovies, capers, ham, tomatoes, cheese and oregano. As always, these are combined into a deep-pan crust to bring mouth-watering delight to you.

Senza formaggio: All of our Pizzas can be made specially without cheese for customers who are allergic to dairy products.

Figure 2.1   A leaflet example, prepared with a word-processor and a 24-pin dot-matrix printer

2   A printer does not correctly reproduce the text and graphics seen on the screen. Which of the following is likely to be incorrect?
   (a) screen driver
   (b) printer driver
   (c) DOS
   (d) DTP program

Essential facilities of DTP software

The easiest way to understand the essentials of DTP is by comparison with word-processing. For producing straightforward text that can be read, replacing the use of a typewriter and duplicator, a word-processor program would do all that was required. Once there is a need to make use of different shapes and sizes of lettering and graphics effects it becomes less likely that a word-processing program can cope. Even quite simple requirements in this respect can make it necessary to have a word-processor that is far from cheap, probably costing as much as a full-scale desktop publishing package. In order to create pages that look like newspaper pages or advertisement leaflets desktop publishing is the only sensible way to go. That said, there is no doubt that many of the top-price word-processor programs are making more and more use of desktop publishing techniques – but at a high price.

OUR NEW PIZZAS

1. Quattro Stagione.

This is the famous Pizza with all four seasons of vegetables incorporated into the delicious deep-pan crust. Ours contains tomatoes, artichoke, mushrooms, olives, cheese ham and bacon to provide that four-season flavour - a dash of Vivaldi in cooking, and at a very special price for you on Mondays, too.

2. Margherita.

The classic Pizza that was named for the first Queen of Italy, this colourful Pizza displays the Italian national flag in the colours of the vegetables. Another deep-pan speciality, it uses tomatoes, cheese and basil - delicious.

3. Napoletana.
The classic Pizza, using anchovies, capers, ham, tomatoes, cheese and oregano. As always, these are combined into a deep-pan crust to bring mouth-watering delight to you.

Senza formaggio
All of our Pizzas can be made specially without cheese for customers who are allergic to dairy products.

Figure 2.2 The same leaflet, also printed with a dot-matrix printer and making use of the different type sizes that are available

An illustration shows very much better what the differences can be. Figure 2.1 is a simple piece of text which we can imagine is a leaflet from the local pizza supplier. This has been produced using a word-processor and printed on a 24-pin dot-matrix printer. The text is fully justified, meaning that the lines of text have an even right-hand margin rather than the ragged margin that you get with a typewriter, in addition to the normal even left-hand margin. It is an acceptable piece of text, but is no more visually interesting than a letter from a solicitor. The only effects are the use of underlining and bold (dense black) type, effects that any word-processor can produce with any printer, but because of the use of a single **font**, there is no variation in the print size or style. This, I should point out, is not inevitable, because you **can** get other type sizes and shapes on a dot-matrix printer, often by very simple methods such as switch selection. This demands the use of a word-processor which will put commands in with the text for controlling your printer, and this in turn requires you to use a 'standard' type of printer. This is a fiddly process, though, and it's worth remembering that a suitable word-processing program will be an expensive program by modern standards.

Now take a look at Figure 2.2. This makes use of the same text, but has

33

been composed so as to be printed using more of the resources of a modern 24-pin dot-matrix printer, in this example the Star LC24-10. It is considerably more eye-grabbing, with the use of the large wide lettering on the headline, the smaller bold print for sub-titles, and the smallest print for the actual text. If this is as much as you need, then why use desktop publishing? The answer is simple – work like this on a word-processor can take a remarkably long time to set up. You have to remember that with all but a few word-processors what you see is not, alas, exactly what you get. My word-processor does not show any of the different text sizes, so that centring the headline (Our New Lines) was not simply a matter of pressing the centring key. Instead, a bit of 'cut and try' had to be used, along with calculations based on the size of letters. The main text is printed using 12 characters per linear inch, but the headline uses 5 per inch, so that each large character takes the space of 2.4 normal characters. Until you have considerable experience, you will be forced into a long session of trial and error each time you want to produce something new.

In addition, there is a lot that cannot be done. The use of the 24-pin printer is satisfactory, but if you use a 9-pin dot-matrix printer the quality of the lettering is not really very good, particularly on the headline. The fact that you cannot see the appearance of the finished page on the screen makes it difficult to decide how the work is going without printing a test page. You can easily end up with four test pages for each final version. Above all, though, you simply cannot make the work look anything like a printed page; you can only make it look like something from a rather superior typewriter. This is because printers, like typewriters, normally use even spacing between letters. Letters vary in width from slim (like **i**) to fat (like **m**), and using a uniform spacing makes the **i**'s too far apart and the **m**'s too close. We can read the words with no problem, but the effect is unsatisfactory. Some word processors allow you to adjust the spacing (proportional spacing), but many do not. Even if you **can** use proportional spacing, with the space between letters varying with the width of the letters, the letter **font** is often unsatisfactory, particularly from a 9-pin dot-matrix printer. Incidentally, producing such text from a laser printer is not always a solution, because to be compatible with the output from the word-processor, the laser printer may simply emulate the dot-matrix printer, giving an output of comparable quality.

One of the most important differences between word-processing and DTP lies in the use of fonts. Font is a word that is rather poorly defined, and you will read several different definitions. To avoid conflicts, we'll use **font** in the sense that Aldus PageMaker uses it. A font is a letter set,

34

comprising the full set of letters and other printable characters in one size and all of one design (the typeface). Design in this sense means the shape of letters, and it's something that you probably have never been aware of unless you have taken an interest in printing. You will, however, have noticed the difference if your daily paper changed its font (as the *Guardian* did in the latter years). Each font design can exist in several **styles**, such as normal, bold and italic. The letters of the alphabet have no real fixed shape, and over the years many typographers and designers (notably Eric Gill) have had very strong opinions as to how these letters should look. A few minutes spent with some old newspapers (from 1940 back) will soon convince you that fashion plays quite a large part in our preferences for type fonts. Each typeface consists of a collection of fonts of different sizes, with each size existing as normal (or Roman), Italic and Bold style. A complete typeface can therefore consist of several fonts. Note that some DTP programs use the word **font** to mean what we have described as a typeface, a set of sizes and styles all in one design.

Basically, leaving aside Gothic and other fancy fonts, you will be using fonts that are either normal or sans-serif. The serif is a tiny foot or hook at the tips of letters, and omitting this serif leads to a type that looks plainer (more like typewriting) and, to some eyes, more modern. Others claim that the sans-serif types tire the eyes, and that they are unpleasant unless used sparingly. This illustrates an important point: typography is a matter of taste, and no-one can give more than the vaguest of pointers to good taste in this respect. What we shall try to do is to show what is very definitely not good taste; it is regrettable that most of the worst examples are to be found in advertisements prepared using desktop publishing in the magazines that deal with computing. On the other hand, if your readers like your entire newsletter to be in a decorative font, who am I to suggest otherwise?

Now take a look at Figure 2.3. This contains the same information, but the style is noticeably different. The pizza illustrations are eye-catching, and suggest the topic of the leaflet. The headline is large, much larger than could be obtained by word processing techniques, and the text is of a much more dense black than would be normal from word processed output. This copy is of a quality that could be used as 'camera-ready copy' by a printer to make thousands of copies at a low price (because the master copy has already been prepared).

Until you have some experience, some of the other changes are less obvious. This example has used three different type faces or fonts. One has been used for the headline, another for the sub-headings (names of fruits)

OUR NEW PIZZAS

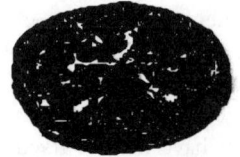 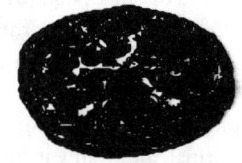

1. Quattro Stagione. This is the famous Pizza with all four seasons of vegetables incorporated into the delicious deep-pan crust. Ours contains tomatoes, artichoke, mushrooms, olives, cheese ham and bacon to provide that four-season flavour - a dash of Vivaldi in cooking, and at a very special price for you on Mondays, too.

2. Margherita. The classic Pizza that was named for the first Queen of Italy, this colourful Pizza displays the Italian national flag in the colours of the vegetables. Another deep-pan speciality, it uses tomatoes, cheese and basil - delicious.

3. Napoletana. The classic Pizza, using anchovies, capers, ham, tomatoes, cheese and oregano. As always, these are combined into a deep-pan crust to bring mouth-watering delight to you.

Senza formaggio: All of our Pizzas can be made specially without cheese for customers who are allergic to dairy products.

Figure 2.3 The leaflet produced with the aid of desktop publishing, showing the use of graphics and different type fonts. This has been printed with the T.I. MicroLaser printer

and a third for the main text. This is not just a matter of size, though three different sizes have also been used. The letter shapes are different for the three fonts, and until you have some experience with fonts, it can be difficult to see these differences. In each size, you can usually have the three styles, normal, italic and bold (some offer also bold-italic), and the bold has been used for emphasis. Some typographers would say that the effects have been overdone here, but in a piece of advertising throwaway like this, a little over-emphasis is justified.

We can sum up the differences between desktop publishing and word-processing, then, by saying that word-processing is a development of typing, but desktop publishing is a development of printing. When you work with desktop publishing, you are creating copy as it would in times past have been created using metal type, but with a fraction of the effort. The example of Figure 2.3 was completed in rather less time than the word-processed example of Figure 2.1, because so many of the items that need cumbersome adjustments when you use a word-processor are done automatically by a good desktop publishing program.

Questions

3 The word *font* is used of printed characters to describe:
   (a) size
   (b) design
   (c) spacing
   (d) use of serifs
4 The main advantage of DTP over word-processing is:
   (a) the use of different type sizes (b) simplicity (c) ability to use a wide range of fonts and graphics (d) true WYSIWYG operation

---

Activity

Print out a simple sentence of one or two lines in as many different fonts of the same size as your DTP package allows. Note which fonts are serif types and which are sans-serifs, and see if you can classify type in books, magazines and newspapers into these two forms.

Supplying text – WP and OCR

In conventional printing, the printer does not provide the text, it is supplied in either typed or written form, often heavily edited along with instructions about the use of fonts, underlining, bold type, headings and so on. The text for DTP follows along the same lines, but the editing work is often done as the text is being prepared or by use of the DTP program. The text itself, however, is always supplied in machine-readable form, meaning as a disk file or set of files.

This is not absolutely necessary because all DTP systems will allow text to be typed. There are, however, several very good reasons for not doing this:

- The page size as seen on screen may be so small that the characters are greeked and hence cannot be read.
- DTP programs do not generally allow for such refinements as spelling checkers and thesaurus programs.
- It is very difficult to check text adequately on the screen, particularly in some font types.
- Some DTP programs cannot accept characters from the keyboard at the speed which a fast typist can achieve.

The normal procedure is therefore to prepare the text as a disk file, using a word-processor, either alone or in combination with a scanner and OCR software. OCR means optical character recognition, and the use of OCR along with a scanner allows the scanner to read typed or printed text which the software then turns into conventional ASCII code form, one byte per character, suitable for use with a word-processor or DTP program. If OCR is **not** used, the characters can still be scanned, but only as graphical images – they cannot be used by a word-processor, edited, rearranged, hyphenated nor any of the other requirements that a word-processor can fulfil. Note that OCR software is useful only along with its scanner; it has no application otherwise.

OCR software is still not as advanced as other, more established, parts of a DTP system, which is why OCR is not yet considered an essential part of DTP. The main drawback is that only certain fonts can be read, and the simplest OCR software is very limited in this respect, reading only Courier 10 or 12 point (as produced by typewriters) and a few sizes of Times Roman. At a considerably higher cost, a larger range of fonts and sizes can be read, but few OCR systems can cope with the range of fonts and sizes found in newspapers. No OCR program has ever been devised that can cope with the huge variations in handwriting, which is why the use of post-codes is still limited – each post code seen on a letter has to be typed again by the sorter in order to print the dot codes on to the envelope that ensure it can be automatically sorted for fast delivery, and even the Post Office OCR machines can cope only with monospaced printed fonts.

The quality of OCR software is steadily improving, and, in common with all computer-related items, its price is falling. This means that the ability to read a good range of fonts and sizes will soon be available even for low-budget systems, provided that the scanner is of sufficient quality (as most are), and this could eventually lead to the establishment of OCR as a normal part of DTP software.

Whether the text originates from direct typing or from other documents by way of OCR, it needs to be word-processed before being fed to the DTP program. Spelling can be checked, headings adjusted, hyphenation used or rejected according to taste – all facilities that are generally unavailable on the DTP program. Most important of all, the text can be printed in draft form and proof-read. This will show errors that were not so readily noticed on the screen and allow the proof-reader to make editing marks in the margin to indicate the layout that is to be used when the DTP version is produced.

The principle used is that text which is finally fed into the DTP system should be as far as possible perfect, requiring no further correction of grammar, spelling or punctuation. This is particularly important when a piece of text forms part of a book or a newspaper or magazine article which will be widely read, and Chapter 7 contains more details of what is required in this respect. Text that has been printed in draft form is considerably easier to check over in a really meticulous way than text on the word-processor screen, and text on the DTP system may be very difficult to check because of its appearance on the screen.

Once the text, whatever its source, is in the form of a checked word-processed file it can be imported into a DTP document. In some cases, the text is placed in the document and all editing is done from then on, altering fonts and styles and creating headings, underlining and so on. Many DTP programs can read text produced by word-processors that contain **embedded** commands for such actions as font changes, underlining, bold print and so on. This allows more of the text preparation to be done using the word-processor and less using the DTP program, and which approach you use is very much a matter of taste – there is much to be said for using the word-processor for bare text only, leaving all editing effects for the DTP program.

Commands, menus and WIMP systems

The way that the operator uses a DTP system can utilise any of three systems – commands, picking from menus, or a full window-icon-mouse program (WIMP) system. Most modern DTP programs allow combinations of all three methods, with a bias to the WIMP system.

A command-driven program relies on you to type a command in the form of a word, and then press the RETURN key. This has to be done for each action that is to be carried out, and it requires you to know the command word for each action. In addition, you have to type each command word with perfect accuracy – if the word is mis-spelled or mis-typed it cannot be obeyed. If the command is COPY, then typing CPPY or CO PY will not have the desired effect. All of the commands of the MS-DOS operating system are of this type. The MS-DOS system provides for making a file (a batch file) of commands that are often used in sequence, so that if this set is correctly typed once they need not be typed again. Using a batch file, the PageMaker program, for example, could be run by typing the letters PM and pressing the RETURN key, without the need to go through the commands for finding the correct directory on the disk, setting up other programs (or removing programs from memory), running PageMaker, and restoring conditions after the program was ended.

The use of commands in addition often requires a *command-tail* or *argument*. A command such as COPY is meaningless unless you specify what is to be copied, where it is taken from and where it is to be copied to. Using the MS-DOS command COPY as an example, you might type:

COPY A:DTPFILE.DOC B:

to copy the file called DTPFILE.DOC from the disk in drive A to the disk in drive B; in this line the portion that follows the word COPY is the command-tail or argument of the command – the parts of the argument are separated by spaces.

Another variation of command uses a different key for each action, and this system used to be quite common in applications programs. Since you need the keyboard to enter text in word-processors or DTP programs, the command keys need to be keys or key combinations that do not occur in text, and the function keys (marked F1 to F12, though only F1 to F10 are normally used) are most commonly used for this purpose. Each function key can be used alone, or along with either the SHIFT key, the CTRL key or the ESC key, giving some 40 combinations for ten function keys.

Another possibility for command keys is to use the combination of the CTRL key with other keys, allowing some 26 possible commands to be used in this way. The ALT key can also be used to permit another 26 commands to be added, so that there is seldom any problem in running out of key combinations.

The disadvantage of this system is remembering which key combination

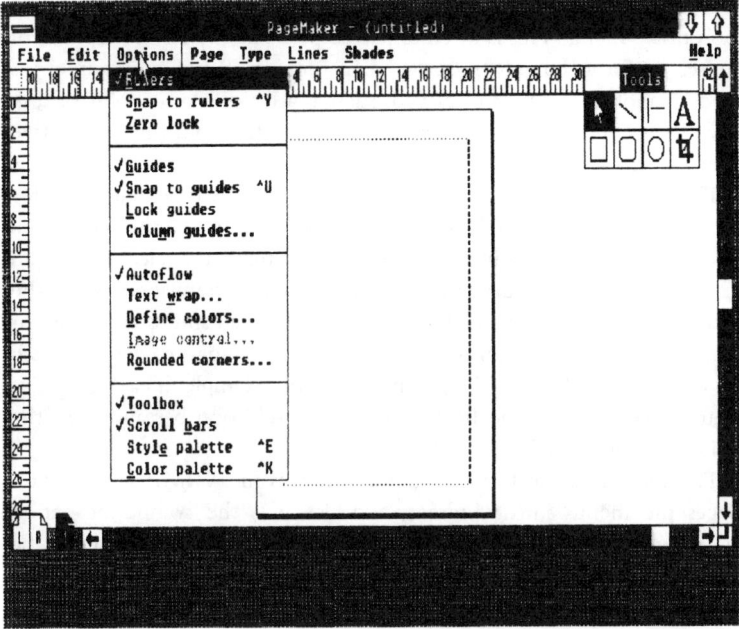

Figure 2.4 A typical drop-down menu. A choice is made by moving the shaded selection bar using the mouse or the cursor keys, and pressing the mouse button or the RETURN key

to use for different purposes. No two DTP programs will be alike, so that if a set of key commands is learned for one system it will quite certainly not be usable on another system. Once the common key combinations are learned, however, the rate of working can be very fast, and some programs overcome the memory problem by using a HELP key (usually F1) which will produce a list of key effects on the screen – the list disappears when any key is pressed. Many fast typists who have used word-processors like WordStar can produce DTP work very rapidly and accurately using command letters.

Another option is the use of drop-down menus. In such a menu, one of which is illustrated in Figure 2.4, the action is obtained either by pressing one of the indicated command letter keys, or by moving the shaded bar (the cursor or selection bar) to one of the options, using the cursor movement keys, and then pressing the ENTER/RETURN key. There is no need to memorize a large number of command key combinations, but you need to know which keys have to be used to produce the appropriate menu. This is often displayed permanently on the top line of the screen for as long as the program is running. When an argument is needed, another menu is displayed, such as a list of files or a list of disk drive letters. This allows these items to be selected from their respective menus in the same way.

This system is not so fast to use as the command key type, but it calls for little or no memorizing of commands and, more importantly, file names. The time needed for the menu to appear and to move the selection bar can be irritating, and many programs which use such a system also provide the option of command letters which can be memorized and used instead for some common requirements. It can be very annoying to have to use such a system for switching bold type on and off, for example, if each time this requires you to press the F6 key, move the selection bar and press the ENTER/RETURN key.

The most extreme form of menu system is the WIMP system. This places the menus into windows, and also puts the computing action (word-processing or DTP, for example) into windows which can be moved about the screen. These windows can be *resized*, meaning that their sizes can be changed, and actions are indicated by icons, symbols which suggest an action (such as a pen for writing text, an eraser for deleting, or a bin for scrapping a piece of text). The other essential part of the system is the mouse.

The mouse is a small trolley, Figure 2.5, which rolls along the surface of a desk and is equipped with two or three buttons. When a suitable *mouse driver* program has been installed in the computer and a program which can make use of the mouse is running, moving the mouse will move a cursor on the screen, and pressing the mouse buttons will cause effects which are determined by the program – often the equivalent of pressing the RETURN key and the ESC key when a two-button mouse is used. Although some DTP programs can be used in a clumsy and limited way without a mouse, it is a necessity for working in any serious way with DTP, particularly when graphics images have to be manipulated. Two particularly important mouse techniques are *pointing/ selecting*, and *dragging*.

The ability to make the movement of the mouse affect a screen cursor allows a screen cursor in the shape of an arrow to be used. This arrow can be pointed at menu items; then pressing a mouse button, usually the left-hand button, will make the menu selection. This is considerably faster than using the cursor keys to move a selection bar, because all of the action

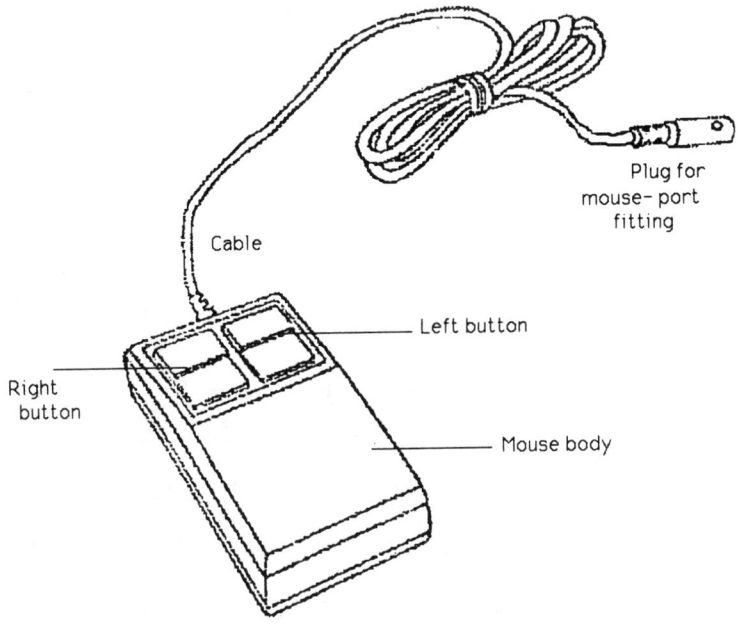

Plug for
mouse- port
fitting

Cable

Left button

Right
button

Mouse body

Figure 2.5 A typical mouse. Movement of the mouse will move the cursor on the screen, and the left-hand mouse button will carry out the action of the RETURN key. The right-hand mouse button may be used for other purposes

is controlled by the mouse alone. The shape of the cursor can be varied (by the applications program) to indicate the type of mouse action that is going to be carried out.

The term *selection* is also used to indicate marking out a piece of text or graphics. The mouse pointer is moved to a piece of text or graphics and the button is clicked, meaning that it is pressed and released rapidly. This has the effect of placing visible markers (shaped like hooks or loops) on part of the text or graphics as seen on the screen, allowing this to be moved, deleted or otherwise worked on. The term *selection* will be used extensively in this sense in the chapters that follow, and knowing how to select text or graphics portions, called *blocks*, is very important.

Dragging is a method that is particularly useful for positioning graphics images into text. The selected image will be contained in a window which has a top strip (the top bar) that is not part of the image. If the mouse is used to move the cursor to this top bar and the left-hand button on the

Figure 2.6 Dragging a window complete with its image, using the mouse with the button held down. (a) The window captured, as indicated by the 4-arrow shape. (b) The window dragged to its new position

mouse is pressed and held down, moving the mouse will then result in moving the whole window and its image, Figure 2.6. With the button held down, the image can be moved to its final position and when the button is released, the window and its image will be fixed in place. This process can be repeated if the position is not correct and it is a very powerful method of working with graphics images as compared to the older methods involving the use of the cursor keys.

In addition, the mouse can be used to change the size of windows using a method like dragging, and to scroll text. When a window appears, positioning the screen pointer with the mouse at one corner or edge of the window and pressing the left-hand mouse button will allow the mouse to be dragged so as to shift this edge of the window in or out, contracting or expanding the window. When text is shown on the screen, one side of the screen (and the foot of the screen also) will consist of a scroll bar, a pair of parallel lines which contain a small box whose position along the lines represents the position of the text from the start. The vertical cross bar marks the position of the text from the first line, and the scroll bar at the foot of the screen marks the position of the text from the left hand side. By placing the mouse marker on a scroll box and dragging the box, the text can be scrolled vertically or sideways so that another piece of text becomes visible. Another option is to place the mouse marker on an arrowhead at the end of the scroll bar and press the mouse button once. This will move the text by one screen height or *page* (vertical scroll bar) or one screen width (horizontal scroll bar).

Aldus PageMaker, like all modern DTP programs can make full use of the mouse that is supplied with machines such as the Amstrad PC range, and it can also use any mouse which is compatible with the Microsoft design. This includes practically all of the well-known mouse designs, whether of the bus or serial type. A bus mouse requires to be plugged into a socket on the machine, and many PCs are not supplied as standard with this socket, nor can it easily be added. The serial mouse connects to a serial port, one of which is supplied on each PC computer. If the serial port is already in use (for a modem, for example), it is easy and also quite cheap to add another serial port. The Genius serial mouse is a low-cost and very effective add-on which works in this way. The convenience of using a mouse for desktop publishing work is such that it is difficult to imagine any user of a DTP program wanting to dispense with it, and in this book, the actions of preparing copy have been described making use of the mouse, rather than making the descriptions cumbersome by adding a non-mouse method each time.

The WIMP system is the most 'user-friendly' method that has been devised to date for using computers. User-friendly in this sense means that the user should not require elaborate instructions to make use of a program, because the methods will be obvious simply from the appearance of the screen. A distinct advantage of the WIMP system is that if all of your software uses the same system (such as Windows-3) then it is much easier to learn to use a new program, since the methods of controlling it are the same as they are for all other programs.

The WIMP system is not perfect, however, and its main drawback is that it can be slow to use because of the time spent in manipulating the mouse. In addition, it is often possible to select or run the wrong command because the mouse has moved slightly when you pressed the selection button. This is why all DTP programs allow a combination of techniques to be used, so that you can, if you like, use fast command letter methods when entering or editing text, and WIMP systems for adjusting the position and size of graphics images.

Machines which use a full WIMP system will generally have very little memory left for applications programs, and in order to load and run an applications program, part of the WIMP system has to be taken out of memory and stored on the disk. All the time a program is being used, then, files are being interchanged between the memory and the disk, which makes a hard disk essential if a full WIMP program is to be used. This continual swapping of files also slows down the action, so that WIMP programs can be infuriatingly slow unless they are used on a very fast machine with a correspondingly fast hard-disk system.

Questions

5 Software which requires you to type words and press the RETURN key is called:
   (a) menu driven
   (b) command driven
   (c) WIMP
   (d) printer driven
6 Which of the following statements apply to OCR at present:
   (a) It is software added to a scanner
   (b) it can recognize only hand-written text
   (c) it can convert typed text into ASCII codes
   (d) it can recognize any typeface.

Activity

Compare some command-driven software (such as MS-DOS) with menu-driven (Lotus 1-2-3, for example) and full WIMP (Microsoft Windows) software. Note the convenience of each (in terms of effort, speed, simplicity) and determine the amount of memory that is needed to implement each system.

Work on text

The work that has to be carried out on text in a DTP system concerns the appearance of the text in the page, since the text should by that time have been corrected for any grammatical, punctuation or spelling errors. The preliminary editing will have determined which fonts are to be used for the main text, main headings and subsidiary headings, so that the text will usually have been read in with the main font in use.

The font that is being used will almost certainly be a proportionally-spaced font, meaning that the spacing between letters will be determined by the width of the letters. Monospaced fonts, such as Courier, sometimes called typewriter or non-proportional fonts, are seldom used for text, but they are valuable for tabulated work because each letter is placed in its own column of uniform width. Using proportionately-spaced lettering for tabular work makes the tables look very ragged.

Some combinations of letters have a poor appearance even with pro-portional spacing and generally require closer spacing, called *kerning*. Examples of such letter combinations are Yo, We, To, Tr and these and many others can be kerned automatically by many DTP programs in the PageMaker class, though this facility is seldom available for low-cost DTP systems. Kerning manually is also possible, but it requires good judgement and experience so that only the automatic system should be used unless you feel that the readability of some words is poor and needs manual adjustment.

The *case* of lettering needs to be considered particularly for headings. Upper case means capital letters, lower case means the ordinary (small) letters, and these terms arose when print was cast in lead and quite literally kept in two sets of wooden cases. The use of upper case (capitalization) for the letter of the first word in each sentence should not require any work, since the text should have been prepared on a word-processor. Decisions do have to be made regarding the use of upper case in headings, in names (such as PageMaker) and for emphasis. Some characters are of fixed size, so

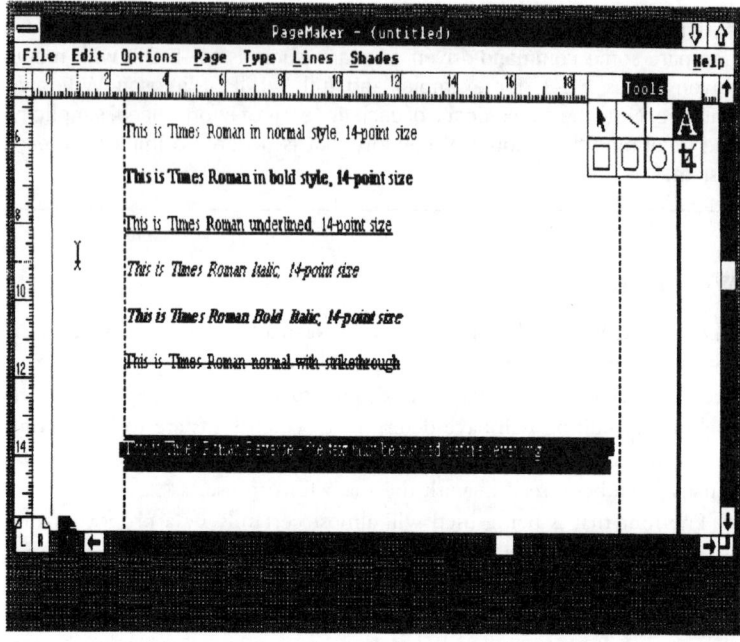

Figure 2.7   The appearance of emphasis effects on typed text, as seen on the screen when Aldus PageMaker is running

that the case is not relevant. Such characters are the punctuation marks, numerals, and signs such as £ $ % & @ and so on.

The use of boldface and italics also needs to be considered. Both are used for emphasis, with the boldface more prominent, and for a long document or book the editor will have to determine a *house-style* on the use of these effects, such as using italic to indicate the use of a new term and bold to indicate an important warning. Other markings on letters are underlining and strike-through. Underlining is another form of emphasis, but strike-through is very seldom used. Figure 2.7 shows examples of these effects as they appear on the screen of Aldus PageMaker during the course of work on a document.

Subscript and superscript are particularly necessary in scientific and mathematical typesetting. A superscript is a character whose baseline has been raised above that of the other letters, and a subscript is a character whose baseline has been lowered compared to others. Both superscript

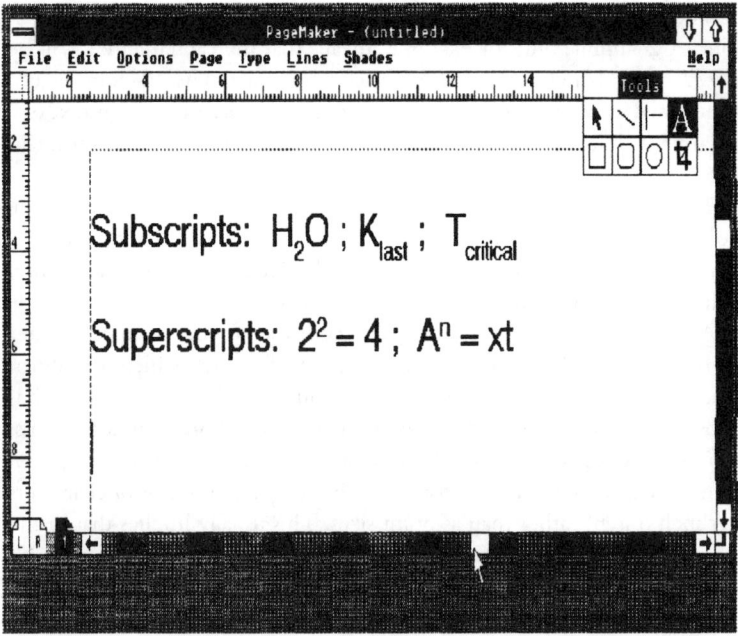

Figure 2.8 Illustrating subscripts and superscripts; these are more commonly used in technical work. Note that the size of superscripts and subscripts is automatically reduced – there is no need to select a different font

and subscript characters are usually in a smaller font. These effects are illustrated in Figure 2.8; they are not common in ordinary text, such as novels, but are very likely to appear in any kind of technical work involving the use of formulae.

Pitch and point size

Because DTP is a development of printing, many of the old terms peculiar to the printing industry have been taken over for DTP use. Some of the most important of these concern units of measurement for which the unit is the point. A point is $1/72''$, a unit which is used for typesetting in all English-language countries, though the Cicero, equal to 4.55 mm (about $9/50''$) is used in many parts of Europe.

The point size of a font means the height of the upper case letters of that font. A 24-point font, for example, means that the capital letters will be 24/72 = 1/3″ high, with the other letters to scale. The 12-point (1/6″) size is used so often that it has a name of its own, pica. The main text of a document, known as *body text*, is usually either 10-point or 12-point in size.

The spacing of text is usually measured in the em unit, equal to the point size for the font. Thus 12-point type would be spaced with letters 12 points apart (approximately the size of the letter **m**, hence the name) before proportional spacing or kerning was used.

Another method of specifying spacing is as the number of characters per inch. This is applied mainly to monospaced fonts (in which a uniform spacing is used) like Courier, in which the number of characters per inch is constant no matter what characters are being used. For DTP documents, monospaced fonts are reserved for tabular work, but when some types of printers are being used some fonts may be specified in terms of characters per inch (pitch) rather than as point sizes. This usually implies that printing will be carried out using built-in monospaced fonts that belong with the printer, and many DTP programs will not show such fonts correctly on the screen.

Questions

7 Classify each of the following characters as upper case, lower case or no case:
a X £ f ″ $ Q j 2 #] 6 T

8 Which of the following letter combinations would benefit most from kerning:
(a) a & l
(b) A & V
(c) B & E
(d) T & o

9 What characteristics are described in each of of the following:
(a) the character height of upper-case letters
(b) the average distance in em units
(c) a unit equal to 1/72 inch
d) the number of characters per inch

Graphics images

Graphics images as applied to DTP can range from the simple heavy underlining or boxing in of a headline to the reproduction of a photograph. The two basic types of graphics images are line vector and dot (or bit-map). Line vector graphics produce what we also know as line drawings, meaning drawings that are made using straight or curved lines, but without any shading or colouring, though some drawings may contain areas that are filled with line patterns that give the appearance of shading. Dot images, as the name suggests, consist of dots which can be black or white (or coloured when colour screens are in use). The importance of a dot or bit-map image is that the number of dots per inch is usually fixed, and this determines the **resolution** of the image, the sharpness of the picture. If an image is described in terms of lines, it can be reproduced in any size without altering the essential parts of the description, only the sizes need to be scaled. When an image is described in terms of dots, altering the size requires the pattern of dots to be completely changed.

Line vector graphics cannot be used to reproduce photographs or any other material that relies on half-tones. Half-tones are shades which lie between black and white, and in photographic processes these can be represented in a dot-constructed picture by using dots that are shaded, neither black nor white. The laser printers that are used for DTP, in common with many other printing methods, cannot reproduce half-tone dots, however; each dot must be either black or white (though clever software inside the printer can sometimes produce the effect of half-tone dots by using, for example, hollow dots).

Dot-patterns that use only black or white dots can convey half-tones (shades of gray) by the process of half-tone screening. In this process, the ratio of white to black dots is altered to give the impression of shading and the impression can be reasonably convincing if the number of dots per linear inch is large, of the order of 300 or more. As it happens, most laser printers can work with 300 dots per inch, though they cannot approach the 2400 dots per inch of some typesetting machines. At 300 dots per inch, the use of half-tone screen is only just acceptable, and the pictures have a very noticeable dot structure. At 2400 dots per inch, the results are very much more acceptable, and this amount of resolution is required if illustrations consist mainly of half-tones. Where illustrations use line-drawings, the lower resolution is completely acceptable. Note, incidentally, that though all laser printers are capable of 300 dots per inch resolution, the actual results depend considerably on the software that drives the printers, and disappointing results can be obtained if this is not suitable.

Scanners also generate dot patterns, and most scanners can be switched so as to reproduce grey-scales on a photograph by using half-tone screening. Dot pattern graphics are also generated by many of the popular paint packages for the PC type of machine, such as DeLuxe Paint II and Publishers Paintbrush. Programs for CAD (computer-aided design) generate line patterns, as also do some business-oriented programs for generating graphs, such as Lotus 1-2-3 or Lotus Freelance which use vector line methods.

The differences between these approaches are fundamental. Vector line-images can be printed and viewed at the highest resolution that is available – if you view a line-image on a screen that permits only a **total** of 320 dots horizontally by 200 vertically, the lines will look ragged, but when the same lines are printed on a printer that is capable of 300 dots per inch the appearance will be very much better with no trace of jagged outlines no matter to what size the image is scaled. By contrast, if a dot-image is created on a 320 × 200 screen, then it will consist of 64000 dots, and printing this on a 300-dot per inch printer will give an image that is just over one inch wide and 0.66″ high. Any attempt to scale up the size of this image will simply print the dots further apart, making the image look insubstantial.

A dot-image, however, can be pixel-edited. This means that a portion of the image can be examined to show the dot structure, Figure 2.9, and individual dots (picture elements or pixels) changed so as to improve the overall appearance. This can be used to tidy up a scanned image, for example, making a line that is slightly squint into a true vertical, or altering the thickness of part of a line. No such editing can be carried out on line-images because the image does not consist of dots, only of descriptions, and a line-image file can be edited only in the program that created it, or a compatible program.

Questions

10 How many of the following statements are true of graphics resolution:
    (a) it is measured in terms of dots per inch
    (b) it defines the quality of a screen image
    (c) it defines the quality of a printed image
    (d) it is always the same on the printer as it is on the screen

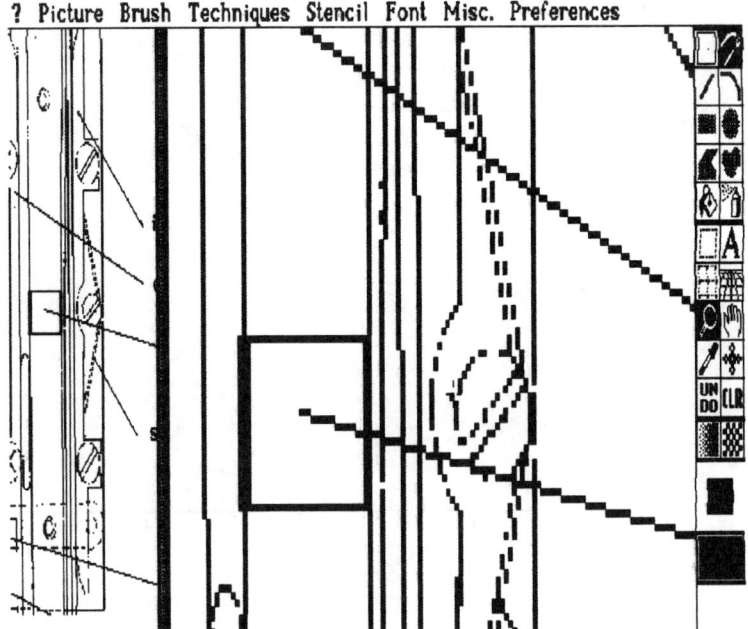

? Picture Brush Techniques Stencil Font Misc. Preferences

Figure 2.9   Pixel-editing being carried out on a dot-image, using a painting package, Deluxe Paint II in this illustration. The left-hand side of the screen shows the normal-size part of the image

11 A photograph in a printed document must be represented using:
    (a) a vector image
    (b) a bit-map image
    (c) a grey-scale image
    (d) a coloured image.

Simple business graphics

The traditional form of graph is the X–Y symbol graph, as illustrated in Figure 2.10. A vertical distance (Y) on this graph represents the size of one quantity, and a horizontal distance (X) represents the size of another quantity so that each pair of quantities is plotted as a point or some other distinguishable symbol. The points can then be joined, if required, with lines. The most useful type of graph is the straight line graph, in which a single straight line joins the points.

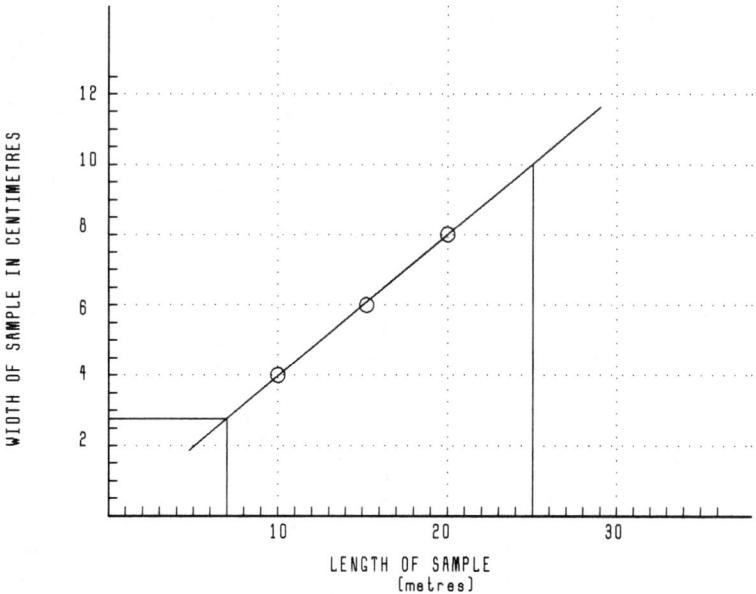

Figure 2.10 An X–Y line graph of the traditional type in which the points can be joined with a straight line. Vertical lines are drawn to show the use of interpolation (at the X-value of 6) and extrapolation (at the X-value of 25)

In the example of Figure 2.10, for instance, it is possible to use the graph to read off values. If you know that the length of a sample is 10 metres, you can read from the graph that its width must be 4 cm. More important, a straight line graph (or *linear* graph) allows interpolation and extrapolation. We can use the graph of Figure 2.10 to find the width corresponding to a length of 7 m, for example (2.75 cm), even though this is not one of the points that was plotted. This range of values lies between plotted points, and this type of reading is called *interpolation*. We can also use the graph to show what values would occur outside the plotted range – for example a length of 25 m would correspond to a width of 10 cm. This is *extrapolation*, and only a straight line graph can be extrapolated with any reliability – some of the worst mistakes made by economists, environmentalists and sociologists are due to extrapolating graphs that are not straight lines. Though the line type of graph is often used to produce jagged lines as in Figure 2.11, the graph is more useful for prediction purposes if its shape is a straight line or smooth curve, or if a line

54

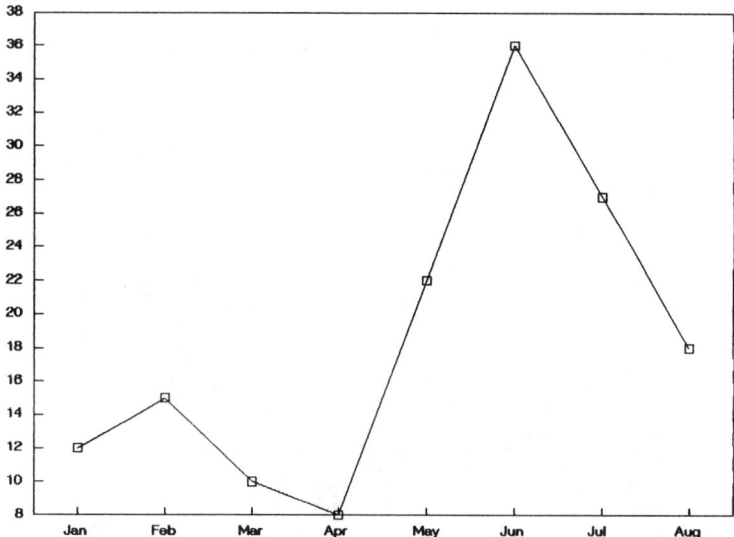

Figure 2.11   Another X–Y graph in which the points do not fit into a single straight line, so that interpolation or extrapolation is impossible

or curve can be drawn as an average of the points (a **best–fit** line). Such a graph is more useful for prediction purposes, using interpolation or extra-polation. The symbols that are used to mark points can be varied, so that several line graphs can be plotted on the same screen or sheet of paper without confusion.

The favourite type of graph for the display of business data is the bar graph, illustrated in Figure 2.12, which also allows more than one set of results to be plotted. In this type of graph, the length of the bar represents a measured quantity such as value of sales and the different positions of the bars are used to show what the quantities relate to, such as which week or month. The bar chart does not imply any type of mathematical rela-tionship between the quantities, and you are free to make the bars rep-resent whatever you like. When a set of bars is used to represent frequency distributions (the number of occurrences of sizes for example), the chart is called a *histogram*. Bar charts are very widely used, and the bars do not need to start from the baseline of the graph – Figure 2.13 shows an example of a bar graph which uses the bars to show holiday dates, a very common use. This type of graph makes it easy to see coincidences (the only word-

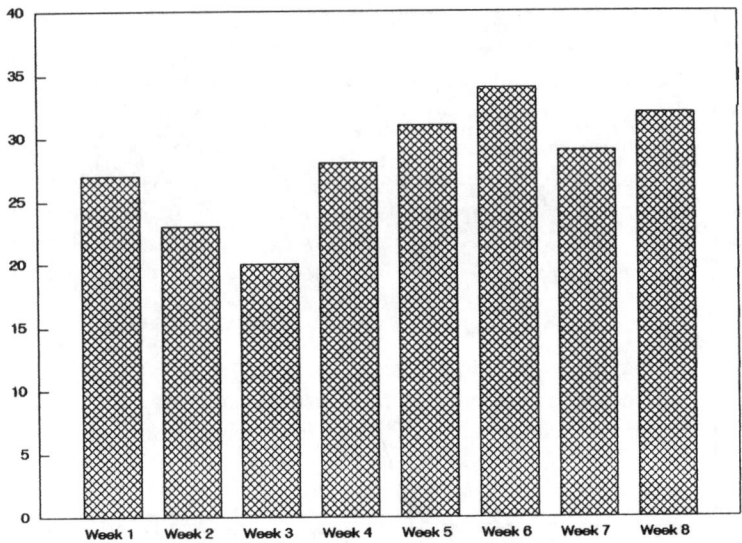

Figure 2.12   One form of bar-graph, a popular type for illustrating business statistics

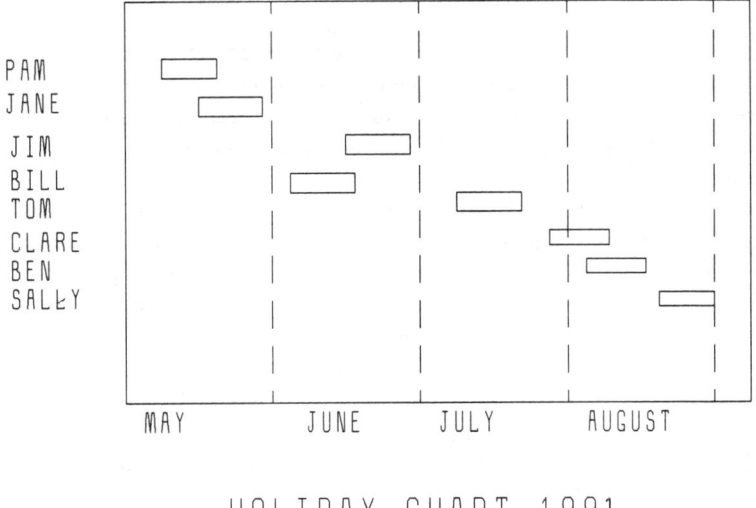

HOLIDAY CHART 1991

Figure 2.13   Another type of bar-graph used for representing holiday periods, stages in a project or ranges of dimensions

56

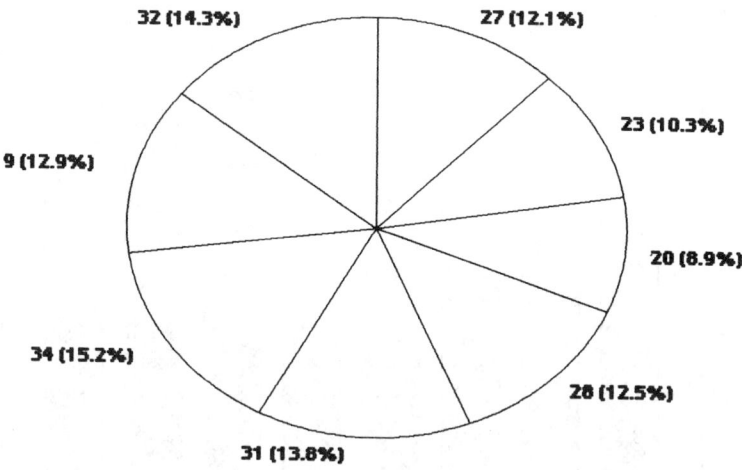

32 (14.3%) 27 (12.1%)

23 (10.3%)

9 (12.9%)

20 (8.9%)

34 (15.2%)

28 (12.5%)

31 (13.8%)

Figure 2.14 The form of a pie-chart which is used for showing relative shares of a whole

processor operator is away at the same time as the legal advisor), and is used extensively as a way of planning large projects where one set of actions can overlap others.

Another form of display is the pie chart, Figure 2.14. The pie chart is particularly useful when you want to show how some global quantity is shared out. You might, for example, want to show the relative contributions of different sources of income to a company or the fractions of the Earth's surface that are covered by water, desert, ice, cultivated land, forest and cities. Pie charts can be printed in simple form, requiring you to guess the relative sizes of quantities, or with more precise percentages indicated in each sector. One problem is that a pie chart can become very cluttered, and no more than 5–7 slices should be shown.

There is another variation on the bar graph, the stacked bar, which allows relative shares of a variable total to be shown. Suppose, for example, that we wanted to show how the relative numbers of sales of different products had changed over the years. A stacked bar chart such as that in Figure 2.15 illustrates this very clearly. The total height shows the total numbers of all sales and the stacked sections show the relative contributions of different items. This type of graph can be more useful than the pie chart for showing distribution when more than one set of shares has to be shown.

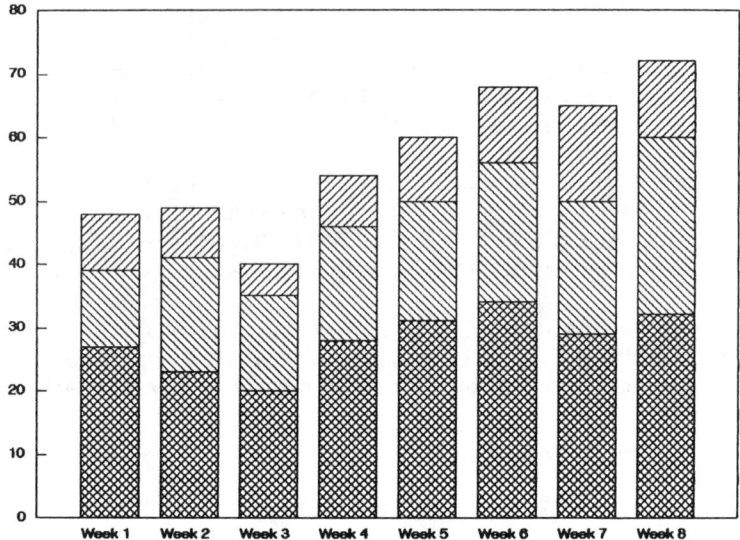

Figure 2.15   A stacked-bar chart allows the change of a quantity to be shown along with the changes in the factors that make up the quantity, so combining bar-chart and pie-chart information

Activity

Draw a graph by hand to show which parts of the C & G 407 course will be covered at what times in the academic year. What type of graph is best suited to this? Is there any computer applications program available which would allow this type of graph to be printed?

Questions

12   Using the graph of Fig. 2.16, what is the profit on the sale of 300 units?
13   Using the pie-chart of Fig. 2.17, what is your estimate of the relative amount of land used for sugar-beet?

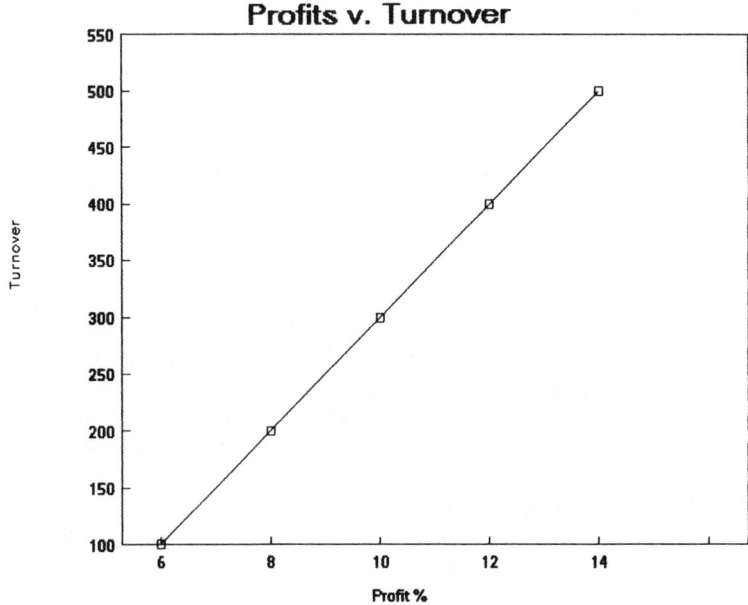

Figure 2.16   A graph to illustrate question 12

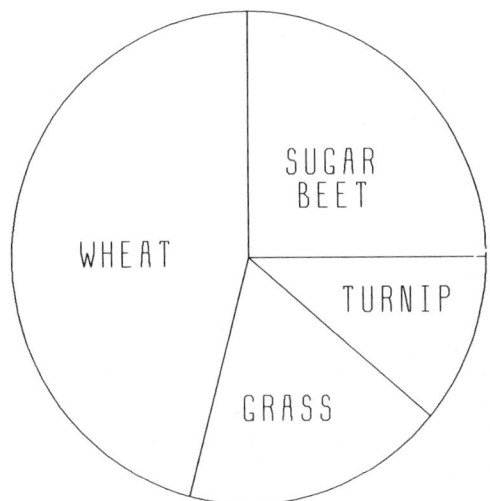

Figure 2.17   A pie-chart to illustrate question 13

Assignment 2

Aldus PageMaker and Xerox Ventura Publisher are the main competing 'midrange' DTP packages. Tabulate their respective features in a word-processed document so that a prospective buyer could assess their relative merits. This document should be kept in file form to be used for DTP work later.

Recap

- The software of the computer system can be of four main types, all of which may be present in the memory together. These are systems software (or DOS), applications software, utilities and drivers, and data files.
- The essential facilities of DTP software are the representation on the screen of a printed page, with fonts and graphics and the ability to print such a page in high resolution.
- OCR software can be used along with a scanner to create ASCII files from printed material in a limited range of fonts and sizes. ASCII files can also be imported from word-processors to be used as DTP text.
- Program control can make use of direct commands, menu selection, or of window, icon, mouse (WIMP) program methods. Of these direct commands are fast and require very little memory, WIMP methods are simple to use but can take longer and require much more memory.
- Type fonts are designs of letter shapes, and each font is available in various sizes and styles. A font can be a serif or sans-serif type. A few fonts are monospaced (non-proportional) with each letter using the same spacing. This is ideal for tabular work, but for readability a proportional font is used, with each letter occupying a space determined by its width. In some cases, strictly proportional spacing is not enough, and appearance can be improved by kerning, reducing the spacing between certain pairs of letters.
- The size of letters is measured in terms of points, 1/72 inch units, with the size of the capital letters used to determine the point size. Spacing can be measured in characters per inch for monospaced (non-proportional) characters, but in ems, an average spacing size, for the proportional type.
- Graphics can be line vector or pixel (bit-map) types. The vector type is less common in DTP work, but has the advantage of retaining high resolution no matter how much its scale is changed. The pixel type is easy to edit, but its resolution is fixed by the resolution of the system that created the image (scanner or screen).
- Business graphs are of the line, bar, pie or stacked-bar variety, and they allow information to be presented in image form.

Answers to questions

1 (c)
2 (b)
3 (b)
4 (c)
5 (b)
6 (a), (c)
7 Lower-case a f j Upper case X Q T No case £ " $ 2 #] 6
8 To
9 (a) point size (b) character spacing, proportional (c) point (d) mono-spaced character spacing.
10 a, b, c only.
11 (c)
12 10%
13 25%

3 Text and graphics layout

Objectives

After reading this chapter you should be able to:
- distinguish margins, tabs and indents
- define the meanings of justification, columns and gutter
- show how to use a master page and style sheets, and alter format and page layout
- describe ASCII files, with or without control codes, and the various types of graphics files
- show how pixel editing of suitable graphics files can be carried out
- show how characters can be represented by a dot-matrix pattern
- describe the use of image scanners
- describe the maintenance of a desk-top publishing system.

Scenario

Your work calls for the detailed design of a document which will form the description of a device within a contract for its manufacture. You are required to undertake the full specification of textual and graphics material. How can DTP make this task easier?

Margins, tabs and indents

The margins of a page are the spaces, at either side and at the top or bottom, which are not used for text, though in some books the side spaces are used for notes or comments. Top and bottom margin spaces are used on many publications for headers and footers. Header text is placed in the top margin and can consist of such items as the title of the book or of the

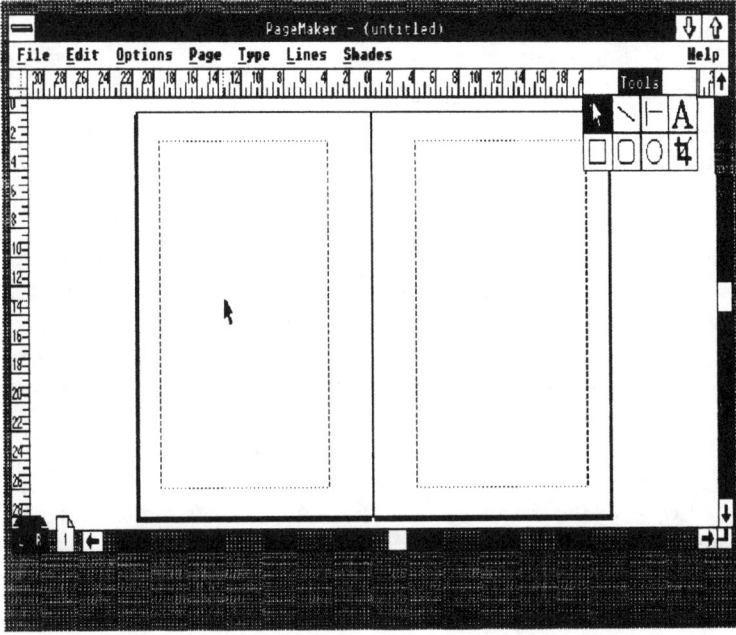

Figure 3.1   Layout of odd and even-numbered pages so as to use a wider margin on the side that will be bound

chapter. The footer space is in the bottom margin and its main use is for page numbers.

Looking at the side margins first, books generally use left and right margins of equal size, so that there is no difference in the margin settings of a page bearing an odd number as compared to a page bearing an even number. Other documents, and particularly single-page documents will normally have a left margin which is larger than the right margin. This allows for binding into a folder and if the document uses both sides of each page, the margins on the reverse sides (the even-numbered pages) will differ from those on the obverse sides (the odd–numbered pages) so as to keep the wider margin at the side which will be bound, Figure 3.1.

DTP programs such as PageMaker provide for the design of either single-sided or double-sided documents, single or multiple pages, and by specifying initially how the pages will be laid out, the differences between odd and even pages will be catered for automatically. Top and bottom

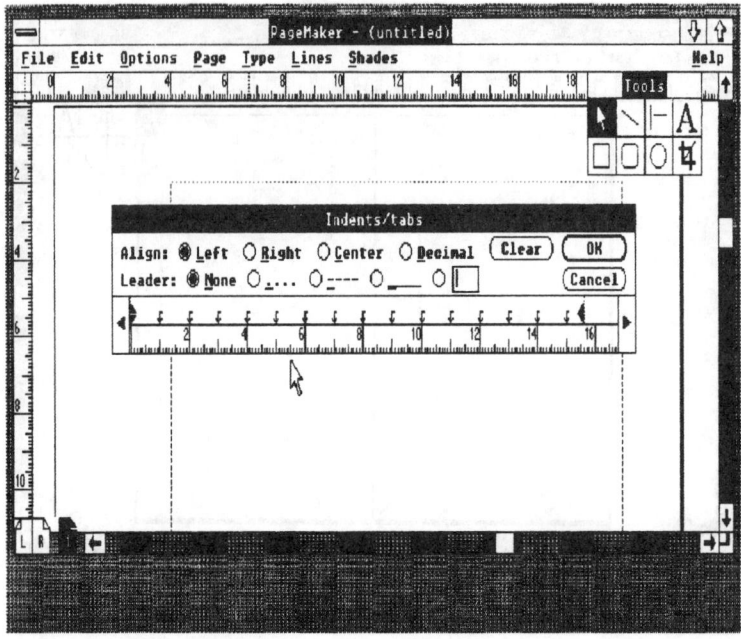

Figure 3.2 Defining tabs, the tabulation stops that allow specified columns to be reached by pressing the TAB key. This uses the Tabs/Indent menu, and tab stops are marked by the small arrows above the rule

margins can also be specified. The bottom margin of a book is normally fixed, but it is common practice for the top margin to be larger on the first page of each chapter – this can be done manually rather than auto-matically, but is often tackled by the use of master page settings or templates.

The left and right margin settings define the normal position of the text in the page, but other spacings may be called for by using tabs and indents. A tab, or *tabulation stop* is a fixed position on a page set with respect to the margin. For example, if tabs are set at each 10 characters, the first tab position will be 10 characters in from the left margin and the other tabs will be 10 characters from the previous tab. This allows tables to be printed with the assurance that text (or, more usually, numbers) will line up correctly, and a tab can also be used to indicate the start of a paragraph, Figure 3.2.

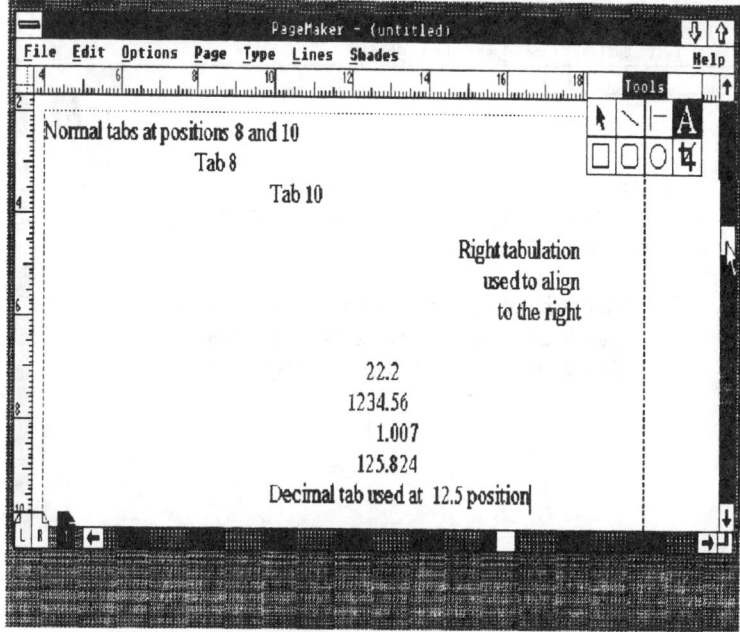

Figure 3.3   Right tabulation used for an address and decimal tabulation used to make figures line up on their decimal points

● If tabs are used for creating tables that contain text (other than head-ings), a monospaced type such as Courier should be used.

● If a proportionately spaced or kerned font is used in tables, text will not be perfectly aligned into columns, causing the appearance of the table to be poor.

● DTP programs should allow you to set tab stops at any position on a ruler line. Tabs are of four main types, plain, right, centre and decimal, of which the plain tab is as already described.

● The right tab allows text to be set so that its right margin is at the tab position – this is widely used in address positioning, Figure 3.3.

● Centre tabs allow text to be centred around the tab position, pro-viding that the text does not extend to another tab position.

● Decimal tabs allow numbers to be typed so that the decimal points will always occur at the tab position. This is particularly useful for numerical tables.

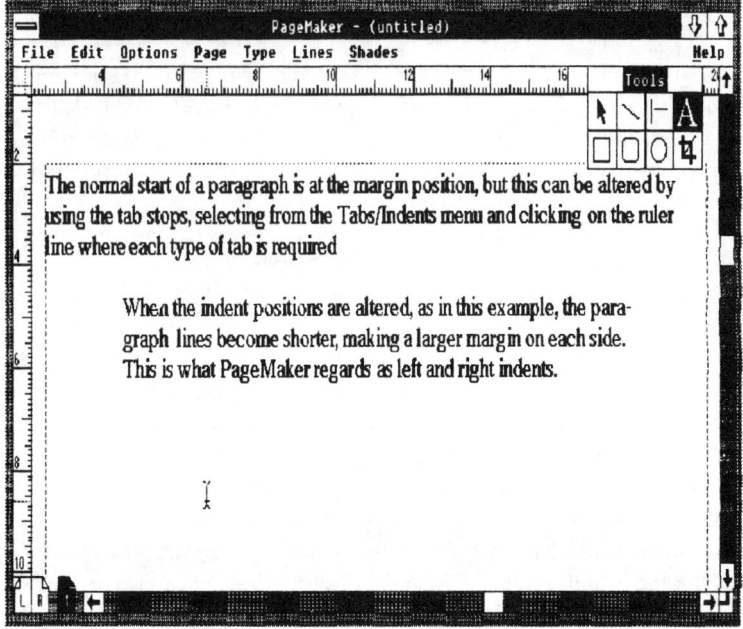

Figure 3.4   A paragraph indented at both margins – this is the PageMaker interpretation of left and right indents

● Most DTP programs allow only for plain tabs, not decimal, centre or right tabs.

The other variation of spacing is indentation. Indentation means that the whole of a paragraph or section is printed with a wider margin, often with both left and right margins increased. For some purposes, the indented section may be in another font or style so as further to emphasize the point that is being made in the section. Figure 3.4 shows an example of left and right margins being indented, and Figure 3.5 shows the effect of a *hanging* indent.

● Note that these effects of margins, tabs and indents are also available on word-processors, and some low-cost DTP programs do not allow these effects to be used on plain text. For such programs, the spacing effects should be put into place by a word-processor before the file is transferred to the DTP program.

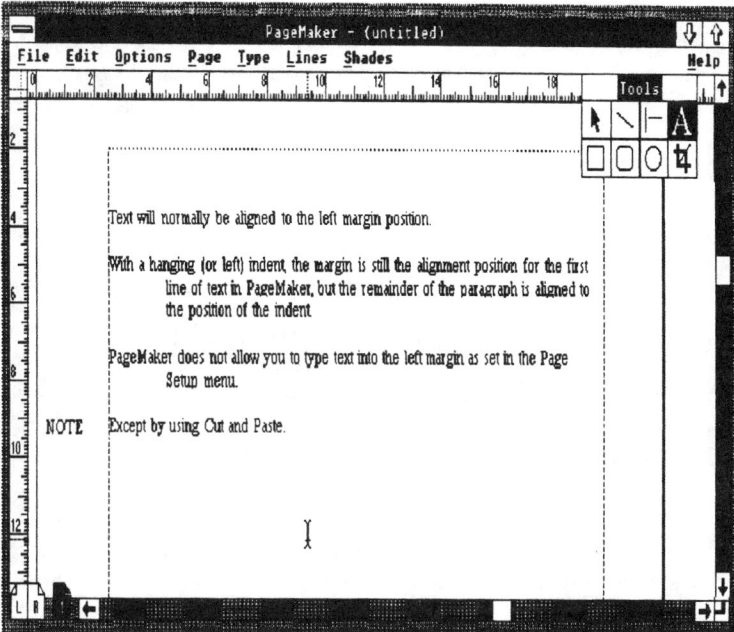

Figure 3.5   Using a hanging indent – this places the first line of a paragraph to the left of the rest of the paragraph. Using PageMaker, the page left-margin must be set to the position of the hanging indent

● An indentation to the right from the left margin position is called a positive indent. It is also possible to use an indentation to the left, making text start in the normal margin space. This is called a *negative* or *hanging* indent.

Justification, columns and gutters

Text that is laid between the set margins of a page need not necessarily take up the full space between margins on each line. In particular, typewriters produce text which is aligned at the left hand side but not at the right, and such text, Figure 3.6, is sometimes referred to as left-justified. Printed work is usually right–justified as well, meaning that each line is of the same length, Figure 3.7, and DTP programs refer to this as full justification, or

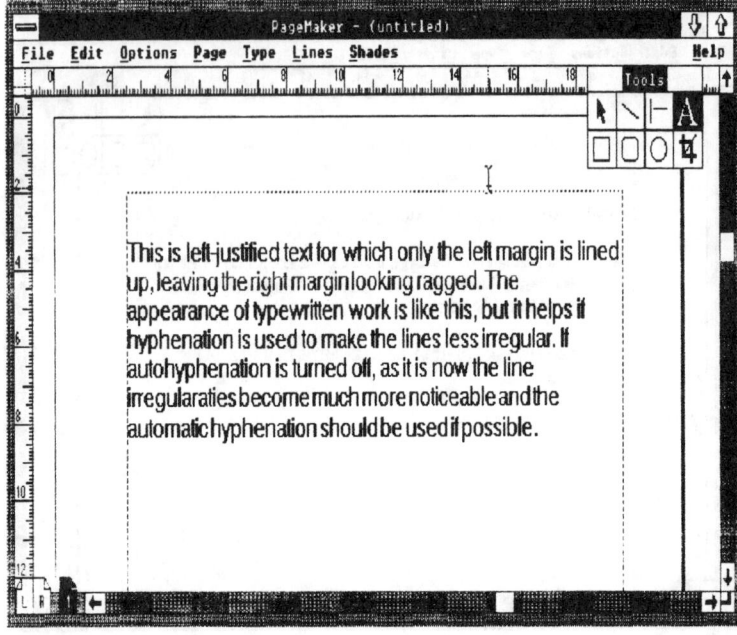

Figure 3.6   Left-justified text as produced by a typewriter. Only the left-hand side is aligned, leaving the right-hand side ragged. The lack of spell-checking is obvious

simply as justification. Justification is carried out automatically by word-processors and by DTP programs by altering the spacings between words on the line so that each line is of the same length.

Justification is applied only to lines of more than a fixed percentage, typically 80%, of the full width between margins. If this limit were not imposed, a final line of, perhaps, two words at the end of a paragraph would have the words spaced out to an unnatural extent, making the line difficult to read. By limiting the extent to which justification can be applied, the use of excessive spacing can be avoided except in narrow columns, see later.

● Justification should never be used on a printed manuscript that is being submitted for publication, because it makes word-counting more difficult.

Book publication normally uses pages containing only one column of

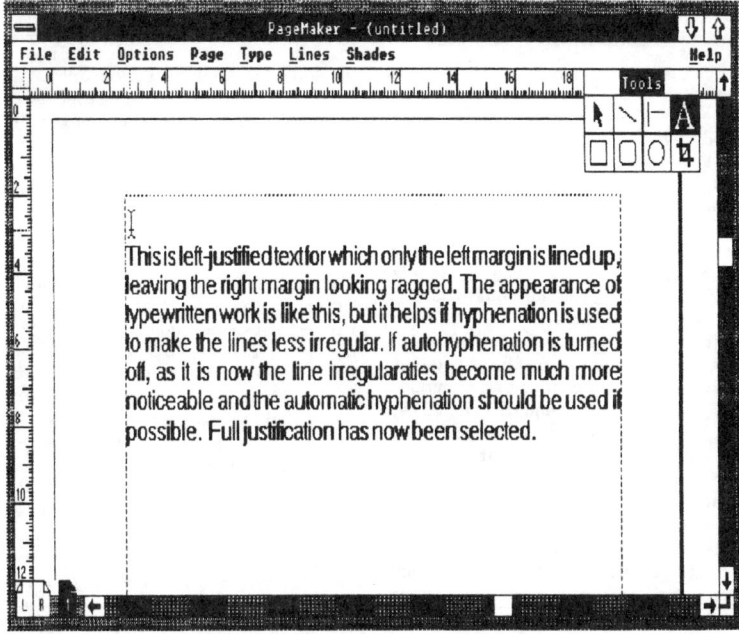

Figure 3.7 Justification (or full justification, right justification) lines up both the left and the right hand sides of the text. This is done by using additional spaces to pad out lines which would otherwise be shorter than the set length

print, and single-column work also applies to many other documents. By contrast, for newspaper work, print is always laid out in several columns running down the page. These columns are not necessarily of full-page height; it is very unusual to have a column of such a size, and the aim is to produce a rectangular block of text that can easily be scanned by the eye.

The space between the columns is called the *gutter*, and the size of the gutter is important as a way of making the division between the columns clear. Too large a gutter makes the columns look as if they are concerned with different pieces of text; too small a gutter makes the text difficult to read because the eye tends to stray from one column line to the next instead of down the column. Figure 3.8 shows text laid out with different gutter sizes.

Newspapers in general use columns with small widths, and this can cause difficulties with justification, sometimes to the extent that a long word may occupy a complete line (if the newspaper is one that uses long

Preface.
Desk-top Publishing is by this time well established, and there are many packages and books for both the large-scale user and the occasional dabbler. As it happens, a large percentage of applications for Desktop Publishing are for minor uses, often a single page or so, consisting of the contribution to the Church Newsletter, the Bob-a-job week leaflets, the menu for the small cafe or the hand-out advertising sheet for the ironmongers. At the other end of the scale, complete books are being produced using DTP at a fraction of the cost and, more importantly, with a fraction of the manpower and resources, of comparable material produced by the methods that were used previously. There are very few areas of printing and publishing that have not been affected by the change to DTP, and some aspects that have changed almost beyond recognition.

The purpose of this book is to introduce a typical modern DTP program for student use, illustrating the capabilities of DTP by using examples which can be applied to a wide range of applications. Since DTP is liable to be used by students whose subjects cover a wide range of disciplines, some care has been taken to avoid using, without explanation, terms that would be familiar to the student of typography. The advent of DTP makes any user to some extent a student of typography, as far as the traditional teachings of typogra-

phy can be said to have relevance nowadays. An important point that this book makers, however, is that DTP does not reduce typography to a set of rules. A well-trained eye for good print appearance is worth any amount of theory, as it always was.

One of the main problems about Desk-top Publishing is that it tends to present the user with a rich choice of styles and fonts, sizes and facilities, graphics and commands. The result of this can be printed work that confuses the eye and is difficult to read. The use of a simple dot-matrix printer rather than the expensive laser printer will always result in work that is rather less visually satisfactory, but if the user resists the temptation to try every special effect that is available, the results can be very satisfying. Though no book can ever teach the art of typography, the emphasis here is on good-looking results, even if this means that many users will never require more than a few of the huge number of facilities that programs such as Aldus Pagemaker can offer. In the course of this book, however, the full range of these possibilities is explored.

Many students who use this book will have had considerable experience with the PC type of computer, but some may not be well versed in the use of MS-DOS and directories. The initial pages are therefore aimed at the newcomer to the use of the PC-AT type of machine, illustration the installation of Aldus Pagemaker on to a typical AT 286 type of machine

(a)

Figure 3.8 Text laid into columns using different gutter sizes. (a) 5 mm (b) 10 mm (c) 15 mm

Preface.

Desk-top Publishing is by this time well established, and there are many packages and books for both the large-scale user and the occasional dabbler. As it happens, a large percentage of applications for Desktop Publishing are for minor uses, often a single page or so, consisting of the contribution to the Church Newsletter, the Bob-a-job week leaflets, the menu for the small cafe or the hand-out advertising sheet for the ironmongers. At the other end of the scale, complete books are being produced using DTP at a fraction of the cost and, more importantly, with a fraction of the manpower and resources, of comparable material produced by the methods that were used previously. There are very few areas of printing and publishing that have not been affected by the change to DTP, and some aspects that have changed almost beyond recognition.

The purpose of this book is to introduce a typical modern DTP program for student use, illustrating the capabilities of DTP by using examples which can be applied to a wide range of applications. Since DTP is liable to be used by students whose subjects cover a wide range of disciplines, some care has been taken to avoid using, without explanation, terms that would be familiar to the student of typography. The advent of DTP makes any user to some extent a student of typography, as far as the traditional teachings of typography can be said to have relevance nowadays. An important point that this book makers, however, is that DTP does not

Phowever, is that DTP does not reduce typography to a set of rules. A well-trained eye for good print appearance is worth any amount of theory, as it always was.

One of the main problems about Desk-top Publishing is that it tends to present the user with a rich choice of styles and fonts, sizes and facilities, graphics and commands. The result of this can be printed work that confuses the eye and is difficult to read. The use of a simple dot-matrix printer rather than the expensive laser printer will always result in work that is rather less visually satisfactory, but if the user resists the temptation to try every special effect that is available, the results can be very satisfying. Though no book can ever teach the art of typography, the emphasis here is on good-looking results, even if this means that many users will never require more than a few of the huge number of facilities that programs such as Aldus Pagemaker can offer. In the course of this book, however, the full range of these possibilities is explored.

Many students who use this book will have had considerable experience with the PC type of computer, but some may not be well versed in the use of MS-DOS and directories. The initial pages are therefore aimed at the newcomer to the use of the PC-AT type of machine, illustration the installation of Aldus Pagemaker on to a typical AT 286 type of machine

(b)

Preface.

Desk-top Publishing is by this time well established, and there are many packages and books for both the large-scale user and the occasional dabbler. As it happens, a large percentage of applications for Desktop Publishing are for minor uses, often a single page or so, consisting of the contribution to the Church Newsletter, the Bob-a-job week leaflets, the menu for the small cafe or the hand-out advertising sheet for the ironmongers. At the other end of the scale, complete books are being produced using DTP at a fraction of the cost and, more importantly, with a fraction of the manpower and resources, of comparable material produced by the methods that were used previously. There are very few areas of printing and publishing that have not been affected by the change to DTP, and some aspects that have changed almost beyond recognition.

The purpose of this book is to introduce a typical modern DTP program for student use, illustrating the capabilities of DTP by using examples which can be applied to a wide range of applications. Since DTP is liable to be used by students whose subjects cover a wide range of disciplines, some care has been taken to avoid using, without explanation, terms that would be familiar to the student of typography. The advent of DTP makes any user to some extent a student of typography, as far as the traditional teachings of typography can be said to have relevance nowadays. An important

Phowever, is that DTP does not reduce typography to a set of rules. A well-trained eye for good print appearance is worth any amount of theory, as it always was.

One of the main problems about Desk-top Publishing is that it tends to present the user with a rich choice of styles and fonts, sizes and facilities, graphics and commands. The result of this can be printed work that confuses the eye and is difficult to read. The use of a simple dot-matrix printer rather than the expensive laser printer will always result in work that is rather less visually satisfactory, but if the user resists the temptation to try every special effect that is available, the results can be very satisfying. Though no book can ever teach the art of typography, the emphasis here is on good-looking results, even if this means that many users will never require more than a few of the huge number of facilities that programs such as Aldus Pagemaker can offer. In the course of this book, however, the full range of these possibilities is explored.

Many students who use this book will have had considerable experience with the PC type of computer, but some may not be well versed in the use of MS-DOS and directories. The initial pages are therefore aimed at the newcomer to the use of the PC-AT type of machine, illustration the installation of Aldus Pagemaker on to a typical AT 286 type of machine

(c)

The appearance of text is not simply a matter of calculation or formulae but of using your typographical judgement in design and layout. . The advantage of DTP is ease of making structural changes on the screen, rather than on type itself.

(a)

The appearance of text is not simply a matter of calculation or formulae but of using your typographical judgement in design and layout. The advantage of DTP is ease of making structural changes on the screen, rather than on type itself.

(b)

Figure 3.9   A short paragraph (a) which has been typed with the automatic hyphenation turned off. Altering the line length (b) can allow some manual hyphenation

words). To some extent, this can be overcome by using hyphens to split up words, and both word-processing and DTP programs will hyphenate either automatically, or with reference to the user.

When fully-automatic hyphenation is used, the results can often be difficult to read, particularly when practically every line contains a word that is carried over to the next line. When hyphenation is not fully automatic, the effect of each hyphenation is shown on screen and the user is asked to confirm or reject the hyphenation. Rejecting hyphenation will mean that the complete word will be carried over to the following line and the subsequent justification of the line may create excessive spacing in the line that has lost the word.

Take a look at Figure 3.9, which illustrates what is meant. The short paragraph in (a) has used the word 'typographical', which is taken over to the next line as you type it. Structural is also treated in the same way. Now you could have inserted hyphenation at the time of typing, deleting back as soon as you saw the part-word 'typogr' move to the next line. You could then type **typo-** and space until the next line was taken, and then continue with the remainder of the word. It's more likely, however, that you will be concentrating on the typing rather than the line appearance at this point.

In example (b), the line length has been increased very slightly, because this allows the whole of the word 'structural' to be brought back. At the same time, 'typographical' has been split. This has been done by inserting the hyphen, and then a space, making the word into 'typo-graphical', and then placing the cursor on to the first letter and deleting backwards, so that the 'typo-' part moves to the line above. You will have to make sure that there is a space between the words 'default' and 'typo-'. This work can be carried out manually, using the delete and the back-space keys, or it can be

The appearance of text is not simply a matter of calculation or formulae but of using your typographical judgement in design and layout. The advantage of DTP is ease of making structural
changes on the screen, rather than on type itself.

Figure 3.10   The use of full justification along with hyphenation

done using a command which will re-align the text. If you have a lot of
such changes to carry out, the use of Realign text is much easier, but you
still have to check back to make sure that the changes have been carried
out as you would want them.

Once the lines have been adjusted, with hyphenation inserted in this
way, you can apply full justification. This, however, may make the words
in the last line space out badly, in an ugly way, unless the DTP program
provides for a minimum length of line to justify (often 80% of maximum
line size). The result of making adjustments is shown in Figure 3.10. Even
this would offend some typographers, who feel that the hyphen should
not count as part of a line, and would take the word 'Structural' left by one
space or place 'typo-' one space to the right. This is, as so often happens, a
matter of taste, and it's *your* taste that counts.

Questions

1 A header is text which is placed in:
   (a) the left margin
   (b) the right margin
   (c) the bottom margin
   (d) the top margin.
2 Tab stops are used for several actions, including (pick more than 1):
   (a) indenting the first line of a paragraph
   (b) indenting the whole of a paragraph
   (c) making a hanging indent
   (d) typing work into columns
3 The space between vertical columns is called the:
   (a) indent
   (b) gutter
   (c) hanging indent
   (d) drain
4 Justified (or fully justified) text has:
   (a) a ragged left edge
   (b) a ragged right edge

(c) all lines other than a last line of equal length
(d) the same number of characters in each line

Master page and style sheet use

In a book, virtually all of the text takes one of two main page layouts, one for an odd-numbered page and another for an even-numbered page – in some cases the formats may be identical other than for page numbers. Where the normal division into chapters is used, however, a different layout will be used for a page that contains the start of the chapter, with the chapter number and title placed very prominently. Typical methods include:

● placing both chapter number and title in large bold print
● using a large top margin
● boxing in the chapter title
● incorporating a graphic into the title

Whatever the differences, DTP programs cater for them by using the device of master pages; a method that is used also in many word-processors.

Some texts confuse master pages with style sheets, and on some word-processors the name style sheet is used for very much the same purposes as a master page. In this book, however, the two terms will be separated and used as they are defined in Aldus PageMaker. A master page defines the margins, headers and footer of each page of a document; a style sheet defines the fonts that will be used for the text.

The essence of a master page is that a framework or template page is created, with the margins, header, footer and other page features set but without text. When a master page is selected, typing or importing (from a file) text will result in that text taking on the layout which has been determined by the template of the master page. Suppose, for example, that a book page contains the page number and chapter heading at the top, with a line and a space separating this from the main text. On a left-hand (even numbered) page this page number and chapter heading will be to the left; and on a right-hand (odd-numbered) page the number and heading will be to the right. Assuming that there are no other differences (same margins to left and to right), then two master pages will be needed, one for each layout.

If you then feed imported text into the first page, you will select the master page for an odd number (page 1), which will have its heading and page appropriately placed, and feed in the text until the page is full. The master is then changed to the even number type and the text is fed in until this page, in turn is full. On some DTP programs, once the masters with their heading and initial page number have been created, this process is automatic, and a full chapter of text will be correctly allocated to the pages.

For a new chapter, a third master page is used. This will contain the layout for chapter number and heading, containing whatever style of heading is being used and with space underneath for text. The words of the heading and the chapter number may be fed in automatically from a word-processor file, or they may be typed directly into the DTP program. The text will be fed in using the normal text font, and if the master page has been correctly created, this text will be put into the correct position under the heading and in the correct font. The new chapter can then use the master pages for left and right pages, with only the heading titles and page number varied as compared to the previous chapter.

The printing of a book is an example of the repeated use of only a small number of master pages, but it would be normal to keep a large stock of master pages in the DTP files. Typical examples might include:

- letter templates on A4 and on A5, possibly with a company logo on the first sheet of a letter
- templates for legal documents, such as conveyancing deeds
- memoranda
- reports
- quotations
- invoices

all of which require a different set format, with only part of the text supplied each time the master page is used.

Many word-processors use this technique under the name of style sheets, and DTP programs can often import text from a word-processed document *together with the style sheet template*. This is by no means universal, and Microsoft Word is often the only word-processor software whose documents can be used directly by a DTP program complete with its style-sheet formats. Most DTP programs allow a restricted number of formatting items such as line spacings, paragraph spacings, use of tabs and indents, to be imported along with documents from some types of word-processors. In general, the more use a word-processor makes of style sheets and fonts the more likely it is that its template information can be imported by the DTP program.

The style sheet, as PageMaker uses it, is a small menu of font descriptions. One font will be specified for the body text, one for a main heading, one for a subheading, one for a caption and so on. Each of these specifications can be quite elaborate, and can take some time to complete, but when a style sheet is used each specification need be done only once. All you need to do once the text has been imported is to specify a piece of text as a heading, body text, caption, or whatever it happens to be, and the correct font and size settings as defined in the style sheet will be applied.

This ensures uniformity in the course of a long document, and makes sure that no errors arise due to mistaken selections from menus. It also ensures that a uniform style is applied to other documents, and allows document templates (skeleton documents) to be held with all of the style sheet ready created. Using such a document is very simple, because the style sheet ensures that the correct fonts and sizes are always used in the right places.

Page display

Subject to the limitations of the screen display, the DTP program will show the page either in full or in part, and you can opt for whichever view is convenient for your uses. When text is being fed in (imported) from a file that has been produced by a word-processor, the best view is of the whole page because this view shows the arrangement of the text and in particular the arrangement of text around any graphics (see later, this chapter). The effects of margins, tabs and indents can also be seen, and if closer examination is needed one of the more magnified views can be used. In general, once the master pages are known to be correct, close examination is seldom needed other than to inspect graphics.

PageMaker allows two facing pages to be displayed on the screen, a very valuable method of showing how text will appear in book form where there are differences between odd and even numbered pages, or for documents that are printed on both sides of a page. When a DTP program does not permit this type of display it will be necessary to check at least one of each type of page.

The display of pages so as to show layout makes it impossible, unless very large typesizes are in use, to show the text. DTP programs overcome this difficulty, caused by the limitations of the screen display, by *greeking* the text, using shapes that suggest the appearance of the text and whose

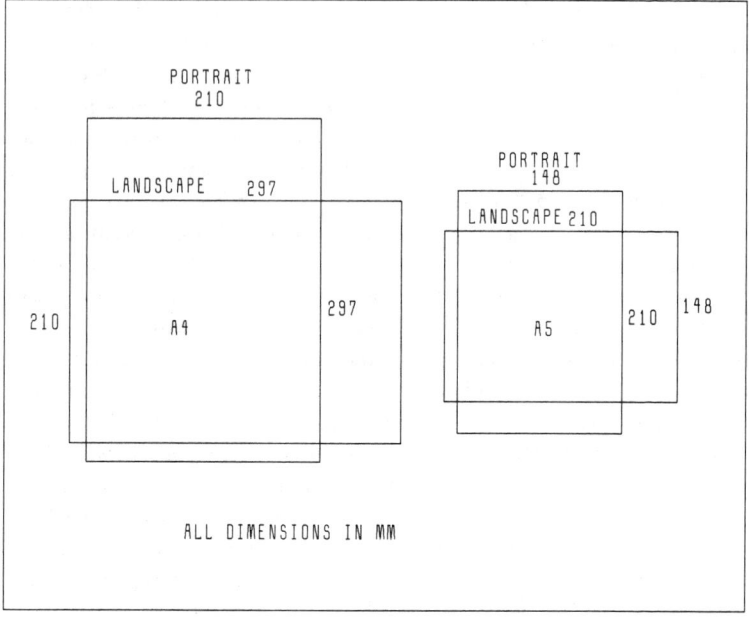

Figure 3.11 Landscape and portrait orientation. Pages are never square, and portrait orientation is much more common

spacing and layout faithfully reflect the text that has been placed in the page(s).

Pages can be planned and printed with either landscape (wide) or portrait (tall) orientation, Figure 3.11. Portrait orientation is by far the more commonly used, though it sometimes requires graphics to be inserted in landscape form so that the book has to be turned through 90° to view the illustration. Landscape orientation is used for books that contain several large graphics, or which require wide tables to be printed. For smaller documents, portrait orientation is used almost exclusively with A4 and A5 sheets unless special requirements, mainly for wide tabular work, require otherwise. Figure 3.12 shows the area left available for printing on A4 and A5 sheets in both orientations, assuming the default margins of Aldus PageMaker.

78

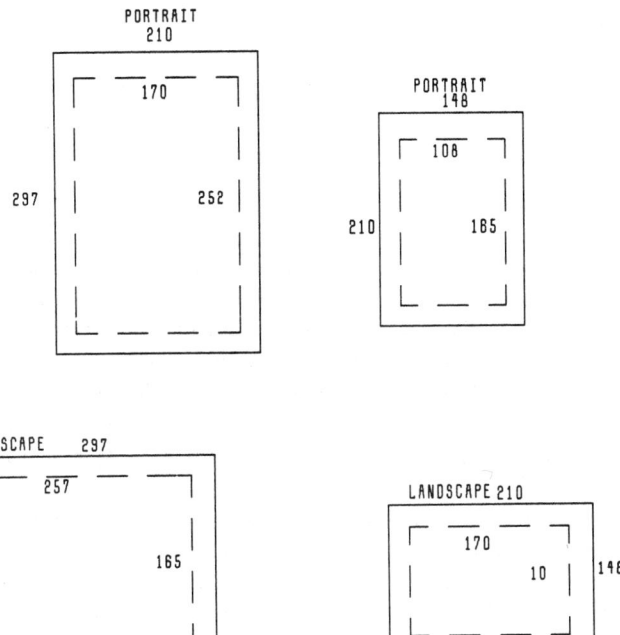

ALL DIMENSIONS IN MM

Figure 3.12   The page sizes left in A4 and in A5 pages for either orientation, if the default margins of PageMaker are used

---

Activity
Draw up on paper what you would expect to use in a master page for:
(a) a book on DTP (b) a letter from a firm of solicitors (c) a leaflet from an estate agent

---

Questions

5 A master page would *never* include:
   (a) a book title
   (b) a page of text

   (c) a page number
   (d) a chapter title
6 A style sheet contains details of:
   (a) header and footer
   (b) page number
   (c) number of lines per page
   (d) fonts and sizes
7 Greeking is:
   (a) reducing the space between characters
   (b) representing characters by small symbols
   (c) making lines of equal length
   (d) reducing the size of a graphic

Using ASCII files

The ASCII form of file, named after the American Standards Committee for Information Interchange, consists of text in which a number in the range 32 to 127 has been used to represent each character of the alphabet, the digits 0 to 9 and the common punctuation marks. The code numbers that are allocated to the lower case characters a–z are 32 more than the codes used for the upper case characters A–Z – for example,' **A**' is represented by the code number 65 and '**a**' by the number 97. The origins of ASCII code in the USA are evident when the codes are printed, Figure 3.13, because there is no code for the £ sign, though the $ and # (hash) signs are represented.

ASCII code of this range is sometimes termed 7-bit ASCII, because it uses only 7 of the bits in each byte, leaving the eighth bit free to be used (often for error checking, using a method called parity). The codes 1 to 31 are used for special purposes, with one (code 27) assigned to the Esc key and the others used for key combinations such as Ctrl-A, Ctrl-B and so on. These Ctrl code numbers are extensively used in word-processors to carry information on margin sizes, bold print, italics, superscript and subscript, fonts, etc.

Several computer manufacturers have extended the ASCII code, using the 'spare' numbers 128 to 255 for characters which could not be catered for in the original set. None of these enhancements is fully standardized, but the set used by IBM in its personal computers, and used also in the multitude of 'clone' computers, is as close to a standard as is ever likely in a fast-developing business. The IBM extension to ASCII code is widely

32		33	!	34	"	35	#
36	$	37	%	38	&	39	'
40	(	41	)	42	*	43	+
44	,	45	–	46	.	47	/
48	0	49	1	50	2	51	3
52	4	53	5	54	6	55	7
56	8	57	9	58	:	59	;
60	<	61	=	62	>	63	?
64	@	65	A	66	B	67	C
68	D	69	E	70	F	71	G
72	H	73	I	74	J	75	K
76	L	77	M	78	N	79	O
80	P	81	Q	82	R	83	S
84	T	85	U	86	V	87	W
88	X	89	Y	90	Z	91	[
92	\	93	]	94	^	95	_
96	`	97	a	98	b	99	c
100	d	101	e	102	f	103	g
104	h	105	i	106	j	107	k
108	l	109	m	110	n	111	o
112	p	113	q	114	r	115	s
116	t	117	u	118	v	119	w
120	x	121	y	122	z	123	{
124	¦	125	}	126	~	127	■

Figure 3.13   The standard ASCII codes, using numbers 32 to 127. An unofficial but widely adopted set also uses numbers 128 to 255. Numbers below 32 represent control codes and are not printed

used by computer printers and also by word-processors and DTP programs, so that it is unusual nowadays to find a program which does not allow the £ sign to be printed and displayed on the screen, though some effort may be needed to achieve this. Some DTP programs which do not exist in an 'English English' version may need the symbol to be created and added to each font.

Simple ASCII text implies that only the codes 32 to 127 will be used in a file, and this type of text is readable by virtually any type of program that can use text; not only DTP programs, but word-processors, spreadsheets and database programs. The advantage of using simple ASCII text is that it will contain no Ctrl codes or (usually) codes in the 128–255 range. This ensures that when such codes are fed into a DTP program or sent to a printer no unwanted effects will be caused. Such effects might include switching to bold type, changing font or size, printing a blank sheet, changing tab sizes and so on; all caused by the effect of Ctrl codes on the DTP program or the printer.

Straightforward ASCII text, however, has several drawbacks:

- it cannot include other symbols like the £ sign
- the spacing between words is usually fixed
- tabs and indents are represented by spaces
- no accented letters such as é and ä, or signs like £ or ¥ can be used

– all of which means that a considerable amount of work may have to be done on ASCII text after it has been imported into a DTP page. The spacing may have to be changed, the tabs and indents reset, and any style effects such as underlining, italics, bold print, etc. will have to be redone using the facilities of the DTP program.

All word-processors can produce ASCII text (WordStar refers to such text as 'non-document' text, implying that it would be used mainly in writing computer programs), but the more useful form of output for most purposes is the natural formatted text of the word-processor. This contains in addition to the ASCII codes a set of control codes, using the number range 1 to 31, and most word-processors for the PC type of machine also make use of characters in the range 128 to 255 so that the accented letters, Greek alphabet, and some box graphics characters can be used.

A file that contains control codes can carry information on tabs, indents, bold type, italics and underlines, subscripts and superscripts, allowing the text to be printed with all of these effects, unlike ASCII text. DTP programs can read text from a limited number of word-processors and convert the control codes of the word-processor into the appropriate control codes for the DTP program, so that much less work needs to be carried out on the document after it has been imported into the DTP page. The bold, underline and strikethrough codes of most word-processor files can be imported by PageMaker, along with subscripts and superscripts, but the transfer of codes for different type faces and sizes is available only for a select number of word-processors such as Microsoft Word and Windows Write.

- An important point to watch is the name of the imported file. A file name consists of a main name of up to 8 characters, followed by an optional extension of up to 3 characters. The extension is separated from the main name by a dot.
- PageMaker, like many other DTP programs, will recognize files from word-processors only if their extension letters are of a particular pattern. For example, WordStar files must use the extension WS, Microsoft Word should use DOC and WordPerfect should use WP.
- If these extensions are not in use, the filename should be changed − see a text of MS-DOS for changing filename on PC machines.
- If files are being transferred from one machine to another along serial cables (including telephone lines) characters other than the ASCII range may be omitted or changed − suitable software must be used if these characters are to be preserved.

Questions

8 If a DTP program requires ASCII text to be imported, which of the following statements is definitely NOT valid:
   (a) The DTP program cannot deal with codes in the range 32 to 127
   (b) The DTP program cannot deal with codes in the range 128 to 255
   (c) The DTP program cannot deal with codes in the range 1 to 31
   (d) The DTP program cannot deal with codes in the range 1 to 255
9 A file which uses WordStar codes is imported into a DTP package using the filename CHAP1.DOC. This proves troublesome because:
   (a) A file called CHAP1 cannot be used; it contains a number
   (b) It uses the extension DOC instead of WS
   (c) No DTP package can import a WordStar file
   (d) Files can only be exported from the DTP package
10 Control (Ctrl) codes are used to:
   (a) define word spacings
   (b) define the formatting of text
   (c) define fonts and sizes of print
   (d) define printer action only

Activity

Prepare two files of identical paragraphs of text, one recorded in a word-processor or DTP format; the other using simple ASCII codes. Name these as TEST.WP and TEST.ASC respectively. Print them by using the DOS command (with no other programs running):

COPY TEST.WP PRN   and   COPY TEST.ASC PRN

and note the difference in the printouts that are produced. What has caused these differences?

Graphics

One of the main differences between DTP and simple word-processing is the provision in all DTP programs for the incorporation of graphics images into text. This can be done in two main ways, assuming that the graphics image is in the form of a file that the DTP program can read.

- The graphics image can be placed onto a blank page, and the text then added. The text will automatically be wrapped round the image so that the image does not hide any text, nor the text hide any of the image.
- An outline frame can be put into a page that contains text, with the text moved to make way for the frame. The graphics image is then placed into the frame.

Designing a page that contains an illustration starts by making a rough sketch, Figure 3.14. This need not be more than an outline, and any text that is to form part of the graphic can be greeked – the main object is to show the *layout* of the graphic as one would show the layout of a complete page. Even if the graphic already exists, it is always helpful to make a sketch of this type to show the scale of the graphic on the page, because if you are to find that the scale is wrong this is the stage at which the discovery should be made, not when the final graphic image is being fitted into the page.

Experience is the main guide to this part of the design process, and it helps considerably to analyse the illustrations in other existing documents, such as public announcement documents, newspapers and magazines, illustrations and text in advertisements, book covers and technical manuals. The style and format of these mixtures of graphics and text will

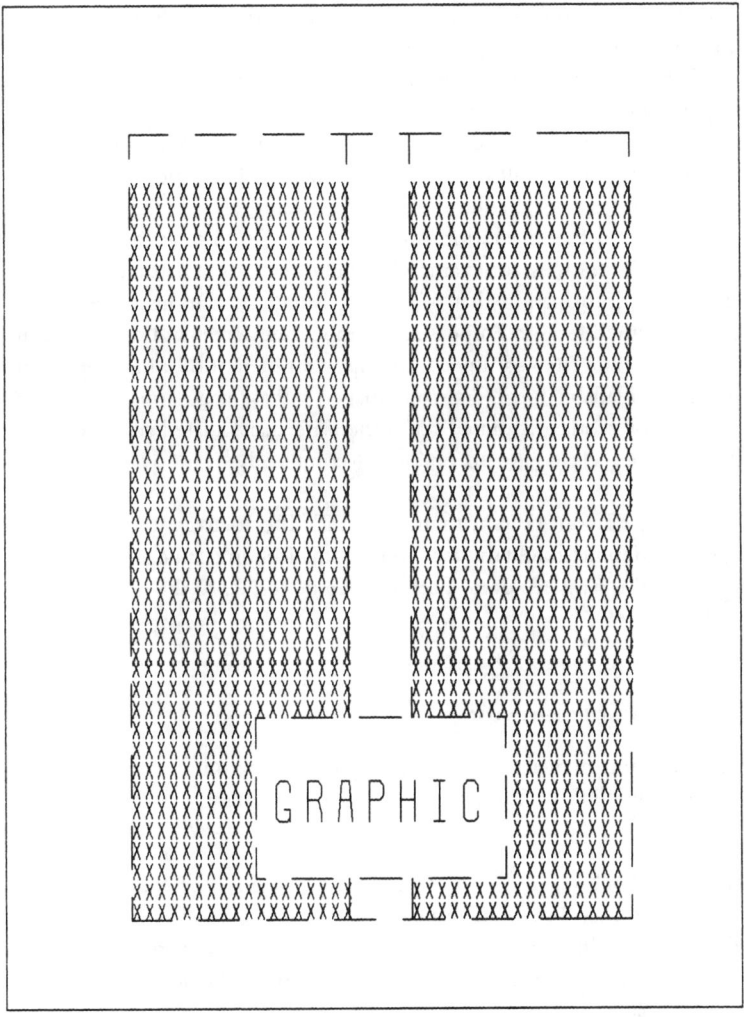

Figure 3.14   An outline sketch for a page that will contain a graphic

all be quite different, but the basis of their design is always that the balance of text and graphic should be visually attractive if possible and at the least, visually bearable.

Common errors are to make the illustration either much too large, leaving only a couple of lines of text on the page, or too small, so that detail

85

is totally lost. In some technical work, an illustration must sometimes take the whole of the page, landscape oriented, in order to be readable. It would be a serious error to shrink such a drawing down to fit into half of a page in portrait orientation simply because this made the balance of text and graphic look good, because in such a case the drawing may carry as much information as all the text of the chapter that contains it.

Even if the size of the illustration is reasonable, about 1/3 to 2/3 of the page area, and the illustration is clear, it may be possible to improve it. Very few illustrations, for example, and photographs in particular, contain exactly the information that is needed. Many illustrations benefit from being trimmed so as to emphasize an important detail, and some need to be enlarged and then trimmed. An important benefit of using graphics in computer-readable form (digitized images) is that images can be trimmed, enlarged or reduced, rotated and otherwise manipulated so as to make their message clearer (or to obscure it completely, if the work is poorly done).

Making a layout sketch, then, is intended to focus your attention on what the graphic should show as well as how it should appear on the page, and once this has been done attention can be turned to the graphic image itself.

Bit-map and line-vector

The two fundamental forms of creating images in computer file form are bit-map and line-vector images, as noted in Chapter 2. The bit-map image:

● consists of a set of dots of equal size, either black or white (coloured dots are used in colour displays)
● cannot readily be scaled up or down without loss of resolution
● cannot show a resolution better than that of the device which created the image
● can be pixel edited to change details or tidy up a 'rough' image
● is obtained from scanners or from 'paint' software packages

The main use of bit-map images is in connection with clip-art and scanned images. Clip-art consists of ready-made images which have been created by artists or by using scanners, and which are often of high resolution. Editing of these images requires the use of a software package which displays only a small part of the image on the whole screen, as if the whole image were much larger than the screen (which it is). Suppose, for example, that a bit image is obtained by scanning a $3''\times3''$ area at a resolution of 300 dots per inch. This gives an image of 900×900 pixels, whereas a high-resolution screen may allow only 800×600 pixels (luminous dots). At any one time, the screen can show at most 8/9 of the width and 2/3 of the height of the picture, though most software packages allow the equivalent of a greeked view to see the proportions of a complete image.

By contrast, if the same image is printed on a laser printer with a resolution of 300 dots per inch, the image should be of its original size of $3''\times3''$. This very different size of the printed image as compared to the screen image makes it difficult to work with graphics until you have had experience of manipulating graphics on screen and on paper. It is particularly difficult to create drawings on the screen because unless these drawings are to look ridiculously small on paper they have to be created to a very large scale on the screen. Not all paint packages, however, allow easy creation of a drawing that takes up more than one screen, and the use of the scanner is a very much better approach.

The alternative method is to use line vector drawings. These are created by programs of the CAD (computer-aided design) type, of which AutoCAD and Generic CAD are well-known examples. These programs work with mathematical descriptions of lines, and such descriptions can be scaled to any dimensions – the resolution of the drawing depends only on the resolution of the display device, so that a drawing which looks of low resolution on a screen can still be of very high resolution on a print-out, particularly using a printer which allows resolutions of 2400 dots per inch rather than the 300 dots per inch of a laser printer. Such drawings:

- can be scaled to any required extent
- maintain high resolution
- can be edited only in the original software package
- can be converted to bit map form
- cannot be pixel edited in their vector form

Line vector drawings are fairly uncommon in DTP work, but they can be important in the production of material which uses technical drawings. By using vector methods, line drawings can be produced that can be scaled to any required extent, and even drawings made with a simple dot-matrix printer can be of excellent quality. If the vector drawings can be converted into PostScript files, they can be imported into DTP packages and will be printed with all the advantages of vector drawings, allowing any scaling to be done with no loss of resolution.

Questions

11 The first step in incorporating a graphic into a publication should be:
(a) to decide the size
(b) to make a vector drawing
(c) to make a pixel drawing
(d) to make an outline sketch.

12 A bit-map image:
(a) is always of high resolution
(b) can be pixel edited
(c) can be scaled to any extent without loss of resolution
(d) is obtained from CAD packages.

Pixel editing

Pixel editing, as used with a graphics package, allows individual dots of a picture, or groups of dots, to be edited by changing the colour of a selected dot, one dot at a time. Since DTP work is largely concerned with mono-chrome (colour images are produced from a set of three monochrome images), the editing consists of either changing a black dot to a white one or a white dot to a black one. The dots are selected by magnifying a portion of an image.

Figure 3.15 shows an image as it appears being edited by the De-Luxe Paint II package running on a PC/AT machine. Like all scanned images, this has jagged edges, and the drawing can be considerably improved by pixel editing. In addition, the use of a drawing package allows captions to be added along with arrows to point out features of the illustration.

Pixel editing with this particular package makes use of the 'side-tool' in the form of the magnifying-glass. These side-tools are located in the small boxes at the right hand side of the picture, and each box carries an image (icon) which serves as a reminder of the action. The magnifying-glass icon lies next to the hand icon which is used to move the picture around on the screen.

When the cursor is moved with the mouse and placed on the mag-nifying-glass icon, clicking the left-hand mouse button inverts the colour of the icon to confirm its selection, and when the mouse is moved, a

? Picture Brush Techniques Stencil Font Misc. Preferences

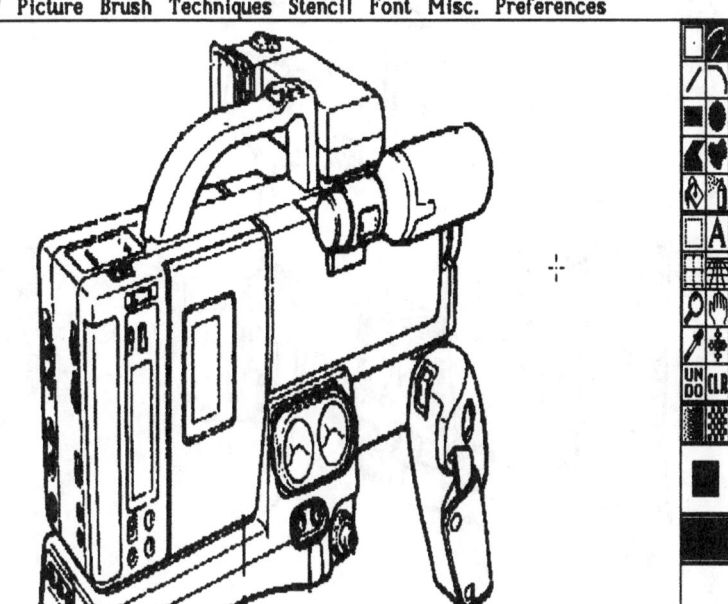

Figure 3.15   A bit-map image as seen about to be pixel-edited by De-Luxe Paint II

rectangular box will move around the screen, controlled by the mouse. This is the magnifying section, Figure 3.16 and when this box is placed over a part of the picture and the left-hand mouse button clicked an enlarged view, Figure 3.17, is seen. This is the pixel-editing view.

Pixel editing then consists of adding or removing the square or rectangular pixels. The precise shape of pixels depends on the type of graphics card that the computer uses, and a rectangle is more common than a square, with the vertical dimension longer than the horizontal dimension. The methods of pixel editing vary. On the Paint-II package, clicking the left-hand mouse button when the cursor is over a pixel will put a pixel in place; the cursor is itself pixel shaped to show the effect. To remove a pixel, the cursor is placed over the pixel and the right-hand mouse button is clicked. A particular advantage of this package is that a line can be cleaned up by specifying the line drawing tool but with a pixel erasing action, so that a jagged line can be made straight.

Other drawing or DTP packages adopt different methods. Some

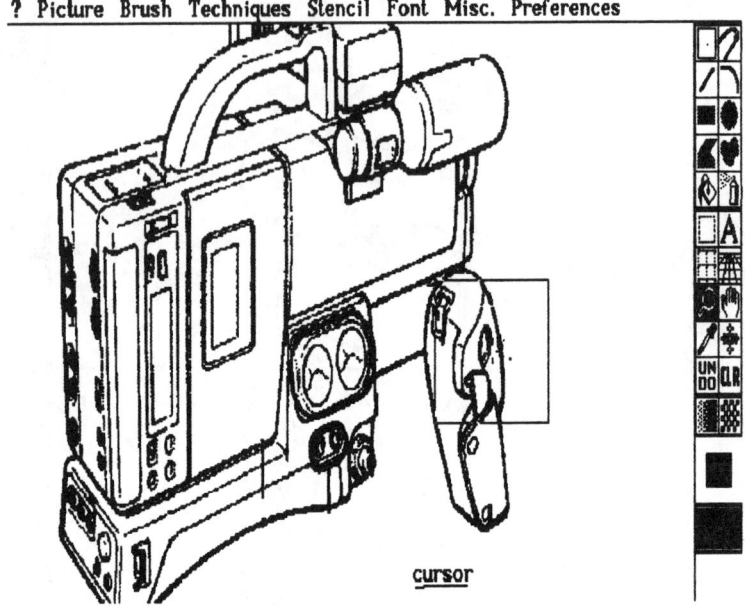

Figure 3.16   The magnifying section placed over a piece of the image

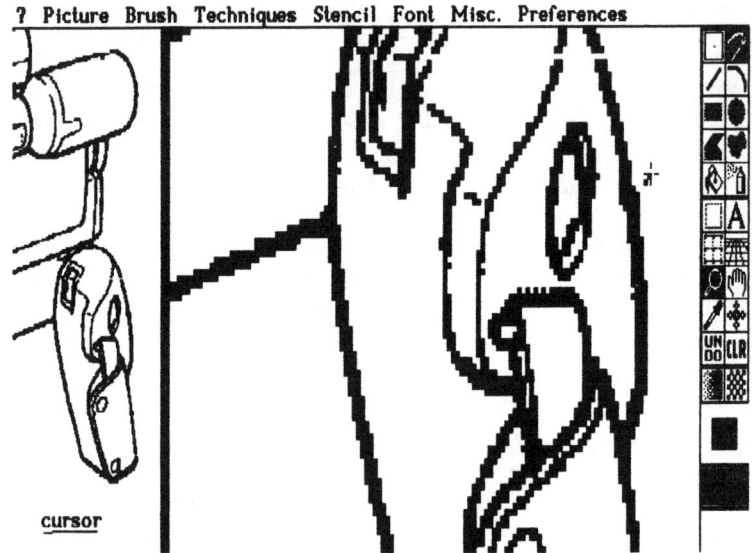

Figure 3.17   The enlarged view – note that the view of the whole image is still seen in miniature form

require a different icon to be used for erasing pixels, so that erasing a pixel requires you to select an eraser icon while you are operating with the magnifier in use. This is tedious if you have to switch frequently between adding pixels and removing pixels, but it can be convenient when a large number of pixels have to be removed. Most packages allow the mouse to be dragged over a set of pixels, either adding or erasing pixels according to the settings used; some packages allow drawing techniques to be used in the pixel editing mode so that drawing or erasure of pixels can follow perfectly straight lines or circles. Another common method for controlling pixel editing is to use one mouse button only. If the cursor is not over a pixel when the mouse button is pressed, a pixel will be coloured. If the cursor is over a pixel, that pixel will be erased. This can be extended to mouse dragging, allowing all pixel editing to be done with one mouse button alone.

While pixel editing is being used on the magnified section of the drawing, the remainder of the screen shows the non-magnified view of the portion that is being edited. This allows you to see the effect on the normal scale and is particularly valuable when the magnified view shows part of a curve in which pixels are missing. Being able to see the overall view allows the missing pixels to be replaced in more or less their correct positions, something that can be remarkably difficult on a magnified view alone.

Some packages, of which De-Luxe Paint II is one, allow several magnifications to be used – typically from $2 \times$ to $16 \times$, so that touching up the image can be done in as much detail as is required. The $2 \times$ magnification is ideal for an overall view of quite a large area of the image, and is good for confirming the effects of work, or for making alterations to a large part of an outline. The $16 \times$ magnification is excellent for working with fine detail and should be used if the drawing is to be reproduced at high resolution.

When a pixel image is to be edited, any size adjustments should be made first. It is always an advantage to create and work on a pixel image that is as large as the software can handle, because the aim will normally be to print the image on a much reduced scale. A pixel image reproduced at screen size would be unacceptably coarse and it is only by using a laser printer set for 300 dots per inch and printing each pixel as a dot that acceptable results can be achieved. The main problems of this method arise when the screen pixels are not square, so that the picture as seen on the screen is not identical to the picture as seen on the paper. Some software will allow the printer to make pixels of the same shape as those on the screen, but for graphics work it is preferable to use a graphics display which uses square or circular pixels to correspond better with the printed shapes. Another option which exists on most DTP and paint packages is to allow each rectangular pixel on the screen to be converted to a square pixel on the printer. This makes the printed version of a drawing possess a different vertical scale (squashed as compared to the screen version) but is often the best way of ensuring an acceptable image. To summarize, pixel editing is used:

● to clean up an image that has been scanned and which looks rough
● to reduce the line thickness on a pixel image which has been reduced in size, by removing pixels along each line
● to touch up an image which has been distorted
● to insert missing pixels into an image that has been magnified (which separates out the original pixels).

Activity
Use a paint type of package to work on an image, such as a scanned image, that is already in file form. Improve the image by pixel editing, save it as a disk file, and print it. Can the file be saved in TIF or PCX format?

Questions

13 Pixel editing can
  (a) make a vector file into a bit-map file
  (b) make a bit-map file into a vector file
  (c) repair flaws in a bit-map image
  (d) repair flaws in a vector image
14 A full-screen image uses 640 × 400 pixels. What size will this become when printed at 300 dots per inch?
  (a) 340″ × 100″
  (b) 1.92″ × 1.20″
  (c) 9.4″ × 7″
  (d) 2.13″ × 1.33″

Assignment 3

Investigate the use of a graphics package of the bit-image type, such as De-luxe Paint or PC Paintbrush. Draw some geometrical patterns and then try to draw a simple picture (desk, VDU, yacht, etc.) using the drawing tools. If a scanner is available, try to obtain a picture from the scanner (assuming it can prepare compatible files) and use the package to work on this picture.

Recap

- Margins, tabs and indents are all spaces and of these only the top and bottom margins are used for text (headers and footers). Left and right margins are set for all the pages of a document, though there may be differences between even-numbered and odd-numbered pages. Tabs are used for the first line of a paragraph or for tabular work, indents are used to set a whole paragraph to different (temporary) margins.

- Justification is about even left or right alignment of text, a full justification means that each full line will be padded with spaces to occupy the same length across the page.

- Text can be arranged in columns, usually justified, and the space separating the columns is called the gutter.

- Before work starts on the text of a document, its layout should be determined by creating one or more master pages, containing the layout of margins, headers, footers, etc. In addition, a style sheet may be used to hold details of fonts and sizes for different parts of the document. Using these methods ensures uniformity of the work with minimum effort.

- Printing can be done with the paper portrait or landscape orientation. Portrait orientation, long side vertical, is much more common.

- ASCII files contain no control codes and will therefore not cause any unwanted effects when imported into a DTP package or sent to a printer. Plain ASCII files, however, do not allow effects such as bold, italic, etc. to be imported by the DTP package.

- The use of graphics should start with an outline sketch to show how the graphics image will fit into the page.

- Graphics can be of the bit-map or the vector type, but the bit-map type is more common. Vector graphics allow scaling without loss of resolution, but cannot be used for such a wide range of images.

- Bit-map images can be pixel edited, allowing each bit of the image to be changed individually.

Answers to questions

1 (d)
2 (a), (d)
3 (b)
4 (c)
5 (b)
6 (d)
7 (b)
8 (a)
9 (b)
10 (b)
11 (d)
12 (b)
13 (c)
14 (d)

4 Practical DTP work

Objectives

After reading this chapter you should be able to:
- describe the loading of program files
- explain the meaning and purpose of screen messages
- describe how to format a data disk
- outline stages in the use of a dtp program
- explain how to create a simple document
- describe how to name and save a document file
- explain how to use the laser printer
- describe how to leave the DTP program.

Scenario

You need to produce a leaflet advertising a seminar. Hand printing will look amateurish and there is no time to get a local printer to do the work. How can the use of a DTP program help you?

Getting started

Getting started is always the most difficult part of desktop publishing, particularly when you are getting to grips with an unfamiliar program. Though Aldus PageMaker makes things as easy as possible, the hardware can cause restrictions that can be irksome at times, but which you have to get used to. Machines which are fitted with the CGA type of screen display, for example, cannot show a well-proportioned view of a page on the screen, and most DTP programs cope with this by displaying the full width and about one third of the depth of each page. An improved view is obtained using the Hercules video card, and the screenviews that appear in this book have been obtained in that way. By far the best type of display for PC machines is the VGA type, preferably with a monochrome monitor (which has better resolution so that it can show fine detail more clearly). The Super-VGA type of screen is even better, but can be used only if your DTP program includes a suitable *driver*. The screen view is never such a limitation as it might appear, because all DTP programs can put up a temporary measuring grille or ruler on to the screen which will show the true dimensions of the work.

Any desktop publication, no matter how simple, must start with planning done on paper and with no reference to the computer. In this book, the examples are necessarily short, and make use of a restricted page width simply to allow for easy reproduction without having to reduce the images too much. For your own work you can expand out, but the maximum size of a single Aldus PageMaker page is about 17″ × 22″, though the printed area will normally be less than this so as to leave a margin on each side and at the top and foot.

- If you are working with a size of page which is larger than your printer can cope with, PageMaker allows you to print in *tiles* – sections that can be fastened together to make up the complete page.
- If you opt for a page size that is much smaller than your paper (such as A5 page on A4 paper) PageMaker can automatically print *crop marks* at the edges of the page to show where you can trim the paper, using a guillotine.

The first example we shall look at is one that uses text only on one side of a single sheet, in the simplest way, so as to avoid the planning complications of multi-page documents for the moment. We shall imagine that this is a single-sheet leaflet announcing the 24th Annual Scrivener Lecture, giving details of venue, time, speaker and topic, and a brief set of comments. Since this is a one-off document, it will not require the construction of a master page. This implies that we shall have a main title with sub-headings for venue, time and speaker and a more emphasized style for the topic. The text of the comments can then follow this in a reduced size of print. The layout might be as in Figure 4.1, with the main heading in large type, 24-point perhaps, the sub-headings smaller, 14-point, and the text in some normal size, perhaps either 10-point or 12-point. If the newsletter is printed on A5 paper, then it will have a printed area close to the limits that this book has required, but on A4 paper you could afford to spread out to a larger width.

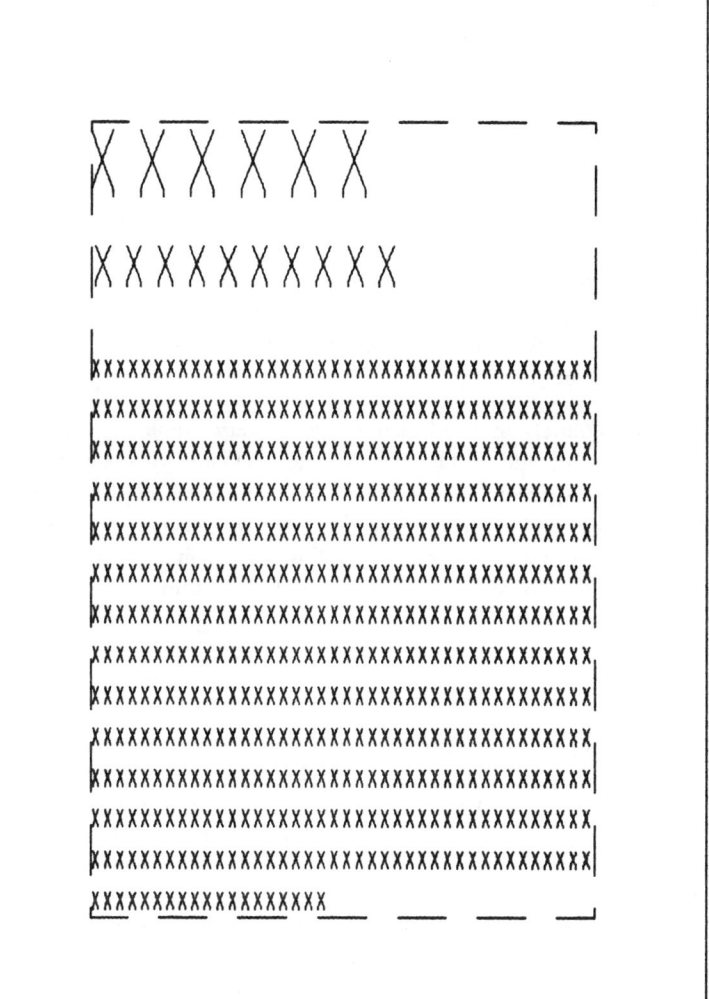

Figure 4.1 A layout for a leaflet advertising an event

The important point here is to know what is available. PageMaker, for example, will not make a font available if your printer cannot cope with it (a problem that restricts older types of dot-matrix printers mainly). You need to know, before you plan in too much detail, what will be possible given the printer you are going to use. PageMaker allows you to use any fonts which are built-in to the printer (the fonts which any word-processor can use with that printer) as well as fonts which are specific to DTP and which are printed as a set of dots controlled by the signals sent to the printer. The built-in fonts will print faster, but may not be of a range that you want to use.

● A point to be careful of is that many DTP programs allow you to specify both screen-fonts and printer-fonts.
● No matter how a document may look on the screen, it cannot be correctly printed if the printer-font is absent.
● You must ensure that a suitable printer font exists for each screen font that can be used.

This is absolutely minimal planning for a very simple example, but it shows what is required. The effort is much the same for a complete book as for a single-page document, because once you have set up for the use of left-hand and right-hand pages by creating two master pages (the main complication in a book (apart from illustrations, and ignoring awkward things like footnotes), the work becomes fairly routine, with PageMaker (or whatever DTP program you are using) automatically placing the text and laying out the pages.

Preparation

The program, PageMaker or otherwise, must be installed to suit the hardware of the computer and printer that will be used with it. The computer, if it is of the PC type, must be fitted with a good graphics card, preferably the VGA type, and with a suitable monitor (monochrome is easier to work with). A mouse must be connected and installed, and printing should preferably use a laser printer.

The use of a program such as PageMaker implies that a hard disk will be used for storage, but a few other types of DTP program can be used from floppy disks. If you are using a smaller program from floppy disks, or if you need to keep your data files (of publications and graphics) on a floppy disk, you will need to prepare some floppy disks for use. On the machines that are best suited to run Aldus PageMaker, these disks will be either the 5.25" 1.2 Mb type or the 3.5" 1.44 Mb type. Other machines will use either the 5.25" 360k or the 3.5" 720k disk systems. The 5.25" 360k disk is not ideally suited to DTP work because of the limited amount of storage space – DTP files are usually large even if they contain no graphics. The only application of 360k disks is for holding files of text from word-processors.

Whatever floppy disks are to be used will need to be formatted, see also Chapter 1. Formatting is the process which tests the magnetic surfaces of the disk and magnetically marks out portions, called sectors, on which data can be recorded. The formatting makes it possible for the computer to locate these sectors and so save or load to or from specified sectors. You never have to specify for yourself which disk sectors are used – if the formatting is carried out correctly the computer can control the whole set of actions automatically. Formatting is carried out typically by a program called FORMAT whose name has to be followed by the disk drive, typically A or B. On a machine which is fitted with only floppy drives, you will need to place the MS-DOS disk copy into drive A to start the process, with the disk to be formatted in drive B. A machine with a single floppy drive is unsuitable for use with DTP programs.

● You must *never* use FORMAT C: on a machine with a hard disk unless you are installing a new hard disk and following instructions for installation.

● For a twin–floppy machine: with a disk in drive B, and the machine using the drive A in which the MS-DOS files are contained, type FORMAT B:

For a hard-disk machine: with a disk in drive A and the machine using the hard drive (usually C) and the directory in which the MS-DOS files are placed, type FORMAT A:

● You should hear the disk start spinning, and the screen will show the progress of formatting in terms of sides and cylinders.

● When formatting is complete you will be offered the chance to format another disk or to end formatting. Format as many disks as you are likely to need.

● From this point on we shall assume that the DTP program is being run from a hard disk and that floppies, if used at all, are used for data files.

On a machine that uses a hard disk, you may wish to hold all data files on the hard disk rather than use floppy disks. Floppy disks are useful in class work as they allow each user of a machine to keep his/her own files separately, with no possibility of another user wiping out files. If you are using a machine which is part of a network, follow the instructions that apply to the network.

When the data files are to be held on the hard disk, it is advisable to create a sub-directory for them. Assuming that the Aldus PageMaker files are held in a directory called PM, the procedure for creating a sub-directory called PAGEFILE is:

● With no program running, type CD\PM (RETURN)
● Type MD PAGEFILE (RETURN)
● Type CD PAGEFILE (RETURN)
● Type DIR (RETURN). You should see a screen message indicating that you are using path C:\PM\PAGEFILE and that this contains no files (the markings . and .. indicate the present and previous directories respectively).
● Type CD\ to return to the root directory ready to run PageMaker or any other program.
● If you are using Windows or DESQview, follow the methods indicated for that system.

Questions

1 Floppy disks need to be formatted so that:
   (a) they are de-magnetised
   (b) they are given a pattern of magnetic markings
   (c) they can store more information
   (d) they are erased
2 A DTP program can:
   (a) work on one page size only
   (b) work with any page size
   (c) work with a range of page sizes
   (d) work only with sizes that the printer can use

Starting up Aldus PageMaker

Once you have some idea of what you want to do, you need to start up your DTP program. The following description applies to Aldus PageMaker, but very similar procedures are used by other programs, though the simpler DTP programs omit several of the steps. Some simpler programs, for example, work with a much smaller maximum page size, so that most of the work that is done will be on the maximum page size.

Throughout the use of PageMaker or any other DTP program, you will

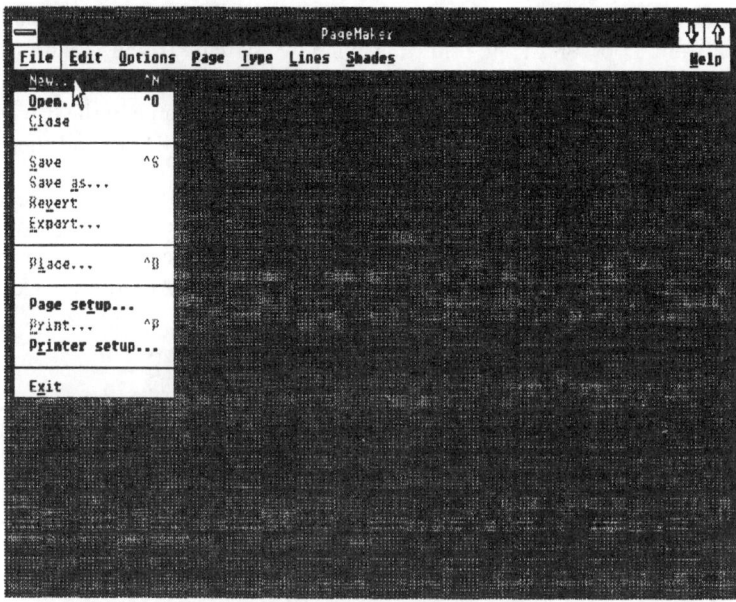

Figure 4.2   The *File* menu of PageMaker from which *New* can be selected

be guided by screen messages that appear either on the edges (top, bottom or sides) of the screen, or by *context-sensitive help*. Context-sensitive help is a particularly useful feature of modern programs which allows you to obtain help on a problem by pressing a key, often the F1 function key. The help message relates to the command that is being executed or selected, so that it is a way of showing you how that command is used. This avoids the problems of the older HELP systems in which you might have to move through many screen pages to find the topic you needed. It also avoids having to thumb through the manual or a set of manuals to remind yourself of the effects of a command.

If we assume that PageMaker has been installed correctly and that its files are in a directory called PM there are three methods of starting the program, but not all three may be available to you.

● If your computer does NOT use windows, type CD/PM to obtain the correct directory, and then type PM (RETURN) to start the program.

● If your computer uses windows immediately when it is switched on, select the PageMaker program from the windows display – see any

101

textbook on the use of windows (such as *Windows: A User's Guide* from Dabs Press) for using the windows system. If you are using DESQview, you should also refer to a book on this particular system.

● If your computer makes use of batch files, type the name of the batch file that starts PageMaker (it might be called PM or DTP) and then press the RETURN key.

When PageMaker starts it displays copyright notices and pressing any key will remove these, leaving a screen which is blank except for a menu of eight items on the top line. These items are File, Edit, Options, Page, Type, Lines, Shades and Help and each can be selected by either:

● typing the first (underlined) letter, or
● by using the mouse to move the arrow pointer to the choice and pressing the left-hand mouse button.

The first step is to notify that a new publication is to be used. The File menu is selected, Figure 4.2, and from this menu window, select New. The other starting option of Open is used only for documents that have already been created and are to be resumed or edited.

Starting a new document brings up another window, Figure 4.3, in which you are asked to provide details of the page set-up.

● Page size shows some familiar **A** sizes along with the envelope B5 size. The letter size, in US program versions, is 8.5″ × 11″ (as used for continuous computer stationery), but for the UK this size is sometimes made equal to A4 (the version being used in the preparation of this book used US letter size); UK versions also use millimetres (by default) as the unit of measurement. The Legal size is 21.59 × 34.56 cm. (approx. 8.5″ × 13.6″) and Tabloid is 27.94 × 43.18 cm. approximately 11″ × 17″.

● You opt for a different page size by pressing a letter key (the letter that is underlined in the menu) or by using the mouse to point to the *button* (the small circle next to each word) for a given page size and pressing the left-hand mouse button. Each size is shown in the *Custom* spaces when you make this option, allowing you to check sizes.

● If you need an odd page size, you can select Custom, place the cursor into each box in turn and type the width and depth that you want to use. This is seldom necessary.

● The orientation of the page is shown as Tall (portrait) or Wide (landscape), depending on whether you want to read it with the long side vertical or horizontal respectively.

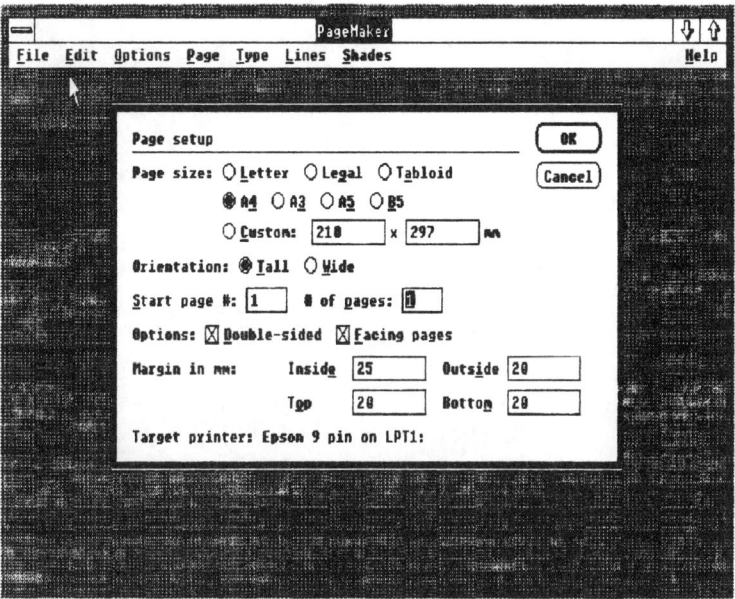

Figure 4.3   The page setup window that appears when a new document is being started

- You are asked to specify the start page number and the number of pages. This allows you to specify that you will, for example, prepare ten pages, and in a subsequent session prepare pages 11 to 20 and so on. The largest possible page number is 9999 and the maximum number of pages that can be specified is 128. You can later insert or remove pages to adjust the number.

- For a single sheet, the check mark on Double-sided is not needed, nor on Facing pages. These are *both* removed when the mouse is clicked on the Double-sided box (or the D key pressed). The Double-sided option is used for multi-page work so that printing can be done on both sides of a page (with the margins in the correct place for left and right-hand pages). The selection of Facing pages allows PageMaker to show both pages in a pair that face each other, such as pages 4 and 5 in any book (even number left, odd number right).

- Finally, the margin has to be specified, using millimetre units in the European versions of PageMaker. The default values that are illustrated, of 25 mm left and 20 mm right, top and bottom, are sensible, and you seldom need to change them.

● The choice of units can be changed, using the Preferences menu of the Edit option. The measurement systems available are Inches, Inches decimal, Millimetres, Picas and Ciceros; with vertical ruler options of millimetres, Picas and Ciceros. The Pica measurement is 1/6″ and the Cicero is 4.55 mm; both are specialized printers' units.

What else do you need to do? When you are starting out in desktop publishing, the less you need to do the better, because it's only too easy to spend so much time in preparation that you never get anything done, and so never acquire the experience. We are using just one column, since this is a leaflet and not a newspaper, so that we do not need to specify the size of columns and of the gutter (the space between columns). On PageMaker, these options are selected from another menu, the Options menu, and for this simple example there is no need to bring up this menu at all. Examples of columnar work will appear later. The only selection we need to be careful about is that we have opted for a single page, and that this page is being worked on, with no master page selected. PageMaker marks its page selection at the bottom left-hand side of the screen.

Questions

3 The quickest method of starting the DTP program is by using:
  (a) a batch file
  (b) Windows or DESQview
  (c) direct commands
  (d) floppy disks
4 The opening menu might require details of the printer and the page size so that:
  (a) the file size will be correct
  (b) the program can start running
  (c) the pages can be numbered correctly
  (d) the pages can be set out for that printer and page size.

Activity

Compare for yourself the time needed to start a DTP program by direct commands, by using a batch file and, if available, by using Windows, DESQview or GEM.

Cursor and selection

If you have ever used a word-processor program, then many of the methods for typing text into Aldus PageMaker will be familiar to you. The position of a typed letter on the screen is indicated by a cursor, a thin vertical line. This cursor can be moved around text that has already been typed by using the mouse or the keys marked with arrows, the PgUp and PgDn keys, and the Home and End keys. Other computer types will have keys that correspond to those. Moving up and down a page of typing can be done either with the PgUp and PgDn keys or, with better control by the 'elevator bar'(scroll bar). This is a vertical narrow box at the right-hand side of the screen, which contains in turn a small square box. Moving this box will alter which part of a page of text you see on the screen. The box is most easily moved by placing the mouse pointer (the curly I) on the box, holding down the mouse button, and moving the mouse up or down (dragging the indicator bar). Releasing the mouse pointer will make the screen change to show the correct part of the page. You can also place the mouse cursor on part of the vertical track for the box and click the button to make the box move to this point, so making the screen change. The indicator bar can also be moved by placing the cursor over it, using the arrowed keys, then pressing the F10 key, moving the indicator with the keys marked with a vertical arrow, and then pressing the F10 key again. An indicator bar type of display is also used in menus of files.

Placing the text

Once the Page setup is completed, PageMaker is ready to accept text (unless the Options menu is to be used). The screen appears as shown in Figure 4.4.

● The top line shows the word 'untitled' because no filename has as yet been allocated to this document.
● The default for text entry is centred – change this to justified or left-aligned.
● The same menu choices appear as in the earlier screen views.
● A ruler, scaled in centimetres in this example, appears across the top of the screen and also down the left hand side. This shows the dimensions of the page *as it will be printed*.
● The paper size and shape is shown in a solid line and the selected page size in a dotted line.

105

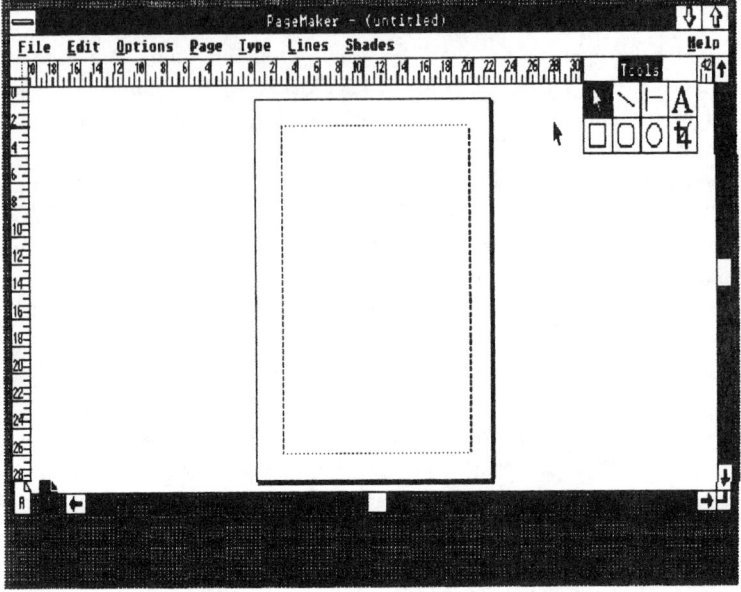

Figure 4.4   The skeleton of the document ready for text to be added

● This size as seen on screen is very small – it allows for viewing two pages per screen. This is not important if you are importing text from a word-processor, but if you need to type small-sized text directly into PageMaker it is difficult to see what is being done. Pressing the right-hand mouse button provides an enlarged view, but this has to be centred by moving the position boxes on the scroll bars at the right hand side and bottom of the screen. Figure 4.5 shows the result of this, which provides a magnified view of the top left-hand corner.

● For headlines, there is nothing wrong in working with the smaller size of image on the screen. Small text will, however, be *greeked*, meaning that it will not be readable; it will consist of a set of token marks which take up the correct space but which are not distinct letters.

● The 75% size, obtained by using this option from the Page menu, is very convenient for short documents, allowing most or all of the document to be viewed and retaining the readability of the text.

The next step is to select a font for the headline. The planning has decided on 24-point being used for this, meaning letters whose maximum height

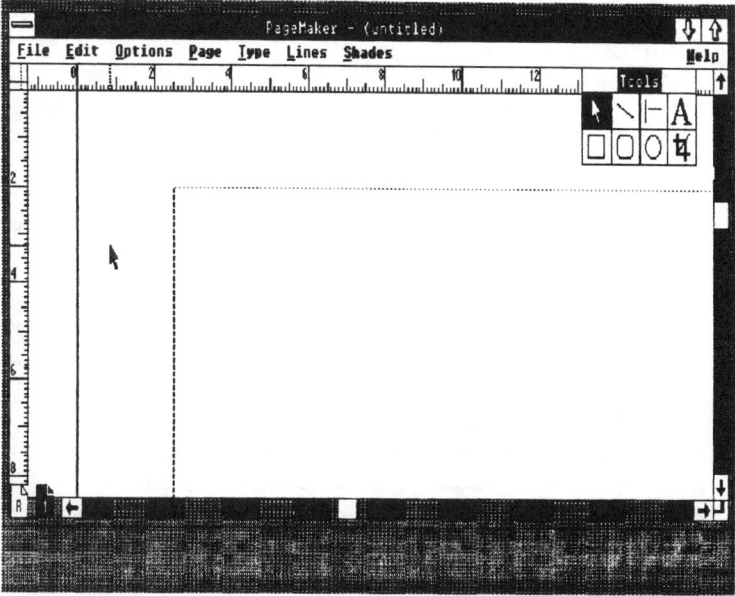

Figure 4.5   The magnified view of the page, a particularly useful feature of PageMaker

will be 24 units of 1/72″, a maximum height of 1/3″. The typeface, size and style will have to be selected. This requires the selection *in turn* of Type, followed by Type specs.

- Remember that what you have available depends on the printer you are using. When you select a dot-matrix printer, you may find that you are restricted to 10 or 12-point text as a maximum size in some typefaces.
- In addition, the type sizes of dot-matrix printers are often shown in terms of characters per inch rather than point size.
- In general, users of dot-matrix printers are better served using the built-in fonts, which will have a greater range of typefaces and sizes.
- Examples in this book have used fonts appropriate to a laser printer so that the screen illustrations will show the choice which will be available for such printers.

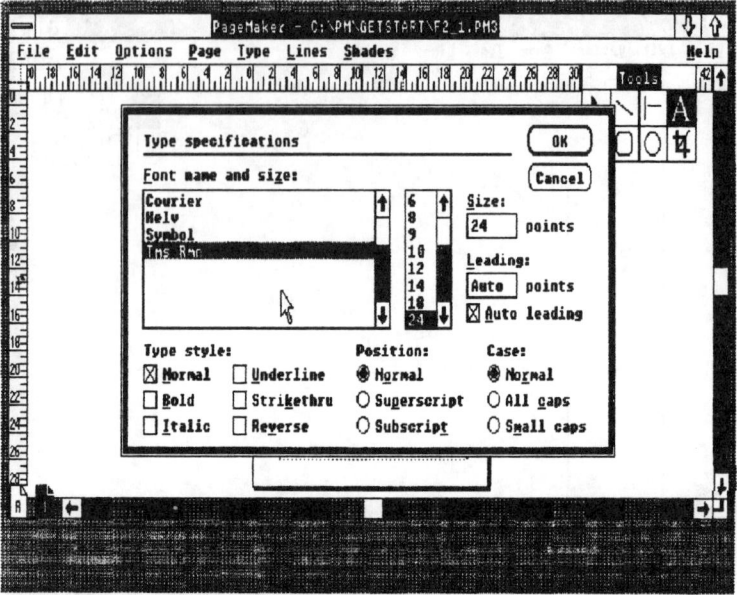

Figure 4.6   Selecting a font for the text from the list of available fonts. This shows part of the list for PostScript printers

- Some printed examples have used a dot-matrix printer, to emphasize the restrictions that this places on the use of fonts.
- Some less-costly DTP programs allow dot-matrix printers to use large fonts and elaborate typefaces, but the quality of these can be poor. PageMaker is designed to produce professional-quality work and it is assumed that laser printers will be used for all but rough drafts.
- You can change the printer by using the Printer Setup option from the File menu. Providing you installed more than one printer, this allows you to specify which printer will be used as the eventual destination for the document.

The font is selected from the list, Figure 4.6. In this illustration, the font is Times Roman in 24-point size. The leading (pronounced 'ledding', and formerly referring to the strips of lead that were used to separate lines of type) is the spacing between lines of print, and is set automatically by PageMaker unless you want to change it. The size of leading is measured in points, and it is common for the leading to be 20% larger than the type.

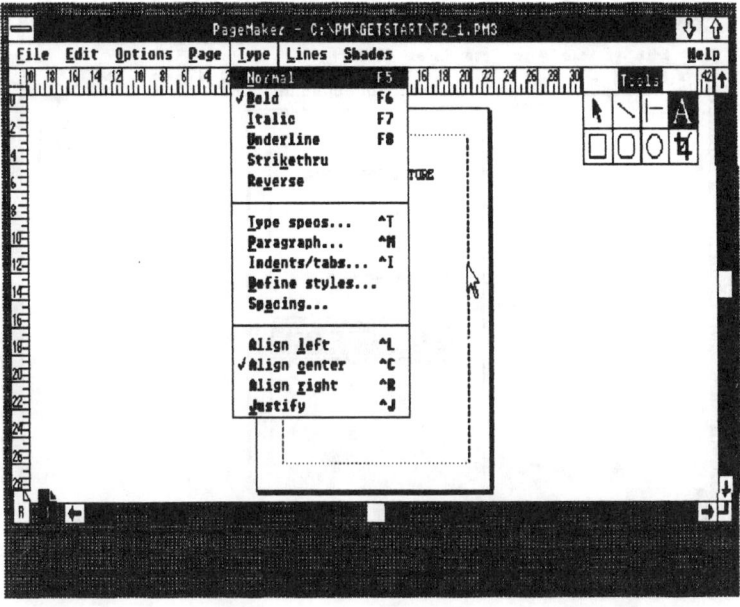

Figure 4.7   Using *Align Center* to centre the heading, which also needs to be in *Bold*

When a printer refers to type as being 10/12 point Times, this means Times Roman font in 10 point size with leading of 12-point size.

The heading will need to be centred on the page. This is done by selecting the Align Center option from the Type menu of PageMaker, Figure 4.7. This same menu allows Bold to be selected, since a heading needs to be in bold (thick black) style to command attention. Large sizes of typeface can look thin and spindly in normal form, and it is quite common to have only the Bold style in these sizes, with the choice of normal, bold or italic available only on the smaller sizes.

The text can now be typed in:

● Remember to select the line arrangement (justified or left-aligned).
● The arrow cursor is moved to the A box in the section marked tools. This selects text (as distinct from drawing actions).
● The cursor is placed near the top of the page, using the mouse.
● The heading THE SCRIVENER LECTURE is typed in capitals.
● The arrow tool is reselected.

109

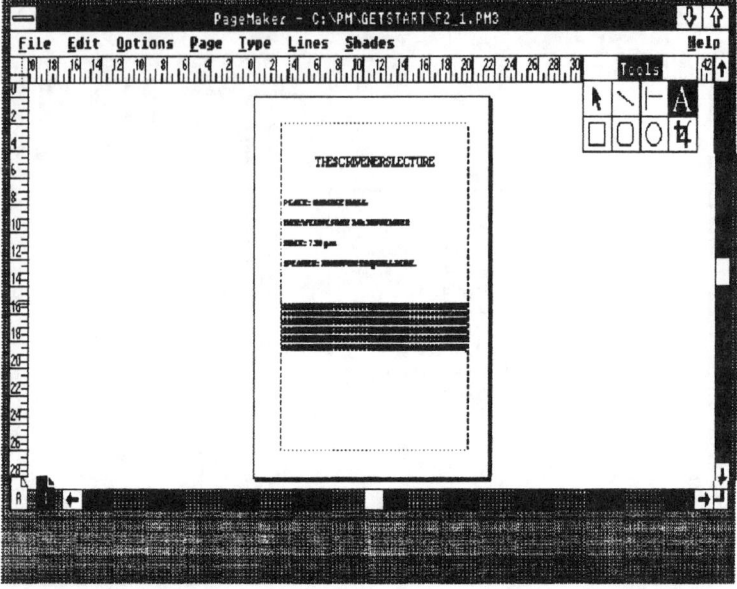

Figure 4.8   The page shown in greeked form, with small symbols indicating the way that the text is arranged on the page

- The 18-point font, bold, is selected along with left alignment and the lines for Place, Day, Time and Speaker typed.
- The 14-point normal font is selected, with justification (each full line of the same length) and the message text typed.
- On the screen, Figure 4.8, this text is *greeked* – it is too small to be shown and is represented by shaded squares.

The work can be checked by using the magnification features of PageMaker, either by pressing the right-hand mouse key or by picking from the five options in the Page menu, which are Actual size, 75% size, 50% size, Fit in window (the default) or 200% size. Figure 4.9 shows a magnified (Actual size) view which allows the smallest size of text to be scrutinized. The missing 'e' in 'these' on the last line can be typed in after the cursor has been positioned with the mouse. The 75% size is particularly convenient for checking over a paragraph of text in 14-point print.

110

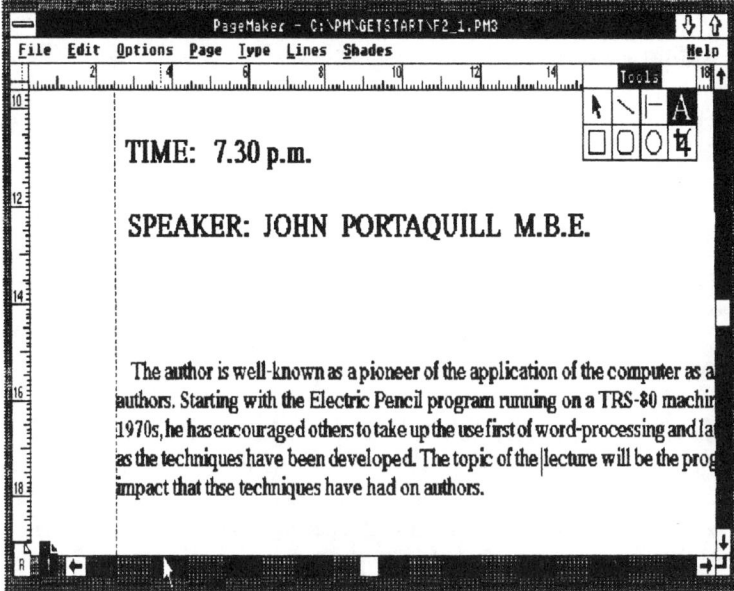

Figure 4.9   A magnified view can be used to show faults in the text – it is always better to prepare text in the word-processor

---

Questions

5   Text typing is selected but the cursor moves at once to the middle of the screen. This is because:
   (a) lines are justified
   (b) centring has been selected
   (c) the cursor is not used to indicate text entry position
   (d) right-justification has been selected
6   You are selecting fonts and sizes and you find that only a few sizes are available, though many were installed originally. This is because:
   (a) only a few fonts are ever available
   (b) you are not intended to use many fonts
   (c) the printer is incapable of using many fonts
   (d) the computer is incapable of using many fonts

Final work

The final work on this simple document consists of checking it carefully. It is unfortunately very easy to overlook spelling and typing mistakes on text that appears on the screen, so that if the document is an important one which will be widely circulated it is worth taking some care over. In particular, watch for mis-use of words, such as mistaking prevarication (telling lies) for procrastination (putting off decisions). This is a very common howler, and there are many others. If you have doubts about words (and reading newspapers is more likely to increase your confusion rather than diminish it) then either use simpler language about which you (and your readers) have no doubts, or check against a dictionary.

When more than a few lines of text are to be used, it ought to be prepared on a word-processor which includes a good spelling-checker. This allows you to prepare a draft with a fast dot-matrix printer and to proofread it carefully – remember that proofreading from paper is much easier than proofreading from a screen. In addition, the author of a piece of text ought not to be the only proofreader because no author ever reads what is on the paper, only what he/she thinks ought to be there.

The final proof of the document arises on printing. If you are using more than one printer, you might assign one printer for draft copies and another for high-quality work. Printing is carried out as follows:

- Select the File menu and choose Print. This produces the menu shown in Figure 4.10.
- This allows you to determine the number of copies; useful if you want to make 20 or so copies with a laser printer rather than creating a master which will be reproduced by offset litho.
- You can opt for all of the document or a selection of pages.
- Scaling is possible only when you are using a PostScript laser printer, allowing you to scale the size of the page by a factor ranging from 0.25 to 10.
- The options that are applicable (in bolder print on the screen) are Thumbnails, Crop marks, Spot color overlays, and Tile. Thumbnails are miniature copies which can be printed only from a PostScript laser printer, and Crop marks are used to guide paper cutting when the print page is smaller than the paper. Spot color overlays allow colour separation copies to be made, meaning that one page will be printed with the image for one colour, a separate page for another colour and so on. This is used when colour work is being created by combining printing in several colours. The Tile option allows for very large pages

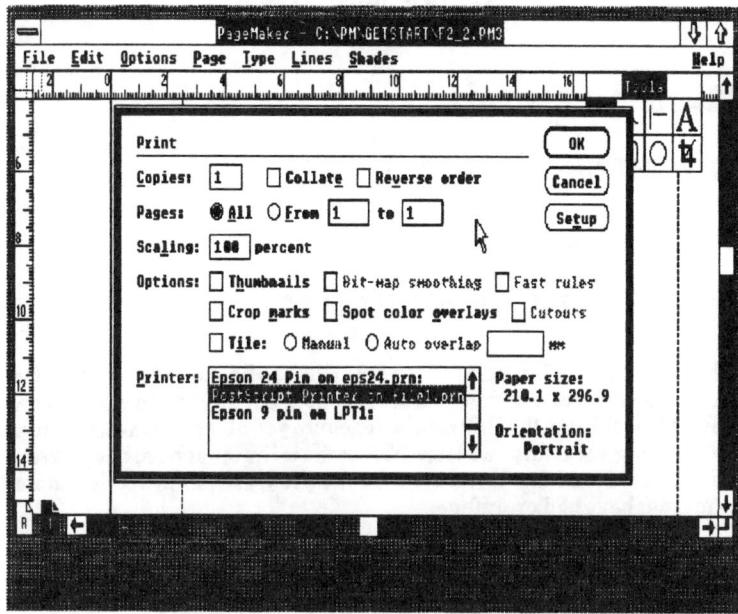

Figure 4.10   The Print menu of PageMaker

being created by joining several printed pages together. You can specify how large an overlap you want between tiles.

● Remember that the printer need not be physically present. The illustration shows only one printer physically present and connected to LPT1. The other 'printers' are, in fact, files which can be used at a later stage to produce print from a printer of the correct type. In the example, a PostScript file is being made for later printing.

● Figure 4.11(a) shows a draft copy made using a dot-matrix printer. This has required the printer to be set-up, and the document re-composed (automatically by PageMaker). The quality indicates why PageMaker does not normally permit the larger fonts to be used by dot-matrix printers. If you need to use a dot-matrix printer, programs such as First Publisher will produce better copy of large fonts from such printers. Figure 4.11(b) shows the output from a PostScript laser printer.

113

THE SCRIVENERS LECTURE

PLACE: HAMBLE HALL

DAY: WEDNESDAY 14th NOVEMBER

TIME: 7.30 p.m.

SPEAKER: JOHN PORTAQUILL M.B.E.

The author is well-known as a pioneer of the application of the computer as a tool for authors. Starting with the Electric Pencil program running on a TRS-80 machine in the 1970s, he has encouraged others to take up the use first of word-processing and later DTP as the techniques have been developed. The topic of the lecture will be the progressive impact that these techniques have had on authors.

(a)

THE SCRIVENERS LECTURE

PLACE: HAMBLE HALL

DAY: WEDNESDAY 14th NOVEMBER

TIME: 7.30 p.m.

SPEAKER: JOHN PORTAQUILL M.B.E.

The author is well-known as a pioneer of the application of the computer as a tool for authors. Starting with the Electric Pencil program running on a TRS-80 machine in the 1970s, he has encouraged others to take up the use first of word-processing and later DTP as the techniques have been developed. The topic of the lecture will be the progressive impact that these techniques have had on authors.

(b)

Figure 4.11   (a) A draft copy made using a dot-matrix printer – the fonts which were chosen in the document are not suitable for this printer, (b) The printout from the MicroLaser printer

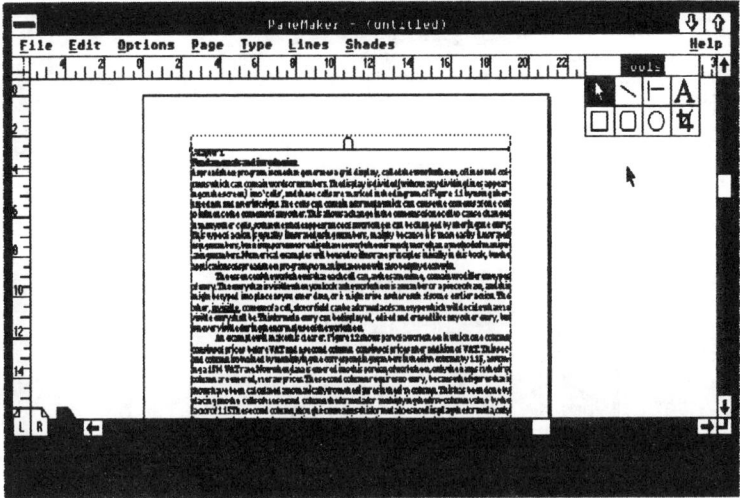

Figure 4.12   Text in place on a page, before adding a graphics image

---

Activity

Start a document, specifying a laser printer, and note the range of fonts and sizes that can be used. Save the document and start another specifying a dot-matrix printer. Compare the range of fonts available. If possible print the same document on both types of printer and compare the versions.

Adding graphics

Each type of DTP program has its own method for adding graphics, but the method used by PageMaker is representative of many. The graphics image must first exist as a file which the DTP program can read. For PageMaker and many others, this might be a file of the TIF (tag image file format) type which can be read directly. PageMaker, like many other DTP programs can read a large variety of other file types, such as the PCX files that are produced by many popular drawing software packages. If a graphics image is not in any of the many formats that PageMaker can read, it must be converted to a suitable form using one of the conversion utilities that are widely available. Note that there are variations – at least two types of PCX files exist, and several TIFF types.

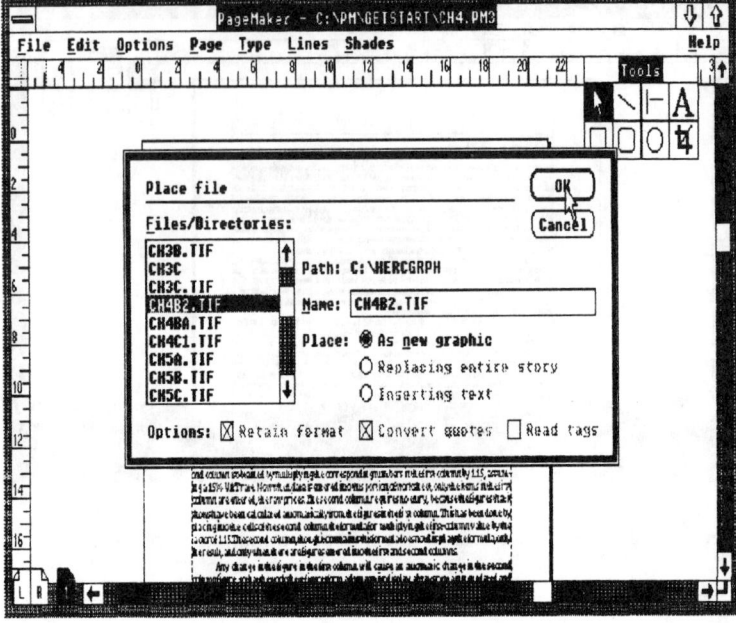

Figure 4.13   Choosing an image from the list of graphics files on the disk

The method of adding a graphic image to a PageMaker page is outlined below – the illustration, Figure 4.12, shows a page from an early draft of the preface to this book with a graphic which is not directly related to the subject matter.

- Figure 4.12 shows the text in place on a page.
- The Text Wrap option has been selected from the Options menu – this allows a graphic image to be put into the midst of text with the text parted to make room for the image.
- Using the File menu allows the selection of Place which is used for importing files. An image is chosen from the list, Figure 4.13.
- The image is placed on the page by steering an icon to the position and pressing the mouse button. The position of the image is then adjusted by dragging it to the required position, Figure 4.14.
- Another option is to place the graphics image on to a blank page and subsequently to wrap the text around the image position.

116

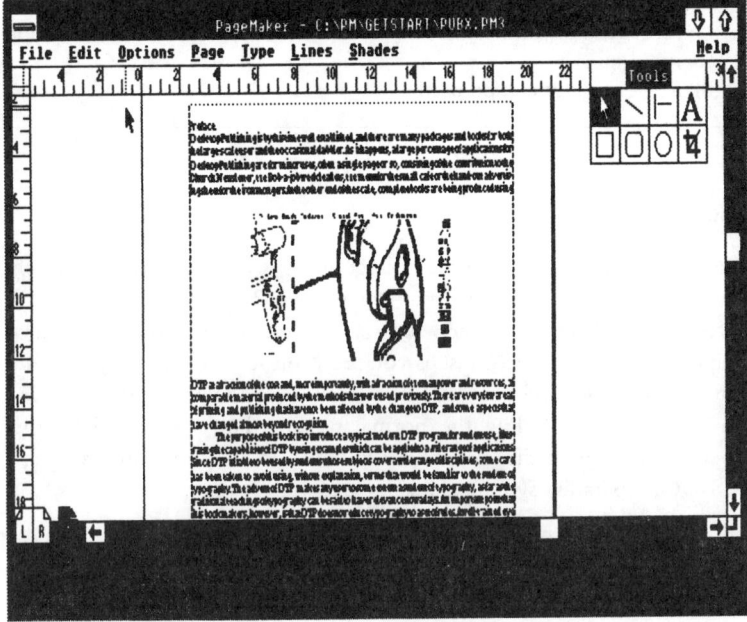

Figure 4.14   Dragging the image to its final position after placing the image, using the graphics icon

● Note that the text is greeked on this scale and even the graphic is not particularly clear – the aim is to see the layout rather than to see the details.
● Looking at the page with a greater magnification is needed to check that the illustration is well placed.

Questions

7 Proofing is NOT for:
   (a) checking spelling
   (b) checking use of words
   (c) checking correct fonts and sizes
   (d) checking number of words
8 Printing to a file is used so that:
   (a) a dot-matrix printer can be used

117

   (b) any printer can be used when the DTP program is not running

   (c) the specified printer can be used when the DTP program is not running

   (d) a laser printer can be used

Naming and saving

Normally when you save a page or a set of pages you do so as a file which will carry a characteristic extension such as PM3 for PageMaker-3. This saves the work in its finished form, complete with layout, fonts, any graphics or special effects, just as you see it on screen and ready to print out. Before a file can be saved, however, it must be named, and the rules for naming a file follow the normal pattern that is enforced by the operating system for the computer. On the PC type of machine using the MS-DOS operating system, the rules are:

● The complete filename can contain a drive letter, path, main name and extension.

● The main name must consist of not more than 8 characters.

● The first character of the main name must be a letter. The other characters can be letters, or you can use the digits 0 to 9, or the symbols

    $ #   & @ ! % ( ) — _ { } ' ~ ^ `

● The following characters **must not** be used:

    * + = [ ] ; : , . / ?

nor can you use:
> the space
> the tab
> the Ctrl character

● There are names that you cannot and must not use. You should not use any of the names that appear on the MS-DOS master disc, because these are reserved for the programs that bear these names.

● In addition, there are 'internal' commands, stored in the memory, whose names you should not use. These are listed in Figure 4.15.

● In addition, if you are working from a hard disk, or with the MS-DOS distribution disk in drive A: you need to avoid the names shown in Figure 4.16.

BREAK	CD	CHCP	CHDIR	CLS
COPY	CTTY	DATE	DEL	DIR
ECHO	ERASE	EXIT	FILES	FOR
GOTO	IF	MKDIR	MD	PATH
PAUSE	PROMPT	RENAME	REM	RMDIR
RD	SET	SHIFT	TIME	TYPE
VER	VERIFY	VOL		

Figure 4.15   Internal command names which must not be used as file names

APPEND	ASSIGN	ATTRIB	BACKUP	CHKDSK
COMMAND	COMP	COUNTRY	DISKCOMP	DISKCOPY
EXE2BIN	FASTOPEN	FDISK	FIND	FORMAT
GRAFTABL	GRAPHICS	JOIN	KEYB	KEYBUK
LABEL	MODE	MORE	NLSFUNC	PRINT
RECOVER	REPLACE	RESTORE	SELECT	SHARE
SORT	SUBST	SYS	TREE	XCOPY

Figure 4.16   Other file names that are usually present in an MS-DOS system and which must also be avoided

Saving a file of a page requires you to specify the main name by typing a suitable name, and to specify the disk drive or directory. Some DTP programs require you to type the drive letter and/or path; others allow you to select, using the mouse, from a menu. PageMaker provides a menu of the last directory used, and you can then use the mouse to move to any other directory (select the name of a sub-directory to move to that sub-directory, or select the item marked as **[..]** to move back to the previous directory). You *must* have some idea of where your directories are placed, and it is very helpful to keep a *tree-diagram* such as that of Figure 4.17, close to the computer. Such a diagram can be produced by several utility programs, notably PC-Tools.

You do not always work on a completely new page, however. If you have previously started work on a page and saved the file under a filename such as PMPHLT1 then you might want to continue work on this document.

● You would start work on this document by specifying its filename – PageMaker uses the *Open* file command for this, not the *New* file command.

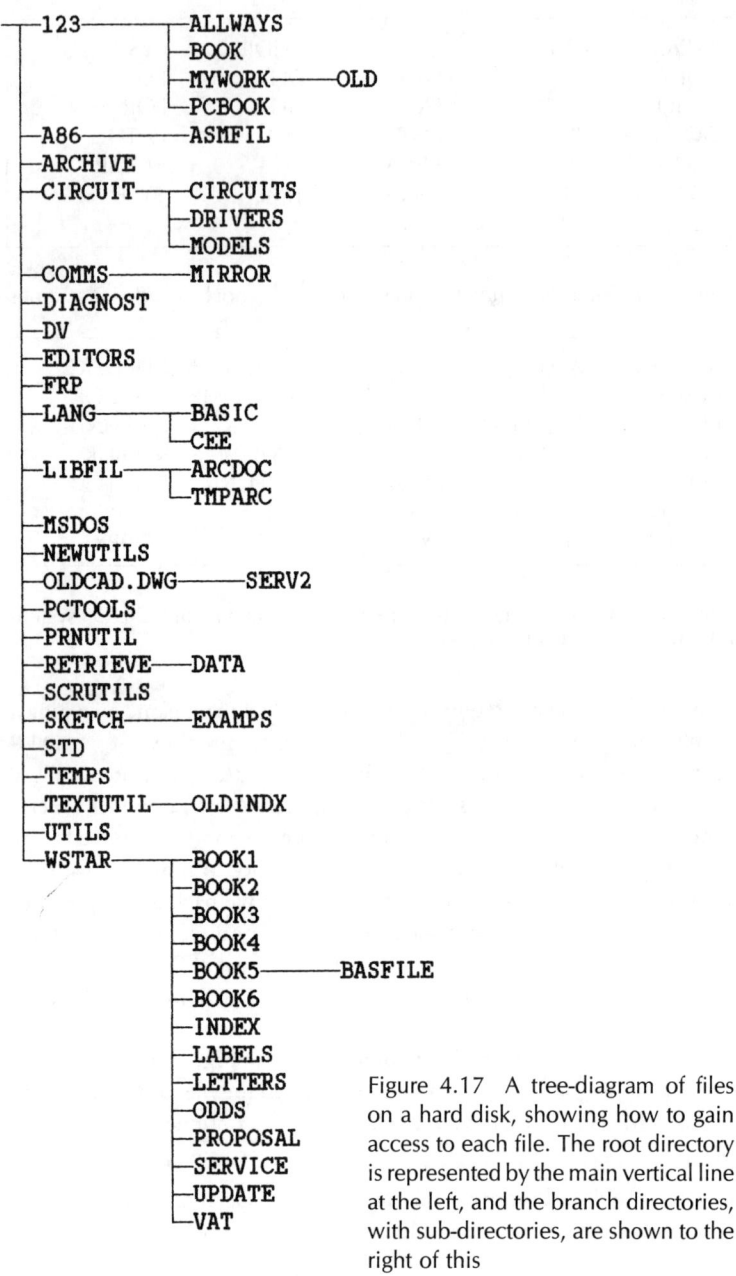

```
┬─123─────────┬─ALLWAYS
│             ├─BOOK
│             ├─MYWORK────────OLD
│             └─PCBOOK
├─A86─────────ASMFIL
├─ARCHIVE
├─CIRCUIT─────┬─CIRCUITS
│             ├─DRIVERS
│             └─MODELS
├─COMMS────────MIRROR
├─DIAGNOST
├─DV
├─EDITORS
├─FRP
├─LANG────────┬─BASIC
│             └─CEE
├─LIBFIL──────┬─ARCDOC
│             └─TMPARC
├─MSDOS
├─NEWUTILS
├─OLDCAD.DWG────────SERV2
├─PCTOOLS
├─PRNUTIL
├─RETRIEVE─────DATA
├─SCRUTILS
├─SKETCH───────EXAMPS
├─STD
├─TEMPS
├─TEXTUTIL─────OLDINDX
├─UTILS
└─WSTAR───────┬─BOOK1
              ├─BOOK2
              ├─BOOK3
              ├─BOOK4
              ├─BOOK5────────BASFILE
              ├─BOOK6
              ├─INDEX
              ├─LABELS
              ├─LETTERS
              ├─ODDS
              ├─PROPOSAL
              ├─SERVICE
              ├─UPDATE
              └─VAT
```

Figure 4.17 A tree-diagram of files on a hard disk, showing how to gain access to each file. The root directory is represented by the main vertical line at the left, and the branch directories, with sub-directories, are shown to the right of this

120

● When you have completed work on the document you have two options for saving it.
● Simply specifying *Save* will save the amended file on the same drive/ directory as it came from, replacing the older version.
● Specifying *Save as* allows you to use another filename, drive, path, etc. so that the new version exists as a separate file, not replacing the earlier version.

For some purposes, however, you might want to save the file in different ways. You might, for example, need to save the text only. This could then be used in a different format (different layout, fonts, graphics) on other pages, or possibly transferred to a word-processor to be printed out in the ordinary way. Most DTP programs provide for saving all the text of a file in simple ASCII form which can be read by any word-processor and (sometimes laboriously) re-formatted into another document or incorporated into another document. Alternatively, such text can be re-imported to another DTP document.

The more elaborate DTP programs such as PageMaker provide several options for exporting text, some of them involving 'filters'. When text is filtered in the course of exporting, it is changed so as to suit a particular word-processor or other program, making the task of working on the text much easier. In some cases, the style sheet for the document can be exported along with the text, assuming that the text is being exported to a word-processor that can use style sheets.

The action of exporting a graphic is usually much more restricted. When the Microsoft Windows system is being used on the computer, it is possible to move graphics from one program to another, using the Cut and Paste options of PageMaker or of Windows. Some other DTP programs allow graphics images to be exported as standard files, notably the MAC format. The usual procedure is:

● the image is surrounded by a dotted line (an envelope) which is created using one of the tool icons
● the Graphics File export option is selected
● you are asked to type a filename, and select a drive/path for the file
● the graphic is copied to the file for use in other applications

Some versions of DTP programs will automatically delete the graphic image that has been exported, others retain the image so that a separate action is needed to delete the image. PageMaker makes no provision for exporting a graphics image other than through the methods of

Windows – and export to other programs will be possible only if the full version of Windows is running. You can, however, save a page that contains only a graphics image so that it can be used later.

Activity

Load a document such as one of the example documents of the DTP program. Now rename this document and save it. Reload this renamed document and export the text to a word-processor. Note the methods that must be used for your DTP program.

Abandoning a page

All DTP programs allow for abandoning a page or a complete document without saving, though this is a procedure which would be done only if the page were hopelessly incorrect and would need to be re-assembled from other files. You can opt to abandon a page of the current document, which means that the page is cleared, though any other pages of the document might not be cleared. The other choice is to abandon a document completely without saving the file, and this can be done either by selecting a new document to work on or by leaving the DTP program altogether.

The methods vary from one program to another, but on PageMaker the Page menu offers the option of Remove Page, and when this is selected you are asked to specify the page number, or a range of numbers if several pages are to be removed. You must then select either to go ahead (the **OK** box) or to Cancel the command. When you opt to go ahead you are given another chance to cancel before the page(s) is/are blanked out. When you take this option, work can start at once on another page or set of pages, and if only one of a set of pages has been removed, the other pages are still available.

The methods of abandoning a document (one page or a set of pages) completely all make use of the Files menu. You can opt to:

● open another existing page file
● create a new page, or
● leave the DTP program completely

and each of these choices will result in the screen displaying a message asking you to confirm whether you want to leave the existing document without saving the file, to save the file and then leave, or to change your mind and work on with the document.

Since abandoning a document can mean throwing away a considerable amount of effort, the decision is never one that can be taken lightly and you should learn the procedures that apply to your own DTP program. PageMaker requires you to select New, Open or Exit from the Files menu, and you are prompted by a window:

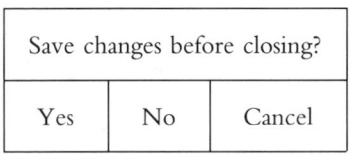

Save changes before closing?		
Yes	No	Cancel

of which the No option will cause the file to be abandoned. The Yes option will save the file before starting on another file or leaving the program, and the Cancel option allows work to continue. You should always save a file that will later be printed.

Questions

9 The SAVE-AS option of a DTP package is used:
   (a) to save any document file
   (b) to save a file under a new name
   (c) to delete a file
   (d) to save a file using its old name
10 A document contains text and graphics. You will find:
   (a) it is easy to export the graphics, difficult to export the text
   (b) you cannot easily export either text or graphics
   (c) it is easy to export the text, difficult to export the graphics
   (d) it is equally easy to export text and graphics

Using the laser printer

The laser printer that is used for DTP work will normally be a type that supports the use of the PostScript language (or a compatible language) and which possesses at least 1 Mb of internal RAM memory. There are many varieties of laser printers which do not use PostScript, and on which some DTP work can be done, but the full range of work of which a program like PageMaker is capable requires a PostScript printer. Many of the lower-cost laser printers are little more than fast dot-matrix printers, even to the extent of emulating the action (and resolution) of dot-matrix machines such as the Epson FX-100. A few laser printers use a Diablo 630 emulation, meaning that they will provide the font of a daisywheel type – but if no other emulation is present, such a printer cannot print graphics or DTP output. At the time of writing, the main alternative to PostScript is the Hewlett Packard PCL language, as used on the very popular Laserjet printers, and many laser printers offer a Laserjet emulation. This is an attractive option (often at attractive prices) but the use of PCL for DTP work requires a large amount of disk space for storing font information. Even if the printer runs PostScript, it is likely that its resolution will be the standard 300 dots per inch, and this can often be improved to as much as 600 dots per inch, or even more, by add-ons.

Assuming that a PostScript laser printer or a suitable compatible printer is available, the steps in printing a document are:

● Ensure that the correct printer is selected from within the DTP package – PageMaker uses the Printer Setup menu for this purpose and this is confirmed by the message:

  Postscript printer on LPT1 (or COM1)

● Ensure that the printer is connected correctly. The AppleLaser printer requires the use of the serial port (COM1), but other printers almost universally use the parallel port LPT1.

● Check that the printer is supplied with paper and that the level of toner is correct. Check that the drum life is not near its end.

● Switch on the printer and allow it to warm up for the time specified by the manufacturers, usually a few minutes.

● At the computer, select the Print option of the DTP program, and answer any questions that appear on the screen. These will be concerned with number of copies, collation (order) or pages when multiple copies are used, page numbers to be printed and specialized options such as crop marks and tiling.

● After making any changes that are needed to this print specification sheet, accept the print action (usually by selecting the OK box).

● The page should now be printed – there may be a delay as data is transferred from the memory of the computer to the memory of the printer, or to arrange data internally in the computer.

● Printing, especially of graphics, can be slow. The speed of laser printers in pages per minute is measured using text only and copies of identical pages (so that new material is being set up in the memory only once). Printing of several different pages that include graphics can be very much slower, several minutes in some cases.

● When the print run is completed, examine the copies and if they are all satisfactory, switch off the printer. If a page needs to be reprinted, select print again and specify that page number only in the print specification menu.

IMPORTANT: Use the laser printer only in a well-ventilated space. All laser printers generate small amounts of ozone, which is a corrosive gas that can cause damage to the lungs.

Leaving the DTP program

As noted above, the DTP program is left by selecting the Exit option from the Files menu – this option is common to practically all DTP programs. If you have forgotten to save the file you were working on you will be reminded. It is better to save the file before printing so that a copy is available on the disk in the (unlikely) event of the file being corrupted during printing. This can happen if there is an interruption in the power supply. Never leave a program, particularly a DTP program, simply by switching off the computer, because this can leave files incomplete (open) and avoid the reminder about saving files.

Questions

11 PostScript or PCL laser printers are preferred for DTP because:
   (a) they are quiet and cheap to run
   (b) other types of printers cannot print graphics
   (c) other types of printers cannot print both text and graphics
   (d) they allow a greater range of fonts and graphics to be printed
12 A laser printer is said to work at 8 pages per minute. You find that it prints the pages of your illustrated book at less than 2 pages per minute. This is because:
   (a) all stated speeds are optimistic
   (b) the stated speeds refer to multiple copies
   (c) printing text slows the printer down
   (d) printers work more slowly after the first page

Assignment 4

Given files of a document and two pieces of art-work, create a document to the following outline specification.

A4 single column, single line border at 1″ from each edge. Title: ASSIGN-MENT 4 to be placed centred inside top border. Rectangular box of almost full width near top of page will be used to contain first graphic. Another box of half that width is placed near the bottom of the page and used for the second graphic. Adjust the sizes of the graphics, run in the text, flowing it round the graphics. Print the result (a second page may be required for the overflow of the text).

Recap

● The DTP program is loaded from disk either by using a set of direct commands, by invoking a batch file or by using 'front-end' programs such as Windows or DESQview.

● The Screen message are used to guide you against making mistakes, enabling you to select from menus and warning against problems.

● Floppy disks need to be formatted so that they are magnetically marked out; several must always be kept ready for data files.

● A document containing text and graphics can be created by preparing a page and then importing text and graphics files in either order.

● A document once created should be named and saved so that there is no possibility of losing it.

● A document should be abandoned only if another copy exists or if it is genuinely useless.

● When a document has been completely edited, it can be printed, specifying the number of pages to print. The printer specified when the document was created must be used – using a different printer will almost certainly cause problems.

● Once all work has ceased on a document you can leave the program by taking an EXIT option – never leave a program simply by switching off the computer.

Answers to questions

1 (b)
2 (c)
3 (a)
4 (d)
5 (b)
6 (c)
7 (d)
8 (c)
9 (b)
10 (c)
11 (d)
12 (b)

5 The design brief

Objectives

After reading this chapter you should be able to:
- describe the stages in designing a publication
- discuss the typographical styles of newspapers and magazines
- use the DTP program to draw rectangles and boxes
- show how to create text in a word-processor and export it to the DTP program
- type text directly into a DTP page, using various fonts
- make use of clip-art, scanned material and screenshots in a page.

Scenario

You are asked to design a two-page advertising leaflet for a device or a service, using illustrations. The leaflet must be eye-catching and informative, and the text must be faultless. How would you go about this?

Making perfect

There is virtually nothing worth doing in which some well-guided practice will not assist in obtaining better results. This is particularly true of desktop publishing, and the more practice you can get, the better able you will be to make effective use of all the equipment and the software. In addition, you need to look at your products critically. Are the points you want to make sufficiently emphasized? Does the page look **interesting**? Would more variation in type face help, or is the page already a mess because of too many different faces? Could graphics be better used? These are all value judgements, things that cannot be resolved by measurement or mathematics.

128

Another aspect to practise is that it may be the only way in which you can become acquainted with some features of the capabilities of a program such as Aldus PageMaker. If, for example, you use desktop publishing to create the menus for a cafe along the road, it is most unlikely that you will learn how to handle the type of work that is required for the Cromwell Club's newsletter. A good principle is to look at other published work, much of which may not have been produced by desktop publishing, and think how you would go about reproducing such pages. Once you learn to think like an old-style inky-fingered printer you are on the way to producing better printed material for yourself. The eye, like the ear, requires education. If you have never heard really excellent hi-fi, for example, you probably have absolutely no idea that such excellence is achievable, but unless you listen to genuinely live music (no microphones, no amplifiers, no loudspeakers) you probably won't appreciate hi-fi because you have no basis for comparison. Similarly, unless you learn to appreciate how the pages of a newspaper have been put together and how emphasis has been made, pictures used, headings and sub-headings placed, etc., you are unlikely to be able to produce pleasing results for yourself.

Good technology, as provided by the PC machine, a PostScript laser printer and a DTP program of the Aldus PageMaker class, helps you along the way, but in the final analysis the appearance of your desktop publishing efforts depends on your own eyes, and how critically you use them. In this book we are considering black and white text and images only. This is difficult enough, and the addition of colour, available only on very expensive packages, is yet another dimension. Many males are partly colour-blind, and you cannot rely on your visual senses to criticize a colour layout unless you are certain that your colour vision is perfect. Unless you can make these judgements, your work is not likely to please you, and if it doesn't please you it probably won't please anyone else.

The design brief

When you are required to design a piece of work for publication, the basis of the work is the design brief, a short description of what is required. This will be supplied by the client, preferably at a meeting in which several vitally important points need to be determined. These are:

● the purpose of the document
● the intended readership

- the size of the budget
- the quantity required
- the timescale for the work
- the need to maintain a house style.

The purpose of the document might be to inform readers that some new facility or product is available, or to go further and point out special advantages. It might need to be a consumer's guide, a technical manual, a price-list, an illustrated catalogue, a short story – the range is endless. The point of this part of the design brief is that the purpose of the document will decide almost every other feature of the document, because it determines how it will be designed. You do not use the same layouts for a story-book for children as you would for an advertising flyer for a new product.

The intended readership is also important. Will the reader have time for a long piece of text? Can the reader cope with the words that might be used – to be brutal about it, are they *Sun* readers or *Times* readers? What age range do you think might be reading the document? What will they expect to get out of it? Do you need to design the document so as to catch attention, and for how long should this attention last?

The budget is important – the difference between the cost of a glossy colour brochure and the cost of a simple but equally eye-catching black and white flyer can be enormous. The client must realize what costs are involved and why there can be such large differences. Equally, you must be able to estimate these costs quickly and point out where money can be saved and what effect the savings might have on the appearance of the document.

The quantities must be agreed. The amount of design work needed to produce one copy is as great as is needed to produce a million, but printing costs on a large number will usually swamp design costs. If your role is purely in design the printing may be the responsibility of the client, in which case quantities have little importance to you, since you are supplying only the master copies. If, as often happens, you sub-contract the printing, you must be aware of how quantities and costs are related. You must, for example, know how many copies need to be printed to qualify for a lower price-per-copy, and how to allow for this in the budgeting.

The timescale is important. If the client has text and graphics already on disk, the DTP work can be fast, but if everything has to be created from scratch the time required can be considerably more. In general, anything that can be supplied will cut the time required considerably, so that if time is short the client should be encouraged to use existing illustrations rather than to commission new ones, and to edit old text rather than supply new. Illustrations are usually more of a headache than text in this respect.

The most important aid to the design brief is a sample, or a set of samples, of existing or previous work. This can show a house style to which the new document must adhere, and it can show attitudes that are never made clear by meetings and specifications. It is possible that the client might want to break from the existing style, in which case it is important to know what should be avoided. It may be that the existing documents are ineffective (no-one reads them) and the client will welcome any views on why they have failed. Even if the client is commissioning printed work for the first time, it can be helpful to look at other work that has been done for other clients. Very few people have clear ideas on the appearance of documents, and many will rely on you, the publisher, to provide help.

The design brief should be agreed at a meeting, and the first part of the work is creative and manual – no machine can assist in this stage. Working from the design brief, thumbnail sketches should be produced; a form of greeked text and graphics page outline. These can be used to produce a 'visual', a sketch layout to be submitted to the client. Nothing can proceed until these have been approved, and it is possible that alterations may have to be made. Remember, however, that most clients do not have fixed ideas of how a document should look, and you are supposed to be the expert and the guide. If there appears to be no chance of compromise, you might eventually have to part with the client, but this is a desperate measure when you have spent so much effort already. Remember that the design stage is the expensive stage as far as you are concerned – the DTP part is the semi-automated low-cost part.

Starting the design

The design brief might be in more general terms than the summary above or it might be more detailed, but it will nearly always leave you with the crucial decisions on the final appearance of the published document. These are:

● the amount and content of text
● the number and size of graphics
● the size and number of pages

- the page orientation, portrait or landscape
- the page format in terms of columns, margins, headers, footers, etc.
- the fonts and styles to be used
- the layout of the text and graphics – presentation style
- the paper quality.

Some thought has to be given to the text and graphics for the document. The text may have been supplied by the client, or it may have to be written. It is possible that you might tackle some writing yourself, but for a lot of work a specialist writer will be required, particularly for technical text. Choice of a writer is important, because the writing must be suited to the readership. Some technical writing looks rather like quotations from a manual, with no attempt to explain or, even worse, with incorrect or misleading explanations. Writing good advertising copy requires experience, and such experience is costly. For general work, some contacts with a local newspaper are very valuable. Journalists can often supply some copy very quickly, or can lead you to a freelance writer who specializes.

Even if text is supplied, some editing is likely to be needed. Authors are never well-equipped to criticize their own work, and text is often supplied from very inexperienced authors. You will need to read the text critically, removing unnecessary repetition and correcting spelling errors. You may need to cut the text if it is unnecessarily verbose, or expand it if it looks too concise. You may also need to alter the arrangement of text – some contributors may not even divide their text into paragraphs. You will probably have to supply headings and sub-headings, and this may require either some knowledge of the subject matter or consultation with the author. If the text is very technical material, you should never take the decisions on headings entirely on your own.

Graphics may consist only of an existing logo which can be scanned into a file and edited ready for use. If there are any existing line drawings to be incorporated these also can be scanned into a file. Photographs are the most difficult material to deal with, requiring a high standard of scanning work and a lot of space on a disk. The use of photographs also rules out the use of a laser printer unless the client realizes and accepts the comparatively poor standard of reproduction. If no artwork is supplied, drawings will have to be made or photographs taken.

If new drawings can be made using CAD rather than paper and pencil, a considerable amount of time will be saved, because many CAD files can be imported directly or converted into a suitable form for import. The same applies to drawings produced using paint packages, particularly for those that produce the PCX type of files. If only work on paper can be obtained, this will have to be scanned and edited before use. If photographs have to be taken, this will cause a very considerable increase in costs, and the client must have been made aware at the design briefing.

Once again, a good set of contacts is essential. It is easy enough to find freelance draftsmen and artists who work on paper, but much more difficult to find any that can work using computer packages. Once again, contacts with a local newspaper can reveal a few names that can lead you to freelance operators who can supply your requirements in machine-readable form.

Graphics also need to be edited. You may need more graphics, or need to reduce the number. You will have to decide the scale to which the graphics will be printed and where each illustration belongs in the text − try to avoid the need to turn over a page to see the illustration to which text refers. Ideally, a graphic should break up a block of text that is otherwise uninterrupted by headings.

Once the text and graphics have been decided upon, the layout can start. A page size and orientation needs to be selected which will allow the whole of the text and the graphics to fit, whether in one page or many − the size of the graphics will often determine the size of page that has to be used because there is a limit to how far a graphic can be reduced in scale and still be useful. The A4 format is a useful large one for documents, but the US Letter size is sometimes more convenient. What you can choose here is usually determined by the DTP program that you are using, and some low-cost DTP programs allow only the 8″ × 11″ page size. PageMaker allows, as we have seen, the choice of a variety of fixed formats such as A4, A5, US Letter and Tabloid, and also Custom formats whose dimensions you can type in for yourself subject to the limitations of the program. Think very carefully before using Custom sizes, because a laser printer may not be able to cope well with some sizes.

The fonts and styles now need to be marked in. Use a draft copy of the text, and decide on the font that will be used for the bulk of the text − this is likely to be a common font such as 12-point Times Roman. Now note in the margin the fonts that will be used for headings and sub-headings. These will be a larger point size and often in bold style. Note also in the main bulk of the text any emphasis effects that are needed such as underlining, the use of italics or bold type, or the use of super-script or subscript. Use all such effects sparingly − excessive emphasis makes work difficult and tiring to read. Remember that you may have little or no choice if a house style exists, and if this is so, make a stylesheet out of this house style to ensure that you do not deviate from it.

The final, and main, decisions concern the layout of text and graphics. The golden rule of page design is often summarized as KISS – Keep It Simple, Stupid, meaning that a cluttered 'busy' page should be avoided. The other golden rule is that consistency is important. Master pages and style sheets help considerably in this respect, but only meticulous work can ensure consistency, and this task is more difficult when one person is the author, editor, typesetter, layout artist and page make-up operator. Conventionally, page layout was done using cut-and-paste, cutting the text and graphics on paper and pasting them to a sheet of the correct size to show the layout. DTP allows this stage to be automated to a considerable extent, but you should plan the layout in rough form, leaving the detailed layout to the screen as you compose the document. Your DTP program will allow you to scale graphics and to alter the relative positions of graphics and text so as to correspond with your rough layout.

Questions

1 The most useful guide to a client's needs is:
   (a) a statement of the purpose of the document
   (b) a list of the graphics to be used
   (c) a full description of the text
   (d) a sample of a previous satisfactory publication
2 You want to make a short document eye-catching and readable. Would you:
   (a) set it entirely in upper case letters
   (b) make each line of a different font
   (c) emphasise a few key words and keep it all short
   (d) rely entirely on graphics to carry the message

Purpose and style

By the time you read this portion of this book, you should be equipped technically to undertake any kind of desktop publishing with your selected package. Being technically equipped, however, does not mean that you can make a pleasing job of the process. A glance at some computing magazines will reveal advertisements which have been created using desktop publishing by users with an excellent technical grasp of the hardware and the software. They show the use of almost every font and every variation of size and style and they look as out of place among typeset work as an abacus at a computer show. All the technical wizardry in the world cannot prevent work looking amateurish if it is not accompanied by some feeling for what the final product looks like. Excessive use of effects in print is the equivalent of 'go-faster' stripes (also known as 'ape-tape') on cars. The purpose of your publishing efforts is to call attention to a text message, and if the message is confusing to the eye it will not reach the parts that count, which are the parts that think.

Your task, then, is to design your documents, using the sequence that has been outlined above. This has to be done with the computer switched off, because there's nothing quite so seductive as a blank screen which can be written on with a variety of fonts. The design of your publications has to be done on the medium that they will eventually appear on, paper. If you are working with items like business cards which must contain their information within a small and fixed format, then you will find it useful to use squared paper. Most graph paper nowadays is scaled in cm and mm, which is not really useful for print design, but with some perseverance you can still find paper that is scaled in 1/10″ squares. Filofax (TM) owners can buy a sheet called Quadrille which is scaled in various fractions of an inch, and this is ideal for laying out print designs whether you own a filofax binder or not. Whatever you do, don't use completely blank sheets because you need some form of guide even if only ruled lines.

These designs need not be detailed. You do not, for example, have to print by hand every word of each line, but you do need to show how many lines will be used, the length of each line and the distance between lines. At this stage, you should know what you want to say, and knowing the space that is available will help you say it better. A very common fault is to try to get too much in, and this applies particularly to business cards. The essentials of a business card are the name, address and telephone number, and anything else is of secondary importance. A good jobbing printer, asked to design and print your business cards, will ensure that these important features are prominent. If you design your own, the temptation is to be too clever, to have an elaborate logo, to use several fonts and sizes, so that you end up with a messy piece of display with the essential information hidden among the eye-catching trivia.

Activity

Make thumbnail sketches and layout plans for an A4 page in a local magazine to announce the opening of a new fast-food store. Try to use a design for which you can easily find graphics in file form.

Guidelines

No firm set of rules can make you an expert in this business, but a few rules can help to avoid some of the errors that leap out of the pages of magazines so often these days. One of the first rules is that anything that you want to appear in a magazine, or anywhere that will be read by anyone other than yourself, should be well printed. This might seem obvious, but you will see work that has been done on a dot-matrix printer in draft mode, which suggests either the use of a desktop publishing package that was not intended for a dot-matrix printer, or a user who did not realize that better print modes were available.

If there is one rule that might be considered more important than any other, it is that you should not try to put out any *major* piece of publishing single-handed. You might think that this defeats the aims of desktop publishing which, for the first time, allows a lot of printing to be under the control of one hand, but the fact remains that if you write your own text, do your own publishing and printing and check your own work, there will be problems. Working single-handed, you never see your own mistakes because you read what you think you want to see, not necessarily what appears in front of your eyes. The most ridiculous mistakes can pass you by because you happen to be concentrating on something else at the time, and this is particularly true if you are doing all your reading on screen. For anything of more than a few words (and even for a few, if their format is important), make a draft print and read it carefully, away from the computer.

The first thing to be critical about is spelling and typing. It's most unlikely that you don't know how to spell *the* but this does not prevent your nimble fingers typing it as *teh*, and since your brain will reassure you that you can't go wrong with simple words like this, you never notice the mistake unless you read word by word through a printed sheet. Typing errors are a very potent source of mistakes like this, and if you do not use a word-processor that incorporates a spelling checker for your text, then you should type slowly and check a lot. In any case, you cannot rely completely on spelling checkers, because, just to take one example, if you type *that* instead of *than*, the spelling checker will not help you because the word is correctly spelled. This is just another example of an error which only reading will detect, and if someone other than you does the reading, the chance of detection is much greater. Not everyone can read critically, unfortunately, and some of the glaring mistakes that appear in advertising copy are a tribute to the ability of the brain to make sense of things that the eye ought to have rejected.

Bad spelling is unfortunately predominant in a lot of desktop publishing output. In an age when even some road signs appear with mis-spellings, this is probably inevitable, but dictionaries are not expensive, and you can still buy copies of Fowler's *Modern English Usage*, so what's the excuse? It's not trivial, because bad spelling in a publication suggests that it need not be taken too seriously, since the publisher did not bother to check it well. If you know that your spelling is shaky, then, oddly enough, it's more likely that you will make fewer mistakes, because you will check more thoroughly. It's those of us who think that our spelling is perfect who are more likely not to notice mistakes simply because we don't think we could have made any. As Mark Twain noted, 'It's not what you don't know that causes harm, it's what you know that ain't so.'

Questions

3 The most important rule for any major publication is:
  (a) to make a draft using a dot-matrix printer
  (b) to make as much use of the space as possible
  (c) to use as many different fonts as possible
  (d) never to work single-handed
4 To ensure that text is of a good standard, you must:
  (a) put it through a spelling checker
  (b) get someone else to proofread it on paper
  (c) proofread it yourself on the screen
  (d) proofread it yourself on paper

Grammar

Hand in hand with spelling goes grammar. At one time, English grammar, and particularly the topic of parsing and analysis, was taught in all secondary schools. We have now reached the stage at which teachers of foreign languages complain that they cannot teach German or French grammar to students who know nothing of English grammar, and, conversely, overseas students who learn English as a foreign language know more of its grammar than native speakers. The point that seems to cause the most confusion is the apostrophe. This ought to be used to show missing letters, often the letter *i*. In the phrase 'it's clear', the apostrophe indicates that this is a shortening of 'it is clear', and in the phrase 'Harry's book' the apostrophe means that this is a shortened version of 'Harry, his book'. The main source of trouble is the use of the possessive forms of *it*, *who*, *her*, *their*, *our*, *your*. These *never* use an apostrophe, so that the phrase 'It brings its own worries' is correct, whereas 'It brings it's own worries' is not. If you find yourself typing who's, her's, their's, our's or your's, then stop and think, because you are probably doing it wrongly.

The second most common grating grammatical mistake is to fail to realize that the word *me* is the correct objective case of *I* at all times. If you don't know what an objective case is, you are probably a victim of school-induced illiteracy and aged under 40. What I mean is the incorrect use of I and me. People who would never dream of saying 'It was given to I' will quite cheerfully say 'It was given to you and I', as if the use of *you* exempted the *I* from being in its correct form. This type of mistake sounds bad enough in speech, but looks even worse in print because we expect print to reflect a reasonable standard of English (and we are speaking of the standard that was not uncommon for a 12 year old at one time). There are very few rules in the English language, so that it does not seem unreasonable that you should not break them in a printed work.

The third most common errors are nothing to do with spelling or grammar, simply ignorance of what a word means. How many times, for example do you see *less* used in place of *fewer*. Less applies to a bulk quantity, like less coal produced, less grain shipped. Fewer applies to number, like fewer cars, fewer cases of 'flu. You never see *fewer coal* but you do see *less cars* for some extraordinary reason. Also in this class you find fashionable words that seem always to be incorrectly used. One of these is *prevaricate* which means to tell lies, and is confused with *procrastinate*, which means to delay, to put something off until the next day. Confusions like this lose us the use of two words that caused no confusion before. If all this sounds too much like the rule of the schoolmaster of old, remember that it is our language, and when words lose meaning and become confused, then we lose the ability to communicate with them. Can anyone now use prevaricate or procrastinate in the hope that the meaning will be correctly understood? The confusion would never have arisen if it had not appeared in print, and it would never have appeared in print if standards of literacy had not dropped. If our language ceases to serve as a way of communicating precisely what we mean, then it becomes useless. Other nations take care of their languages and there are many compelling reasons for us to do the same, not least the reason that English is a language spoken by a very large number of people.

Spelling and grammar are topics that can be checked, either by yourself or, preferably, by someone else as well, and they are also items for which you have ample guidance in the form of dictionaries and books of style, like Fowler's masterpiece. The appearance of print is a very different matter. You can lay down rules for the way that print should be arranged, and find that you have to break half of the rules within a couple of lines. Rules and guidelines for printing are like rules and guidelines for art, they give you a start, but need to be abandoned if they conflict with what you think looks good. Just as we celebrate the greatness of artists who have abandoned rules to strike out in a direction of their own, we also celebrate the work of typographers who have known when to bend rules in favour of better appearance of text. You can study examples to your heart's content and learn from them, you can learn what rules there are, but the final result depends critically on your keen eye and good taste. These are qualities that you have to nurture and develop for yourself.

Having said all that, might we look at a few rules? Perhaps if we call them guidelines you will feel less inhibited by them. Whatever type of publication you embark upon, you will still have to follow roughly the same methods to obtain something that looks good and will be a pleasure to read. We can set out a set of guidelines for these methods so that you can avoid absurd blunders, and yet at the same time have considerable freedom to develop the work as you think fit. The all-important rule is to look critically at a draft print. Designing the layout of a page when you are looking at a distorted screen picture is asking too much of even an experienced typesetter and even if you are using a PC machine with a VGA graphics card that permits a screen display that is in true proportions you should not attempt to make a final judgement on the basis of the screen image.

The first decision that you will have taken on your printing is the page size. A lot of printed material uses the A4 size, which, being a metric size, does not conveniently fit into the printers' inch scales. Another common format is A5, which is an A4 sheet folded halfway along the longer dimension. Many newsletters are printed in A5 format so as to permit the use of A4 turned sideways and then folded. Whatever size you aim for, you need to remember how margins will be used. If you are working with a newsletter or any other material that extends to more than one page, your margins will have to allow for the space taken up when the sheets are bound together. A few word-processors allow you to alternate the margin width for even-numbered and odd-numbered sheets, but you have to do this for yourself on most word-processors and even with some DTP packages. The rule is that a sheet bearing an odd number appears to the right-hand side of the binding when it is lying open, and will have a large margin on the left-hand side. The even-numbered sheets will lie to the left, and have a large right-hand margin. You might, of course, specify equal margins on each side, but this loses you a lot of text space, so that attention to your even- and odd-numbered pages will normally be needed.

Once the page size has been fixed, you can start thinking about page layout, designing each page on a squared or lined sheet. A few newsletters may require little in the way of such design, but the more time you spend away from the screen the better the results when you start work. In any case, if a newsletter is so straightforward that it needs no design, is it going to be a good read? Now that we have the technical ability to make even the most esoteric newsletter appear well laid out and printed, why should we assume that the subject matter is so gripping that the readers will put up with any old thing? The experience of computer user groups is that readers soon desert a poorly-produced newsletter in favour of more pro-fessional work, and there is no reason why this experience should be unique. If your newsletter does not look good, someone else might do better.

The main item to decide about layout is whether you will go for one or more columns. My own feeling is that most newsletters on A5 paper should use only one column, because two-column work on paper this size looks too fussy. Even on A4, the use of two columns is not really necessary unless the page consists of a lot of very short items. For a newsletter as distinct from a newspaper, the items will probably be longer, and you lose space by having two columns. Provided that the print is broken up here and there by an illustration, there is no real objection to using a single column in A4. If your readers are predominantly elderly, there is a good case for aiming for the largest size that looks reasonable in the font you are using, so as to make for maximum legibility.

Questions

5 Which of these phrases quite definitely uses the words correctly:
   (a) We can prognosticate a better future.
   (b) Prevarication will always gain us time.
   (c) Better be truthful than prognosticate.
   (d) We might prefabricate about the incident.
6 The use of more than one column is reasonable if:
   (a) the columns are narrow
   (b) there are many graphics
   (c) the items are short
   (d) the paper is narrow

Fonts and sizes

Your next decision is that of fonts. Avoid the use of too many fonts, because this is visually confusing. There is no good reason, in fact, for using more than one good font on a newsletter, particularly when you have the range that a font like Times Roman offers. Too much variation in sizes and styles is almost as bad as too many fonts, and you should plan to have at most three sizes in most of your work. This might consist of 24-point for headlines, 18-point for sub-headings, and 12-or 10-point for the main text. Once again, remember that you are not trying to vie with ghosts of Fleet Street. Use bold for emphasis and italics for quotations by all means, but only a few words per page should need to be emphasized, and more than one paragraph in italic becomes tiring to read. Advertising work, of course, needs a greater visual impact. The problem with any advertising is that no-one reads it for pleasure, and everyone has become accustomed to the visual tricks in advertising material. The shorter the message, the more likely it will get across, but putting it into a large size or a fancy font does not guarantee that it will be noticed. Your eye has to be the judge here, and only critical examination of other printed work (newspapers, magazines, advertising brochures, etc.) can help to educate your taste.

   Whatever you do, try to avoid making changes to fonts or sizes in the middle of any piece of text. This is very noticeable, and many readers interpret it as a change from one piece of text to another. This means that half of your readers will read down as far as the change, and the other half will start reading the page at the point of the change. You can use the change deliberately as a means of separating sections, but it is better to confine this to the first capital letter of each new section. You can, for example start each story with a capital letter in a larger size, possibly also of a different style or font, to act as a marker, so that a reader has no problem in identifying the correct start of each section. This is preferable to the common practice in typed newsletters of leaving a large gap between sections.

Large gaps bring us to white space, the appearance of blank paper. Too much white space is an abomination in any publication, and indicates that little or no thought has been put into the design. By contrast, overcrowded text is just as bad, and as much of a deterrent to reading. You should think of white space as a splash of colour on your page, and try to balance it as well as possible. The worst offence is the fully-justified line with two or three short words in it, and a large space between words, but this often appears in newspapers. Some work might even look better with only left justification, using hyphens to split words so that the line lengths, though ragged, are reasonably similar.

You should not, however, be tempted to fill in white space with anything that comes to hand. If you have too much white space, that's a defect of planning, and you will not put it right by afterthoughts. If you have time, then get back to the drawing board; if not, then get to work on the screen so as to make the page more acceptable. Perhaps some editing would help. For newsletter editors, editing only too often means cutting and correcting, but at times a longer headline can be a useful way of balancing up the appearance of a page. White space is more of a problem for a wide-page single-column publication than for a multi-column one, because when you use more than one column you are less likely to have large gaps remaining. Don't, however, be tempted to put anything into the gutter between columns. A few desktop publishing users like to put lines down gutters, but this never looks good and can be very distracting to the eye.

Sometimes, it will be your sad duty to cut text. If you are running an 8-page newsletter, you can't let text spill on to a 9th page, and cutting is the only answer. Even careful planning can't avoid this at times, and you find that you have to pull back a line or two. Some reduction of white space may help, but you may still be left with the need to cut down text. This does not have to be the text that spills over, however. It may be that the article on pages 3 and 4 contained some repetitions that could be edited to a more concise form, and you can then shift text back until the whole newsletter is neatly filled. Making your newsletter of the same size each month (week, quarter, whatever) is an art-form in itself, and you should keep odd items of text around to fill in space if at any time you find that you are short of text. A gross excess will have to be dealt with by leaving an article over until the next issue, and small excesses can be dealt with by cutting text.

Activity

Take a piece of typed or printed text of about 1200 – 1500 words and reduce this to just under 1000 words without loss of meaning. Could you make a considerably shorter synopsis so that the meaning of the text could be seen at a glance?

Underlining and boxing

The use of bold and italic styles of type constitutes the main forms of emphasis that are built into any font, but, like word-processors, DTP packages also allow you to select underlined text. Traditionally, when using metal type, underlining was carried out by placing lead strips under lines, using strips that were wider than the leading strips, so that the line was inked and therefore printed. DTP packages can underline using fine lines by making this selection in the same way as bold and italic styles are selected. In addition, DTP packages can underline using much thicker lines, making use of line graphics. On PageMaker this means the use of the symbols at the top right hand side of the screen, the 'side tools'.

PageMaker can underline with a choice of about 17 different line thicknesses and styles, and you can, of course, merge such lines together to make even thicker lines. Like the other graphics actions, underlining requires the use of the mouse. The example in Figure 5.1 shows a headline with and without underlining. To underline the second header:

● Select from the Lines menu the thickness and style of line that is required.
● Select the side tool that shows a straight (diagonal) line. The reversal of shading in the box will indicate that this has been selected.
● Move the mouse so that the cross-hair marker on the screen is at one end of the phrase to be underlined.
● Press down the mouse button (left-hand) and drag the mouse with this button held down until the line extends right across the phrase.

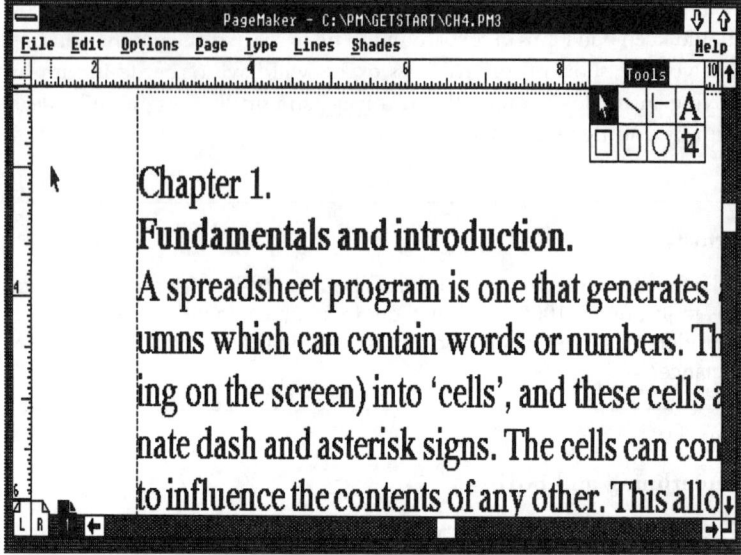

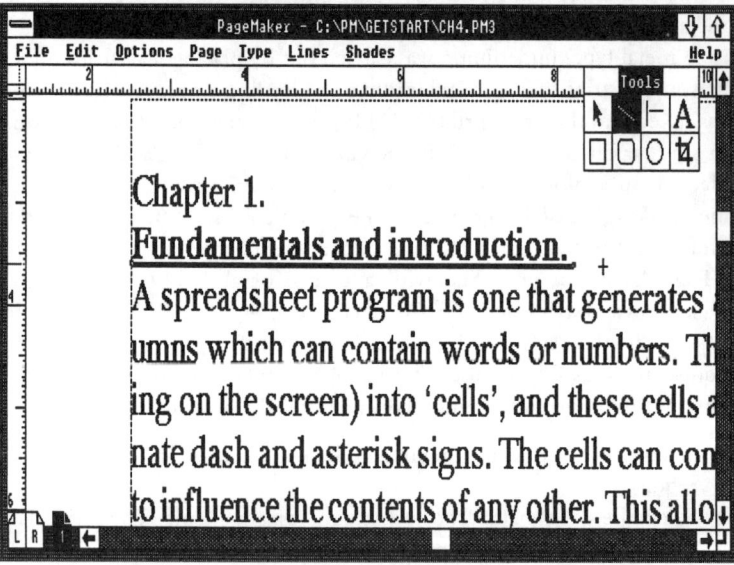

Figure 5.1 A headline shown with and without graphics underlining. In the second frame, the straight line side tool has been selected. The other form, indicated by lines at right angles, is even better for ensuring that lines are either horizontal or vertical

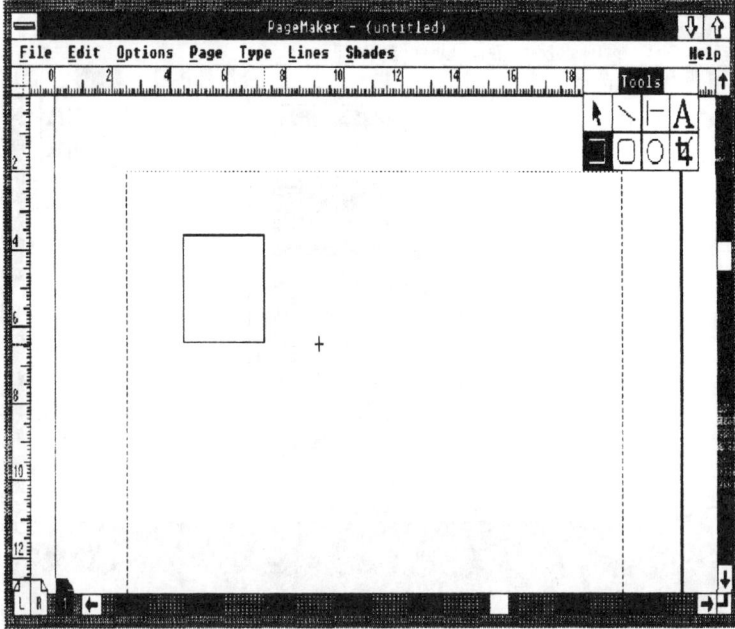

Figure 5.2 A box shape appears on the screen as the mouse is dragged from one corner to the opposite corner – shown here on a blank page for clarity

- Release the mouse button. This leaves the underlining in place.
- If the underlining is incorrect it can be deleted. On PageMaker this is done by pointing to the line (using the arrow tool) and then selecting Clear from the Edit menu.

It is usually possible to move an underline if it has been incorrectly positioned – PageMaker does this when the arrow tool is selected and the arrow pointed to one of the 'handles', small loops, that appear on the line. The mouse can then be dragged to move the line elsewhere. The same techniques can be used to create square or rectangular boxes.

- Select the line thickness and style as before.
- Select the box shape from the side tools.
- Use the mouse to place the cursor at the top left hand corner of the box position.
- Press the mouse button and drag the mouse so that the pointer is in the

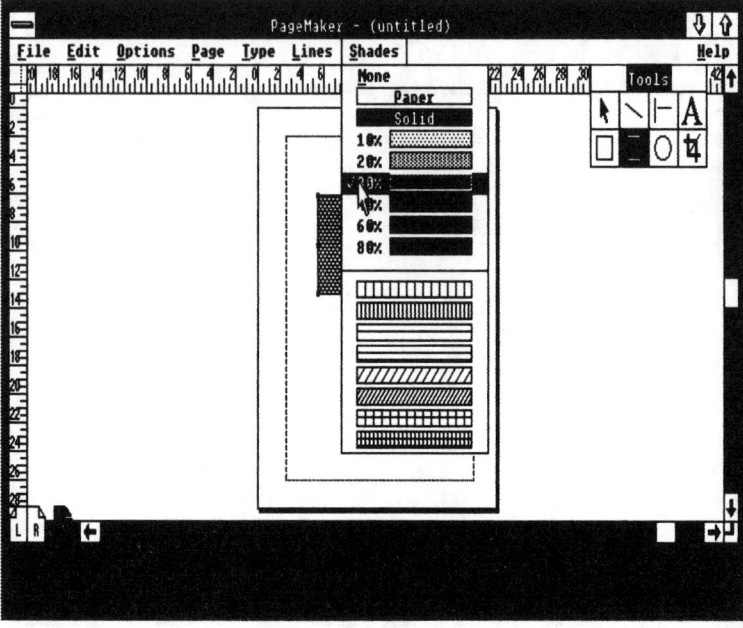

Figure 5.3   The *Shades* menu of PageMaker

lower right hand corner of the box – you will see the box shape develop as you do this, Figure 5.2.

● Release the mouse button.

PageMaker allows the choice of rectangular shapes with sharp or rounded corners, and circles can also be drawn. To draw a circle, the circle tool is chosen and the cursor placed with the mouse to the position for the centre of the circle. The mouse is then dragged with the button held down, and the circle appears – its radius is controlled by the mouse displacement from the original centre.

Any of these closed patterns can be filled, though the lower-cost DTP programs often do not permit the filling of an area. Using PageMaker, a rectangular box (to take an example) can be filled as follows:

● Draw the box as before
● Select the Shades menu and pick one of the shades illustrated, Figure 5.3
● The box will then appear with this shade filling it, Figure 5.4.

146

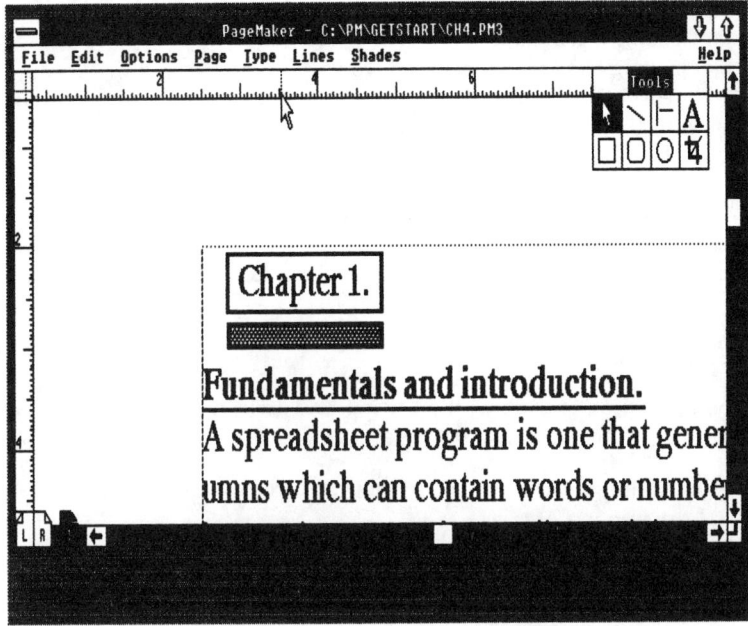

Figure 5.4   The area of an underlining box filled with the selected shade

This area-fill facility is very useful and many DTP programs allow it to be used on any closed shape, using the mouse pointer to indicate the area that is to be filled. One point to watch is that the area **must** be perfectly enclosed – if there is even the smallest gap in the surrounding lines, the filling will spread out through the gap and fill the rest of the page. Such gaps do not appear when the square or circle tools have been used, but are liable to be present on graphics that have been imported, particularly from scanned images. In general, it is better to work on such images first with a paint type of package before transferring them to the DTP program. Some painting packages allow an image or part of an image to be surrounded by an invisible line that will act to contain any filling.

Questions

7   Which of the following is the most useful way of dealing with excess white space:

    (a) adding some words to the text
    (b) adding a graphic
    (c) putting more spaces between words
    (d) replanning the page
8 You might use a box to emphasise:
    (a) chapter headings only
    (b) every important word
    (c) each line in a list
    (d) each important line

Using word-processor text files

For any text other than the most trivial, it is preferable to import from a word-processor rather than to type directly.

- Word-processors allow faster typing and are better suited to handling large amounts of text.
- Word-processor files can be smaller than DTP files.
- A word-processor can check spelling and, sometimes, writing style if needed.
- It is easy and quick to print a draft copy of text from a word-processor, allowing editing to be done before the text is imported into the DTP package.

As an example, Figure 5.5 shows a piece of text that has been created using a word-processor, in its uncorrected and unedited form. By contrast, Figure 5.6 shows this text cleaned up and edited, with the mis-spellings and mis-typings corrected, and headings added where required (only a portion of a longer text is shown here). This revised and edited text has been recorded as a file, and since the word-processor that was used is WordStar, the file is given the extension letters **WS** so that PageMaker can recognize this file as a WordStar file and make the conversions that are needed. The file can then be imported as follows:

- A new PageMaker file is opened, and a font suitable for the main body of the text is selected.
- The Files menu is used to select the Place option.
- This displays a listing of files (on the root directory of the hard disk initially) and from this the correct directory and the correct file are located. The mouse is used to select the file.
- The file is read – during this time PageMaker is inactive.

Chapter 2.
First Steps.
The first step in starting to make use of Masterfile is to decide in what
pattern you want to store the date. This, in trun, is closely tied up with what
use you intend to make of it, and you very often find that you need to alter
your ideas of what to keep in the database as your experience grows.
    The simplest rule to follow is that each item that has to be entered goes
into a separate field in the database. This is not always appropriate, but it
is a very good guide. In particular if you want to keep a list of names that
will be indexed alphabetically it is desirable to make the first field of each
record hold a surname. You can then use a separate field for other names and
for other appropriate items. Each time you enter a set of items that make up
one record about a person, a car, an aircraft, an hotel room, a train journey
or whatever, this data will be filed in the database and will have to be
loaded in again to be used. The usefulness of a database depends a lot on how
easily you can recover data from it, and the Masterfile database is
particularly good in this respect.
    Masterfile works in a way that much more flexible than a paper-based card
file, with each record holding data which need not all be displayed when the
records are viewed. For a full-scale database, a considerable amount of
planning is needed to decide the name of each field, which fields will be used
for indexing, the size and layout, how the data will be viewed and which items
you might want to extract to paste into documents. The most helpful hint is to
design as far as possible on paper rather than on the screen, so that by the
time you start to create a file, you know exactly what you want to see on each
'card'. As a starting example for this book, we shall assume that Masterfile is
going to be used to replace entries in a file about Civil Aircraft which were
formerly kept on card files of the type illustrated in Figure 2.1. We shall go
through the steps that are needed to convert this file from card format into
Masterfile format, because in this way the planning is minimal, we need only
make use of the existing card files as a guide to the Masterfile version. The
important points to note are the number and titles of the fields and the sizes
that have to be catered for.
    The illustration shows that the original card files used up to 20
characters for manufacturer's name, 15 for aircraft type, six for date, and
four for each dimension. Masterfile will not limit the number of characters in
a field, and the only reason for knowing what was allocated as space in the
paper version is so that a screen view can be organised to look reasonably
neat. We do not need to store dimensions as numbers because no arithmetic is
likely to be performed, but it is always an advantage to store a number in
number format. You might, for example, want to know how many aircraft of one
type would be needed to transfer the passenger load of another larger type. In
addition, when you have decided how many fields you will need, it is desirable
to allocate two spare fields. These need not be used right away – they might
never be used – and they need not be seen, but if you needd at any time to
expand the database it can be very useful to have these spare fields which need
only be named and used.
Starting an entry form.
When you have Masterfile installed, starting the program produces the initial
menu which was illustrated in Figure 1.8 CHECK. The actions which you need are:
    1. To establish what drive or directory will be used for data files, and
    2. To supply the information about the new file
and in order to carry out these actions we need to make selection from the main
menu, Menu 01. The drive/directory selection requires you to use Menu 03 wqhich
is reached by taking the Disk finctions option, letter K, from the Main Menu.
From this menu select P - Path/subdirectory and you will see a message at the
fott of the screen asking you to type in the new sub-directory path. You need
not specify drive C: if you start the path name with ther usual backslash

Figure 5.5   A piece of uncorrected and unedited text from a word-processor

Mastering Masterfile

Chapter 2.
First Steps.
The first step in starting to make use of Masterfile is to decide in what pattern you want to store the data. This, in turn, is closely tied up with what use you intend to make of it, and you very often find that you need to alter your ideas of what to keep in the database as your experience grows.

The simplest rule to follow is that each item that has to be entered goes into a separate field in the database. This is not always appropriate, but it is a very good guide. In particular if you want to keep a list of names that will be indexed alphabetically it is desirable to make the first field of each record hold a surname. You can then use a separate field for other names and for other appropriate items. Each time you enter a set of items that make up one record about a person, a car, an aircraft, an hotel room, a train journey or whatever, this data will be filed in the database and will have to be loaded in again to be used. The usefulness of a database depends a lot on how easily you can recover data from it, and the Masterfile database is particularly good in this respect.
Masterfile.

Masterfile works in a way that much more flexible than a paper-based card file, with each record holding data which need not all be displayed when the records are viewed. For a full-scale database, a considerable amount of planning is needed to decide the name of each field, which fields will be used for indexing, the size and layout, how the data will be viewed and which items you might want to extract to paste into documents. The most helpful hint is to design as far as possible on paper rather than on the screen, so that by the time you start to create a file, you know exactly what you want to see on each 'card'. As a starting example for this book, we shall assume that Masterfile is going to be used to replace entries in a file about Civil Aircraft which were formerly kept on card files of the type illustrated in Figure 2.1. We shall go through the steps that are needed to convert this file from card format into Masterfile format, because in this way the planning is minimal, we need only make use of the existing card files as a guide to the Masterfile version. The important points to note are the number and titles of the fields and the sizes that have to be catered for.
The cards.
The illustration shows that the original card files used up to 20 characters for manufacturer's name, 15 for aircraft type, six for date, and four for each dimension. Masterfile will not limit the number of characters in a field, and the only reason for knowing what was allocated as space in the paper version is so that a screen view can be organised to look reasonably neat. We do not need to store dimensions as numbers because no arithmetic is likely to be performed, but it is always an advantage to store a number in number format. You might, for example, want to know how many aircraft of one type would be needed to transfer the passenger load of another larger type. In addition, when you have decided how many fields you will need, it is desirable to allocate two spare fields. These need not be used right away - they might never be used - and they need not be seen, but if you need at any time to expand the database it can be very useful to have these spare fields which need only be named and used.
Starting an entry form.
When you have Masterfile installed, starting the program produces the initial menu which was illustrated in Figure 1.8. The actions which you need are:
    1. To establish what drive or directory will be used for data files, and
    2. To supply the information about the new file
and in order to carry out these actions we need to make selection from the main menu, Menu 01. The drive/directory selection requires you to use Menu 03 which is reached by taking the Disk functions option, letter K, from the Main Menu. From this menu select P - Path/subdirectory and you will see a message at the

Page 2.1

Figure 5.6   The text cleaned up and edited, with headings added

150

- When the file is ready, the normal arrow point changes to one that resembles a book. This indicates that the text is ready.
- The pointer is moved to the top left corner of the PageMaker page, and the mouse button is clicked. This loads in the text – some time is needed for this action.
- The text can now be dealt with in PageMaker.

For the sake of illustration purposes, little has been done with the text of Figure 5.7 because it has been printed on a dot-matrix machine which allows very few fonts to be used. The headlines use a different font (a larger size is not available with this printer) and the main body of the text is Times Roman 12-point. Figure 5.8 shows the text printed with the MicroLaser Printer.

As the text is read in, it will be placed into PageMaker with a single font (unless a style sheet is also imported), so that font changes have to be added later. The important point is to ensure that the main body of the text has the correct font, because once this is established only minor portions will require changes, often only for chapter headings and sub-headings. These changes of font are carried out by marking a block of text which is to be changed, and this technique is described in more detail in Chapter 6.

Direct entry of text

All DTP programs allow for the direct entry of text from the keyboard, and the screen will show the words as they are typed, using the selected font. This method of entering text should be used only for short pieces of text, for corrections to a text that has been entered by way of a word-processor, or for small additions to an existing text.

- Many DTP programs cannot accept rapidly-typed text efficiently, so that fast typing will result in the screen display lagging behind the typing or, even worse, omitting some characters.
- On the scale of the whole page, text is greeked and cannot be read as you type.
- On a scale that allows you to read the text easily, you cannot usually see the whole of a line without scrolling sideways.

If you need to add text, however, the methods are not difficult. When text has to be added to a piece of existing text, the addition will automatically use the same font as the existing text. If you need the additional text to use

Chapter 2.

First Steps.

The first step in starting to make use of Masterfile is to decide in what pattern you want to store the data. This, in turn, is closely tied up with what use you intend to make of it, and you very often find that you need to alter your ideas of what to keep in the database as your experience grows.

The simplest rule to follow is that each item that has to be entered goes into a separate field in the database. This is not always appropriate, but it is a very good guide. In particular if you want to keep a list of names that will be indexed alphabetically it is desirable to make the first field of each record hold a surname. You can then use a separate field for other names and for other appropriate items. Each time you enter a set of items that make up one record about a person, a car, an aircraft, an hotel room, a train journey or whatever, this data will be filed in the database and will have to be loaded in again to be used. The usefulness of a database depends a lot on how easily you can recover data from it, and the Masterfile database is particularly good in this respect.

Masterfile.

Masterfile works in a way that much more flexible than a paper-based card file, with each record holding data which need not all be displayed when the records are viewed. For a full-scale database, a considerable amount of planning is needed to decide the name of each field, which fields will be used for indexing, the size and layout, how the data will be viewed and which items you might want to extract to paste into documents. The most helpful hint is to design as far as possible on paper rather than on the screen, so that by the time you start to create a file, you know exactly what you want to see on each 'card'. As a starting example for this book, we shall assume that Masterfile is going to be used to replace entries in a file about Civil Aircraft which were formerly kept on card files of the type illustrated in Figure 2.1. We shall go through the steps that are needed to convert this file from card format into Masterfile format, because in this way the planning is minimal, we need only make use of the existing card files as a guide to the Masterfile version. The important points to note are the number and titles of the fields and the sizes that have to be catered for.

The cards.

The illustration shows that the original card files used up to 20 characters for manufacturer's name, 15 for aircraft type, six for date, and four for each dimension. Masterfile will not limit the number of characters in a field, and the only reason for knowing what was allocated as space in the paper version is so that a screen view can be organised to look reasonably neat. We do not need to store dimensions as numbers because no arithmetic is likely to be performed, but it is always an advantage to store a number in number format. You might, for example, want to know how many aircraft of one type would be needed to transfer the passenger load of another larger type. In addition, when you have decided how many fields you will need, it is desirable to allocate two spare fields. These need not be used right away - they might never be used - and they need not be seen, but if you need at any time to expand the database it can be very useful to have these spare fields which need only be named and used.

Starting an entry form.

When you have Masterfile installed, starting the program produces the initial menu which was illustrated in Figure 1.8. The actions which you need are:

  1. To establish what drive or directory will be used for data files, and

  2. To supply the information about the new file

and in order to carry out these actions we need to make selection from the main menu, Menu 01. The drive/directory selection requires you to use Menu 03 which is reached by taking the Disk functions option, letter K, from the Main Menu. From this menu select P - Path/subdirectory and you will see a

Figure 5.7   The text printed on a dot-matrix machine

152

<u>Chapter 2.</u>

First Steps.
The first step in starting to make use of Masterfile is to decide in what pattern you want to store the data. This, in turn, is closely tied up with what use you intend to make of it, and you very often find that you need to alter your ideas of what to keep in the database as your experience grows.

The simplest rule to follow is that each item that has to be entered goes into a separate field in the database. This is not always appropriate, but it is a very good guide. In particular if you want to keep a list of names that will be indexed alphabetically it is desirable to make the first field of each record hold a surname. You can then use a separate field for other names and for other appropriate items. Each time you enter a set of items that make up one record about a person, a car, an aircraft, an hotel room, a train journey or whatever, this data will be filed in the database and will have to be loaded in again to be used. The usefulness of a database depends a lot on how easily you can recover data from it, and the Masterfile database is particularly good in this respect.

Masterfile.
Masterfile works in a way that much more flexible than a paper-based card file, with each record holding data which need not all be displayed when the records are viewed. For a full-scale database, a considerable amount of planning is needed to decide the name of each field, which fields will be used for indexing, the size and layout, how the data will be viewed and which items you might want to extract to paste into documents. The most helpful hint is to design as far as possible on paper rather than on the screen, so that by the time you start to create a file, you know exactly what you want to see on each 'card'. As a starting example for this book, we shall assume that Masterfile is going to be used to replace entries in a file about Civil Aircraft which were formerly kept on card files of the type illustrated in Figure 2.1. We shall go through the steps that are needed to convert this file from card format into Masterfile format, because in this way the planning is minimal, we need only make use of the existing card files as a guide to the Masterfile version. The important points to note are the number and titles of the fields and the sizes that have to be catered for.

The cards.
The illustration shows that the original card files used up to 20 characters for manufacturer's name, 15 for aircraft type, six for date, and four for each dimension. Masterfile will not limit the number of characters in a field, and the only reason for knowing what was allocated as space in the paper version is so that a screen view can be organised to look reasonably neat. We do not need to store dimensions as numbers because no arithmetic is likely to be performed, but it is always an advantage to store a number in number format. You might, for example, want to know how many aircraft of one type would be needed to transfer the passenger load of another larger type. In addition, when you have decided how many fields you will need, it is desirable to allocate two spare fields. These need not be used right away - they might never be used - and they need not be seen, but if you need at any time to expand the database it can be very useful to have these spare fields which need only be named and used.

Starting an entry form.
When you have Masterfile installed, starting the program produces the initial menu which was illustrated in Figure 1.8. The actions which you need are:

  1. To establish what drive or directory will be used for data files, and
  2. To supply the information about the new file

and in order to carry out these actions we need to make selection from the main menu, Menu 01. The drive/directory selection requires you to use Menu 03 which is reached by taking the Disk functions option, letter **K**, from the Main Menu. From this menu select **P** - Path/subdirectory and you will see a

Figure 5.8   The same text printed from a laser printer

another font, you will have to ensure that the font is changed (by selecting another font) before typing starts. It is simple enough to change the font **after** typing, but this creates more work.

● Select the new font if you need a change of font.
● Select the text-typing tool if this is required (select the box labelled **A** if you are using PageMaker).
● Place the cursor to the place where you want to add or insert text – you may need to press the RETURN key to create a blank line if you are creating a heading.
● Type the text. It is advisable to type one letter and wait to see the effect before typing the rest of the text, since (particularly if there is a change of font) it can take some time to place this first letter on the screen.
● When the text has been typed, go back to the normal pointer tool.

Remember that when you add text to existing text, the font that was in use for the original text will be applied to the new text that you add, unless you deliberately change to another font. The use of style sheets ensures that fonts are used systematically, so that text will always be in one font, main headings in another and sub-headings in a third. Such style sheets can be created by most DTP programs and by some word-processors and require you to fill in the details of the font to be used for each part of the document, and then to mark the parts of the document where the exceptions (headings, sub-headings, notes etc.) occur, using codes that refer to the style sheet. The style sheet is then saved in the file along with the document.

Questions

9 You would normally create text using a word-processor so as to ensure:
  (a) that the correct margins and column layout are used
  (b) that the text is correct before it is imported to the DTP package
  (c) that the correct fonts are being used
  (d) that the final appearance of printed text is checked
10 When you type text directly into a DTP page:
  (a) it will always appear greeked
  (b) it will use a Times Roman font
  (c) you cannot control the size and font of the text
  (d) it will take the size and font of the surrounding text

Using clip-art

The simplest form of graphic to use is **clip-art**, meaning graphics images which are held in the form of computer files which can be read by the DTP program. These clip-art images are available in large numbers and in a variety of formats and, as the name suggests, consist of images which can be extracted from a set and edited to suit your applications.

The main limitation on the clip-art that can be used is the type of graphics files that the DTP program can read. This is indicated by the extensions to the filenames, of which the most common are MAC, PCX and IMG and if your DTP program will read none of these then very little clip-art will be available. The images that are available cover a wide range, including:

- animals, including dinosaurs
- company logos
- cartoon characters
- religious images
- symbols for engineering drawings
- maps, flags and other national symbols
- commercial images such as waiters, shop fronts, etc.

The MAC types of file often contain a large number of images in one file, and the DTP program should be able to extract one image and store it separately. When images are obtainable in PCX format they can be edited using a wide range of commercially-obtainable programs before being used by the DTP program. This allows images to be resized, edited, colour-inverted, transposed (upside-down or left-for-right), or otherwise worked on before use.

Clip-art is by far the easiest way of using graphics images in DTP work, and the wide range of images that are available, particularly in the popular formats such as PCX, make the use of clip-art a first choice when graphics images are needed. Some clip-art is very elaborate and would take a very considerable time and great artistic ability to create from scratch. Even if your DTP program does not accept one of the popular formats for clip-art, it is often possible to obtain conversion programs which will convert from a PCX (for example) file to other formats; such conversion programs are obtainable from the Public Domain Software Library (Appendix D).

Even if a piece of clip-art is not entirely suited to your purposes, fairly simple editing in a program such as Deluxe Paint II may be enough to make the image as you wish it to be, and if the only editing that is required is the addition of lettering this can be accomplished in the DTP package.

Activity

Select a piece of clip-art from a disk and import it into a DTP page. Type in some text to surround the clip-art, using either direct typing or importing from a word-processor.

Scanned material – line drawings

If no clip-art is available for the type of illustration that you need, one solution may be to scan existing images on paper. For small illustrations up to 4″ wide and 6″ long, a hand-scanner can often be used, but a full A4 scanner will be needed if the images on paper are larger. Remember, however, that the size of file required to store a graphics image of an A4 page can be very large. The simplest form of scanning is of line drawings, but even these can present difficulties, particularly when hand scanned.

The most difficult line drawings to scan are those which feature long prominent horizontal or vertical lines. Whether the scanner is a block type, a rotary type or a simple hand scanner, it is very difficult to ensure that the direction of scanning is perfectly aligned with one of these prominent lines in the drawing, and the result is that the line looks jagged when seen on the screen. This can be corrected by erasing such lines and redrawing them, or by rotating the image slightly (if a suitable Paint program is being used) until the lines are perfectly straight on screen.

A very recent development is the Mitsubishi MH216-400 scanner package, which consists of an A4 handheld scanner with paper-feed for desktop use, an interface card and scanning software. The software allows scanned images to be converted into vector images which can be further edited by a CAD package. If the CAD package allows, such images can be converted to PostScript form and used for high-quality image reproduction by laser printers or Linotronic machines. This is probably the best method of reproducing and manipulating graphics images for DTP so far devised.

Another difficulty arises when a drawing contains coloured lines, particularly red lines. Many scanners use red light in their scanning action, and red lines on a drawing simply do not scan – they do not appear on the scanned image at all. A few scanners overcome this by using a yellow scanning light which will allow red lines to be scanned with success. Drawings which include areas that are filled with colour also present

156

difficulties when scanned, and some editing is often needed to remove patchy shading in the filled areas.

When line drawings are being scanned, the scanner should be set for a resolution (if this is adjustable) that will be suitable for the final printed image. If a laser printer working at 300 dots per inch will be used, then setting the scanner to this resolution will ensure that the printed image is the same size as the original image. Scanning at other resolution figures can result in changing the scale of the image, and this can also be achieved by editing in a paint type of program.

Scanning photographs

Some scanners are specifically intended for use with photographs rather than with line drawings, but it is more common for scanners to allow either type of image to be scanned by setting a switch to line or photo. Scanning photographs requires the system to be able to reproduce a grey-scale (a set of shadings between black and white), and this is a much more difficult requirement than the scanning of a line drawing.

The usual method is to scan as a set of dots, placing dots closely together in dense black areas and spacing them more widely in light grey areas. On small hand-scanners, this system is called 'dither' and can be switched in for scanning photographs and out for line drawings. This can look unacceptably coarse if the dots are not very small, and a resolution of 300 dots per inch is only marginally acceptable for such purposes. The images obtained in a fax machine (which uses a scanner action) indicate the type of work that can be obtained at such resolution levels. For publication, much higher resolution must be used for photographs.

- Scanners are not a perfect solution to graphics problems, though they produce excellent results on line drawings.
- Unless a scanner is capable of good greyscale rendering, scans of photographs will usually be disappointing.
- An indication of an unsuitable scanner is the appearance of bands on scanned photographs, or of 'fishnet' appearance.

Geometrical patterns

Many DTP programs allow simple geometrical patterns to be created, usually lines, boxes and circles, and some allow for filling closed patterns with shading. Paint programs allow a much greater range of effects, but if technical drawings are to be created, a CAD program such as AUTOCAD or the simpler and very effective Generic-CAD is required. If less ambitious work is required, there are lower-cost packages such as Turbo-CAD and EASY-CAD, along with many excellent shareware programs which can be used. You must, however, ensure that the drawing program can produce files that can be read directly by the DTP program, or which can be converted to suitable files.

One method of making CAD files readable is to convert them into PCX files or TIF files, but when this is done, the precision of the original drawings will be lost and their resolution will depend on the screen rather than on the printer. If the files can be imported *as vector files* they will retain the ability to be scaled without losing resolution. Another option is to convert the files into PostScript form, the variety known as Encapsulated PostScript (EPS files), which can be read and manipulated by all the leading DTP packages.

Other sources

Two other important sources of artwork are screenshots and video stills. Screenshots, used extensively to illustrate this book, make use of software that allows the appearance of the VDU screen to be stored into a file. The software is of the resident type, meaning that it remains in the memory even while other programs are running, and is activated when a particular combination of keys is pressed. The file that is created can either be read into a DTP package, or converted into a form such as TIF or PCX which can be read by the DTP package. Screenshots are particularly useful when writing about the use of computers or when use is made of computer software to generate diagrams.

● The main problem concerning screenshots is the type of software to be used.
● Some screen-capture software works only on a few screen types, or produces files which cannot be read by any DTP package.
● Some software packages cannot co-exist with screen-capture software and will cause conflicts.
● The output files, even if stated to be PCX or TIF, may not be readable by the DTP package.

It is unusual to find that one screen-capture utility is capable of dealing with all of your requirements, and, in particular, you will often find that one utility is needed for graphics screens and another for text screens. The package used for this book was Pinch and Punch, which is excellent for capturing graphics screens (modified versions are needed for best results on Hercules graphics screens) and can capture text from VGA and some other screen types. Other well-known packages are HotShot and Hijaak.

Still video

The other option for graphics is the still video. Using a modern video camera is as simple as the use of a still camera, with the considerable advantage that the image can be seen while the camera is being used. A suitable combination of hardware and software allows the video camera to be set up to film so that any frame can be captured to a disk file. This is a particularly useful way of creating artwork without the need for drawing or painting skills, and is much faster than the use of a still photograph and a scanner. At one time, the use of black and white Polaroid film with a scanner was used, but it is now quite difficult to find suitable film, and colour Polaroids do not scan well. The main drawback of the video still is that the resolution is only that of the video system. Such shots look better if they are reproduced on a small scale, so that illustrations made in this way should not contain a lot of detail. Like any other artwork, the results from video stills can be edited to any required extent.

Questions

11 Scanning is particularly useful for:
  (a) colour photographs
  (b) black and white line drawings
  (c) coloured drawings
  (d) mixed text and drawings
12 Photographic images are always a problem for small-scale work because of
  (a) the limited resolution of a laser printer
  (b) the limitations of all scanners
  (c) the difficulty of editing a scanned file
  (d) the difficulty of importing a scanned file

Assignment 5

Prepare a visual layout for a client who wishes to produce a document to the following outline specification:

Purpose: to advertise, using a flyer, a car-spares shop, open all hours
Aimed: at car owners with a DIY interest
Budget: £500 for black and white pages
Quantity/Timescale: 2500 copies in 30 days
Samples: None available

Recap

- The design of a document starts with a briefing meeting with the client. This meeting must settle the purpose of the document, the intended readership, budget, quantity and timescale, and examine any previous work that might be used as a pattern or to indicate a house style.
- Style is not easily learned, it depends on considerable experience along with critical examination of books, newspapers and magazines.
- Some graphical effects can be provided by the DTP package itself. These include the use of thick underlining and the use of boxes, either hollow, surrounding text, or filled with pattern.
- Text files should be created in a word-processor, so that they can be fully proofread before importing into the DTP pages. Direct entry should be used only for minor work as it cannot be spell-checked and often is difficult to read.
- For graphics, as much use as possible should be made of clip-art and of scanned material. Clip-art is particularly useful as it already exists in file form and can be edited to suit. Scanning is most effective on line drawings, least effective on colour photographs. Screenshots and video stills are also useful sources of artwork.

Answers to questions

1 (d)
2 (c)
3 (b)

4 (b)
5 (a)
6 (c)
7 (d)
8 (a)
9 (b)
10 (d)
11 (b)
12 (a)

---

6 Image and text manipulation

Objectives

After reading this chapter you should be able to:
- describe how a graphics image can be scaled
- show how a graphics image can be cut, cropped or deleted
- describe how to move, copy and re-orient graphics images
- explain how text can be arranged around the image
- describe how fonts for text can be changed
- show how to change line spacing and carry out kerning
- describe how to correct errors in text
- show how text can be boxed with line patterns.

Scenario

You have text for a promotional booklet on file and also a set of graphics images. How can you now construct the booklet, scaling the images to the correct size to fit the page and placing them correctly in the booklet?

Positioning text and graphics

When a document is likely to consist of several pages, a master page layout should be used to ensure consistency. In addition to holding margins, headers and footers, the master pages can also hold *ruler guides* which are particularly useful for ensuring that text and graphics are correctly placed on the pages. In addition, these ruler guides can be put on to any other page as a way of ensuring that positioning of text or graphics is according to plan.

A ruler guide is a dotted straight line which is horizontal or vertical and seen only on the screen. It is normally drawn at specified distances down or across the page, using the permanent side-rules to provide a measure of the distances from the top of the page or the left hand side of the page. A horizontal ruler guide can be used to show where text is to start in each page if not immediately under the margin, and a pair of crossed horizontal and vertical guides can be used to show where the top left-hand corner of a graphic will be placed on the page. Some examples of ruler guides will be seen on the screen images in the following chapters. PageMaker allows such lines to be generated when the cursor is placed on a side-ruler line and dragged across or down the screen.

Scaling a graphics image

Scaling means altering the size of an image, using a scaling ratio such as 0.5, which would mean that all dimensions were halved. Scaling is used when an image is of the correct shape (correct ratio of height to width) but not of the correct size, so that it will not fit the space allocated to it. A scaling factor less than unity implies that the image is to be reduced in size, a scaling factor greater than unity implies that the image will be increased in size. A unity scaling means that the image is unchanged.

When scaling is applied in the course of a DTP program, it is usual to specify both X and Y scaling separately. If the image is correctly proportioned, the scaling factor should be the same in both directions, but it very often happens that the process of creating the image, whether by drawing or by scanning, makes the image distorted and this requires rescaling using a different scaling factor for the Y direction than for the X direction.

● In this respect, remember that it is the appearance of the final image **on paper** that is important.
● If you rescale an image simply because it appears to be stretched in one direction (usually vertically) on the screen, the result of the rescaling will almost certainly turn out to be incorrect on paper.
● To ensure that rescaling is correct, use the side and top rulers of the DTP program to measure the X and Y dimensions of any part of the image which is known to be a circle, a square, or a rectangle whose ratio of width to depth is known.
● By using the screen rulers, the correct scaling can be applied to make the dimensions correct.
● For example, if a circle appears on screen with its X diameter measured on the rulers as $1''$ and its Y diameter as $0.8''$, then the

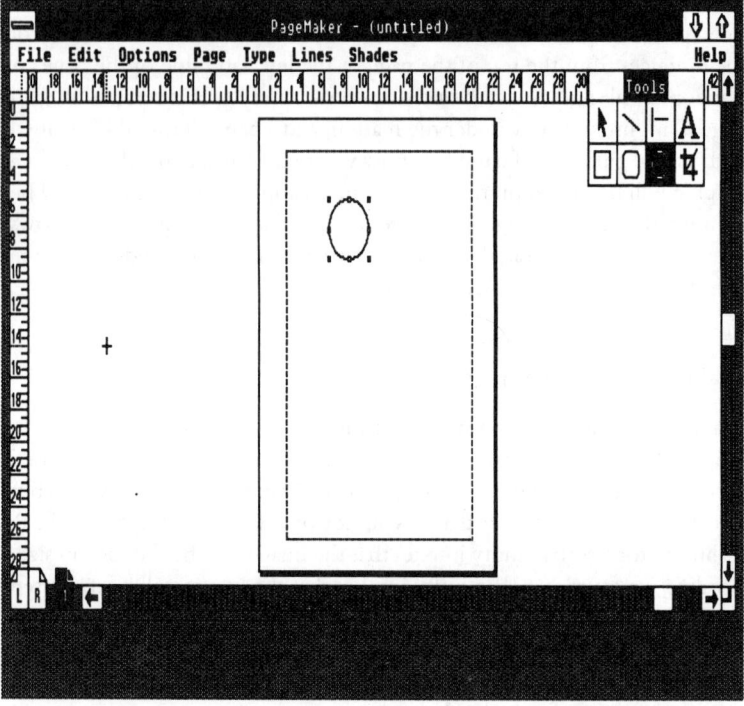

Figure 6.1 A circle drawn into a page by using the circle-drawing tool of PageMaker. The handles of the selection box are visible

rescaling must be such that the Y scale is greater than the X-scale to compensate for this.

● In this case the ratio is $1/0.8 = 1.25$, so that if the X scaling is 0.5 then the Y scaling must be $0.5 \times 1.5 = 0.75$.

● REMEMBER that the dimensions must be measured using the rulers that the DTP program places on the screen, NOT by measuring the dimensions from the screen using an external ruler. The DTP ruler display takes account of the distortion caused by the screen (because the number of dots per inch horizontally is greater than the number of lines per inch vertically).

Rescaling is typically carried out when the image is placed on the screen. At this time, the image will be surrounded by a window or selection box,

164

a frame of dotted lines which also define how near the text can come to the image. If the image has been placed in the text earlier and the window is no longer present, it can be put around the image by selecting the graphics window option of the DTP program. PageMaker allows a graphics image to be marked in three ways, by using the pointer (with the SHIFT key), by drawing a selection box, or by a Select-All command.

● Using the pointer recreates the original selection box that was used when the image was imported. It is most useful when each image has been imported in its own selection box.

● Drawing a new selection box is particularly useful when you want to work on several separate images or parts of an image.

● Selecting All is useful when all of the imported images need to be rescaled.

Rescaling, in virtually all DTP packages, involves using the 'handles' of the selection box or window. These appear when an image is created on screen and also when an image is imported. They also appear when a selection box is placed around an image.

Figure 6.1 shows a circle that has been drawn on the screen using the circle-tool of PageMaker. The circle appears in its selection box (invisible on this scale), but the handles of the box can clearly be seen as four dots around the circle. The pointer tool is then selected, and if this removes the handles they can be restored by clicking the mouse button on the edge of the circle.

If the pointer tool is then placed on a handle, the result is to allow rescaling by dragging. In the PageMaker example of Figure 6.2 the pointer has changed to a double-headed arrow to indicate that movement of the mouse will now cause rescaling of the image. This rescaling will be identical in both X and Y directions.

● PageMaker puts eight handles on imported images, four at the corners and four half-way along each side.

● Pointing to a corner handle and dragging the mouse will rescale the image with the same scale factor in both X and Y directions.

● Pointing to a top, bottom or side handle and dragging will re-scale either the X or Y dimension. The choice of top or bottom handle will rescale the Y dimension; the choice of a side handle will re-scale the X dimension.

● Some other DTP programs allow you to type in the amount of re-scaling required in the X and the Y dimensions.

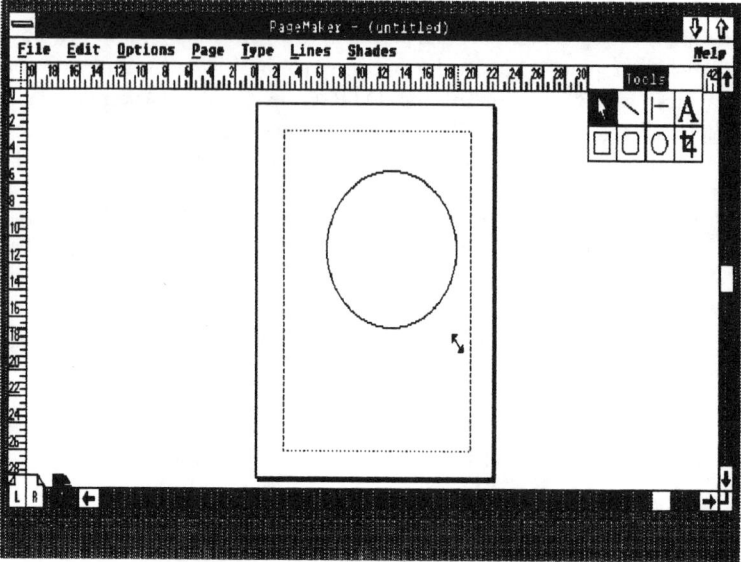

Figure 6.2   The pointer tool changes to a double arrow when placed on a handle to indicate that mouse movement will cause rescaling

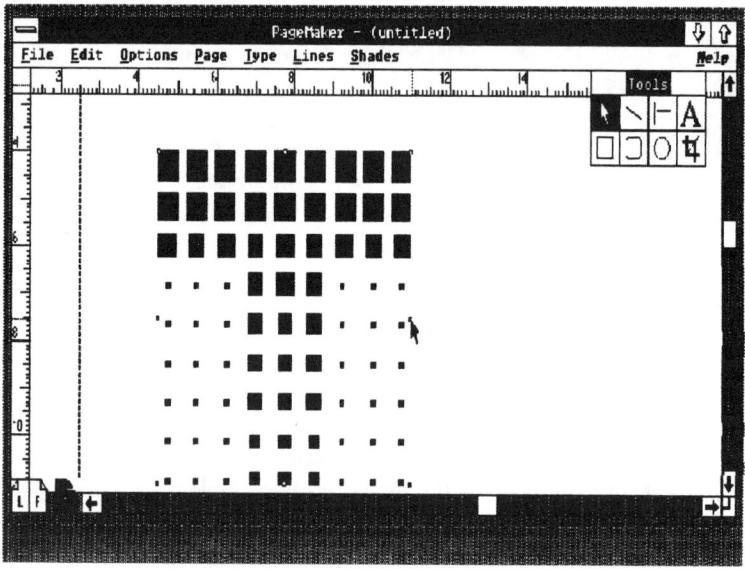

Figure 6.3   The pointer placed on a side handle of a logo pattern

166

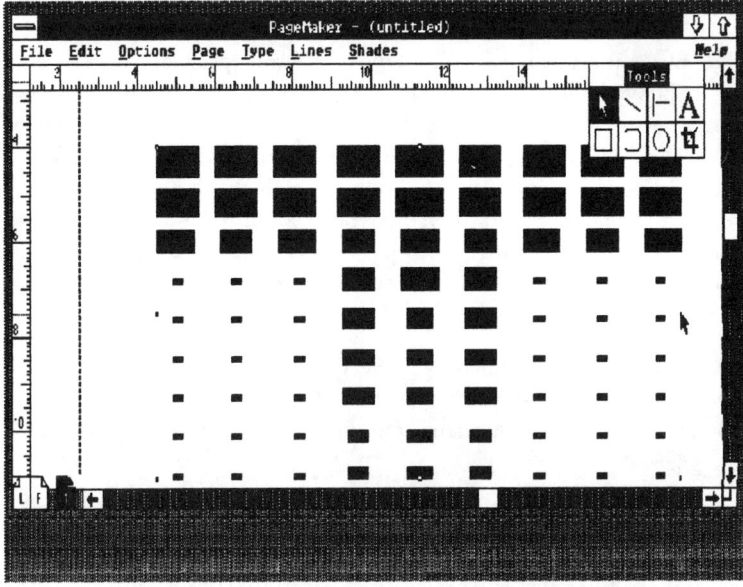

Figure 6.4 The pattern distorted by increasing its X-dimension while keeping the Y-dimension constant

● Figure 6.3 shows the PageMaker pointer placed on a side handle of a logo pattern. Figure 6.4 shows the results of dragging the pointer to increase the X scale while keeping the Y scale constant.

Questions

1 Scaling is used:
   (a) to improve the resolution of a graphics image
   (b) to check what size of graphics image will be printed
   (c) to increase or decrease the number of dots per inch
   (d) to make the image fit into a selected space in the text
2 A graphics image will have to be rescaled with different X and Y factors if:
   (a) circles look squashed on the screen
   (b) the on-screen rulers show that a circle has different X and Y diameters
   (c) circles look circular on the screen
   (d) the image has to fit into a rectangular box

Deleting the image

If an image is created or imported into the wrong place in a document it can be moved, but if the wrong image has been created or imported then it is necessary to delete it. Most DTP programs provide for this by way of the selection box, allowing a simple command to delete the image in the selection box. A point to watch, however, is that if all images have been selected all will be deleted when this type of command is used. The Delete action normally uses either a menu selection such as Delete or Clear, or the use of the normal text–delete key when a graphic has been selected.

Using PageMaker:

- the image is surrounded by a selection box in the usual way
- the delete or backspace key is pressed
- alternatively, the Edit menu is brought down and the Clear option is selected

Deleting an unwanted graphic is not always necessary, particularly when PageMaker is being used, because an unwanted graphic can be replaced. Replacement in PageMaker is particularly useful because if the unwanted graphic has been scaled to fit part of a page, it can be replaced by another graphic which will be scaled *automatically* to fit the same space. This makes replacement a better option than deletion and placing a new graphic, and it is done as follows.

- The original, unwanted, graphic is marked with a selection box. This is VERY important – if this is not done the new graphic will be placed over the old one (which allows the merging of two graphics).
- The Edit menu is selected, and the Place option used.
- The new graphic is selected from the directory list.
- The option of Replace Old Graphic is taken, Figure 6.5.
- The new graphic will now replace the old one in the same position and using the same size.

Activity

Import a clip-art image and rescale it so as to fit into a smaller or a larger space. Show the effect of using different X and Y factors.

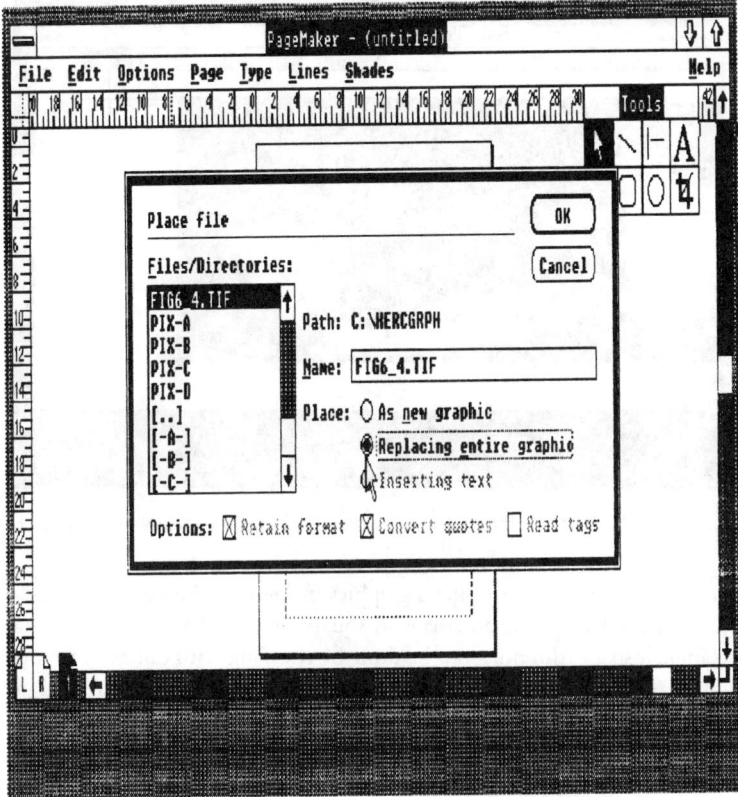

Figure 6.5 Using the *Replace Entire Graphic* option of PageMaker to re-place one graphic with another which will be scaled to fit automatically

Cutting and cropping

Cutting and cropping both mean the process of reducing the size of an image by clipping pieces from the image. In photography, cropping a print means using a guillotine to remove unwanted pieces of background when the print is to be mounted in a frame. During the photographic enlargement process it is also possible to place only the wanted portion of an image on the printing paper so that subsequent cropping will not be needed.

Cutting or cropping on a DTP image is normally used for the same purposes – to remove irrelevant or distracting backgrounds from an

169

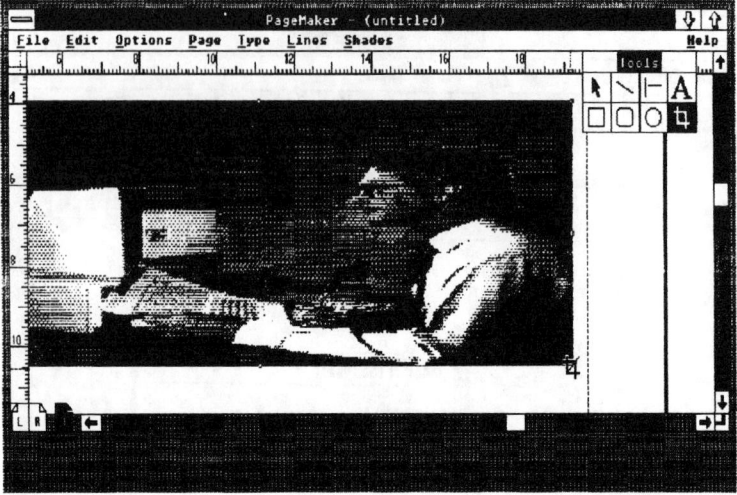

Figure 6.6   Placing the cropping tool on to a handle of the selection box

image – and also to ensure that a graphics image is of the same shape as a space reserved for it. If an image is square and has to be fitted into a rectangular space, this must not be done by rescaling with different factors (which will distort the image), but by cropping the image so that it becomes rectangular. This ought to have been done before an image was imported, but if a scanned image is imported into the DTP package directly it is necessary to carry out the cutting/cropping (both words are used) in the DTP package itself.

Some of the simpler DTP packages make no special provision for cropping an image, and on these packages cropping is done by placing a selection box around the part of the image that is to be cropped and deleting this part of the image. PageMaker and comparable DTP programs allow cropping to be carried out in a much more flexible way.

● The process starts by selecting the graphic image, and then a cropping tool and placing the cropping tool on to one of the handles of the selection box, Figure 6.6.

● The corner handle can be used to crop both X and Y directions, but the handles at the top, bottom or sides will crop in one direction only.

● Dragging the cropping tool across will show a cropped image, Figure 6.7, but it is only the framing that is changed – the cut part of the image is still available for use.

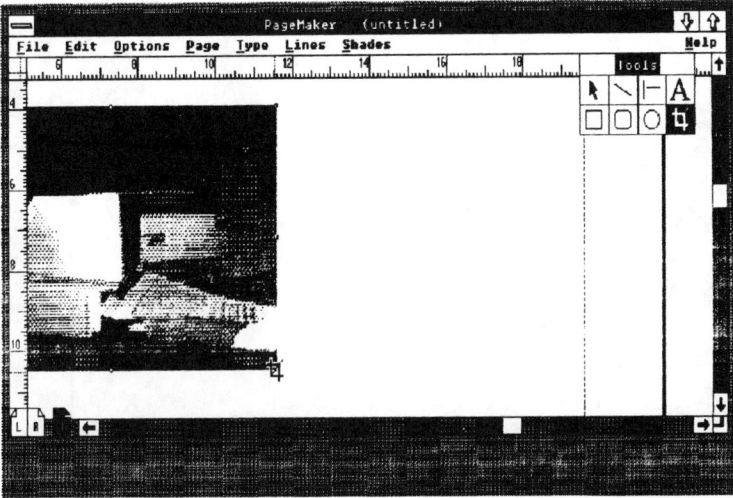

Figure 6.7   Dragging the cropping tool will crop the image using a framing method – this can be reversed and other parts of the image can be revealed

● For example, placing the cropping tool into the image and pressing the mouse button changes the cropping tool into a hand. This can be used to drag the image over the cropped frame to expose a different part of the picture, Figure 6.8.

● Cropping is therefore not so final as deletion – the image can still be adjusted after cropping.

● NOTE that PageMaker uses cropping only for imported images, graphics shapes created by PageMaker's own line, box and circle tools cannot be cropped.

Moving graphics images

Any graphics image, imported or drawn using the built-in tools of the DTP package, can be moved about a page. The important point is that the movement of the graphics image should not cause the text to be interrupted. If the text wraps around the graphic, as is normal, then when the graphic is moved text will occupy the space that has been vacated and the text will wrap correctly around the new position of the graphic.

● Figure 6.9 shows a page that contains a graphic image in the top one third of the page.

171

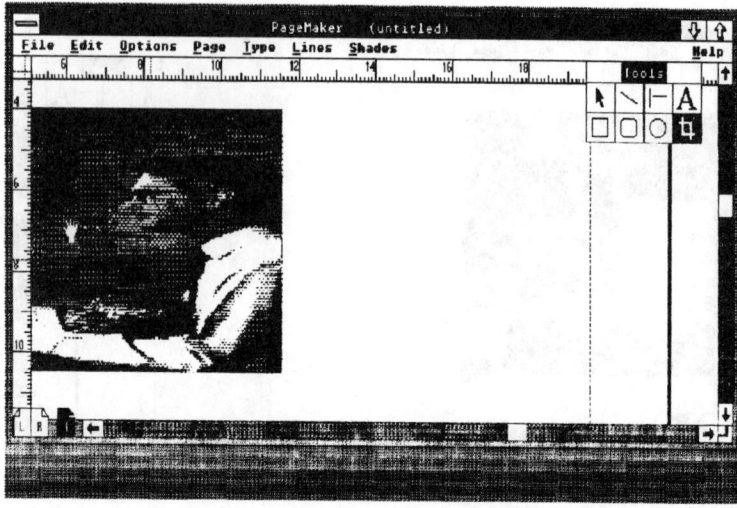

Figure 6.8   Dragging the image over the frame to alter the effect of cropping

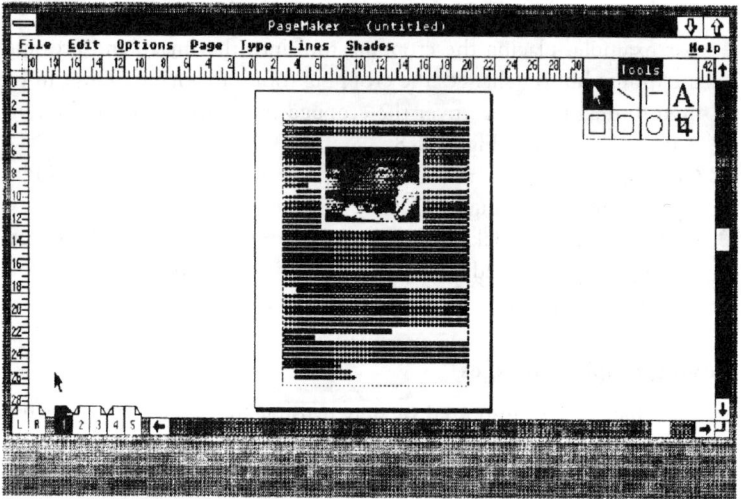

Figure 6.9   A page which contains an image in the top part of the page

● The graphic is then selected using the pointer tool.
● The graphic is dragged to its new position. Using PageMaker, pressing

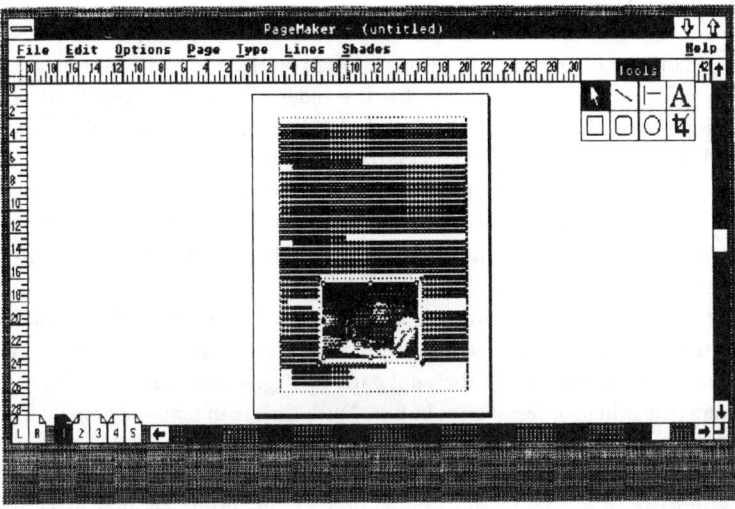

Figure 6.10   The graphic dragged to a new position with text still wrapped around it

the Shift key down as well as the mouse button will ensure that the dragging can be either perfectly vertical or perfectly horizontal, so preserving the column or row position of the image.

● When the mouse (and any other) key is released, the graphic can be seen in its new position, with text filling the old position and the graphic in its new position, with text wrapped around its boundary, Figure 6.10.

Some care is needed if a program does not automatically wrap text, or if the text-wrap has to be selected before moving the graphic image. If, when the image is moved, you find that the text does not correctly flow into place you may have to delete the text (not the image) and reload the text, taking care to see that the options for automatically flowing text around the graphic have been correctly selected.

When a graphics image is moved in this way, the position of the image should be gauged by the ruler lines that the DTP programs places against the page, or by the use of ruler-guides that have been placed into the page. If positioning is critical, you may have to look at a magnified version of the page in order to see exactly how the image is positioned.

Copying images and text

The copying of an image or of text is often referred to as a cut-and-paste operation, following the name for the older method that was used on galley proofs. The portion to be copied is marked, using a selection box, and the Cut command of the DTP package is used to remove the portion of image or text. Another page or piece of the same page is then selected and the Paste option is used, placing the cursor to where the material has to be pasted in. The text or graphic will then be placed at the new cursor position.

PageMaker, in common with many other DTP programs, uses a piece of memory to hold the text or graphics that has been cut. This piece of memory is referred to as the clipboard in PageMaker, other DTP programs use other names, such as buffer. Once a piece of text or a graphic has been cut and therefore stored in the clipboard, it can be pasted into more than one place – you can continue to paste in the same piece of text or graphics until it is replaced in the clipboard (by cutting another piece of text of graphics).

The extent to which this facility can be used depends on the DTP package. PageMaker allows the clipboard to remain active while a document is closed and a new document opened. The content of the clipboard can then be pasted into the new document. In addition, if your PC machine uses the full version of MicroSoft Windows (now Windows-3), the clipboard remains active even after you have left PageMaker, so that the contents of the clipboard can be pasted into any program that will accept them, such as paint packages or word-processors which are designed to use Windows. DTP packages that do not make use of MicroSoft Windows are rather more limited in this respect.

Questions

3 An image might have to be deleted because:
  (a) it is the wrong image
  (b) it is too small
  (c) it is the wrong shape
  (d) it is too large
4 When a graphics image is moved:
  (a) it will leave a blank space
  (b) text should still flow around it

Figure 6.11   An image created with First Publisher using clip-art

(c) text can be seen through the image
(d) the image hides the text

Re-orienting images

Re-orienting images means such actions as lateral inversion (making a mirror-image), turning the image upside down, or revolving the image. The provision for making such adjustments to an image varies considerably, and some DTP packages, PageMaker notably, make no provision for such effects, assuming that all of this kind of manipulation will have been done before an image is imported.

Figure 6.11 shows an image created from the low-cost DTP package, First Publisher, using one of the many clip-art images which has been duplicated in this page. The penguin image on the right hand side has been selected, as indicated by the dotted line. When the Art menu of this program is selected, Figure 6.12, the re-orienting options shown are Flip

Figure 6.12 The Art menu of First Publisher, showing the useful options

horizontal, Flip vertical, and Rotate. There is also the Invert option which means colour inversion – exchanging black for white on a monochrome image.

Figure 6.13 shows the result of the horizontal flip action. The image is now the mirror-image of the original version, making this a very useful method of creating 'book-end' images. The result of the vertical flip is shown in Figure 6.14, and Figure 6.15 shows the image rotated through 90° – this program permits only 90° rotation each time the Rotate action is specified. Note the distortion of the image on the screen when the 90° rotation is used because of the difference between horizontal resolution and vertical resolution – the image prints correctly on paper.

Activity

Create a letter heading which uses 'bookend' graphics images (one turned horizontally) so as to frame a title.

176

(a)

(b)

Figure 6.13 (a) The on-screen result of a *Horizontal Flip* action on a dupli-
cate of the image. This creates a 'bookends' effect. (b) The laser-printed
version

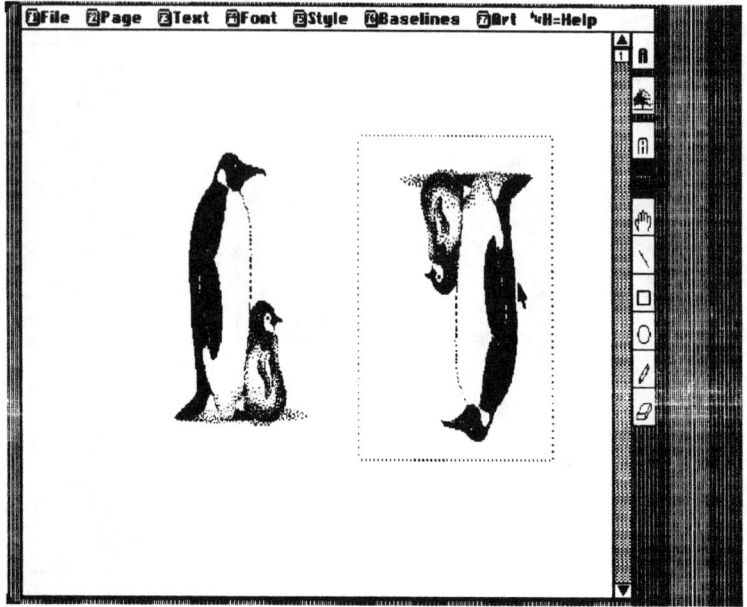

Figure 6.14   A vertical flip will turn an image upside down

Line type and infilling

When simple geometrical graphics are created using the tools of the DTP package, several variations in format are usually possible. Once again, some of the lower-cost packages offer more in this respect because it is assumed that all of the work of preparing graphics will be done using the DTP program. Because of this, there is usually an eraser tool which allows portions of lines to be deleted by moving the mouse pointer.

The more expensive packages assume, once again, that these actions will be carried out in a separate graphics program, but they provide for considerable variation of the pattern of the images that are produced by the line, box and circle tools. Lines can, for example, be dotted or dashed and created in a variety of thicknesses. The method of use is:

● Select the straight-line tool for drawing.
● Now select the Lines menu and the width/pattern options(s) that you want.
● Move the cursor with the mouse to the starting point for the line.

178

Figure 6.15 The *Rotate* action will turn an image clockwise by 90° each time the command is used. Note the different size of the rotated image because of the difference between horizontal and vertical screen resolution

- Press the left-hand mouse button and drag the mouse to the end-point of the line. Be careful about the positioning of the mouse at this end-point if you want to make lines that are exactly horizontal or vertical, see later.

- Release the mouse, leaving the line, which will be marked with handles.

- Alternatively, draw the line first with the default 1-point size of solid line and select the line width/pattern after drawing.

Note that for precisely vertical or horizontal lines, PageMaker uses another tool marked by two lines at right angles.

Figure 6.16 shows some lines drawn with PageMaker in a variety of patterns, along with the Lines menu which shows the variety of line patterns that can be used. These patterns are not so readily seen on the screen as on paper, and the Hairline can be printed only with a laser (or inkjet) printer, not with a dot-matrix printer. The Reverse line will change the line from black to white if the line is to be drawn on a dark background. PageMaker offers (with a laser printer) the choice of eight

179

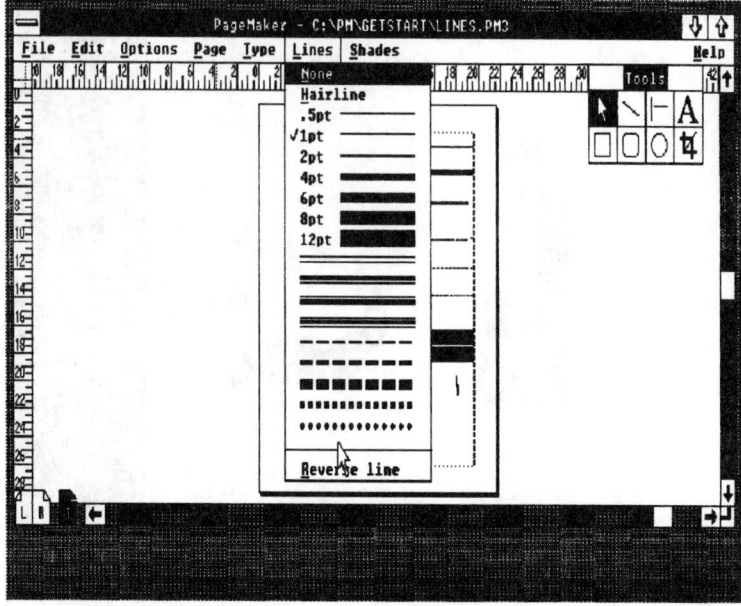

Figure 6.16 Some lines drawn on screen using the Lines menu of PageMaker

different thicknesses, four sets of double or triple lines and five sets of dotted or dashed lines, as well as the Reverse line facility.

The lines do not necessarily display clearly on the screen when the page is fitted inside the window, and to see the lines as they will appear it is often necessary to look at a magnified view of the page, Figure 6.17. When the whole of the page is visible, the thicker lines will often appear to be of the same thickness as the thin lines because the screen image will show a line to indicate position even if the thickness of the line cannot be represented.

For example, if the screen can show 400 lines for a vertical distance of 7″, this corresponds to about 57 lines per inch, so that the line thickness on the screen is 0.017″, 1/57 inch. A 1-point line, by contrast, corresponds to a thickness of 1/72 inch, but since the line must be shown on screen it has to be shown by using the thicker screen line. A 2-point line should be, on paper, of 2/72 inch, which is 1/36 inch. On the screen, using two screen lines would make this appear to be too thick, so that, again, only one

180

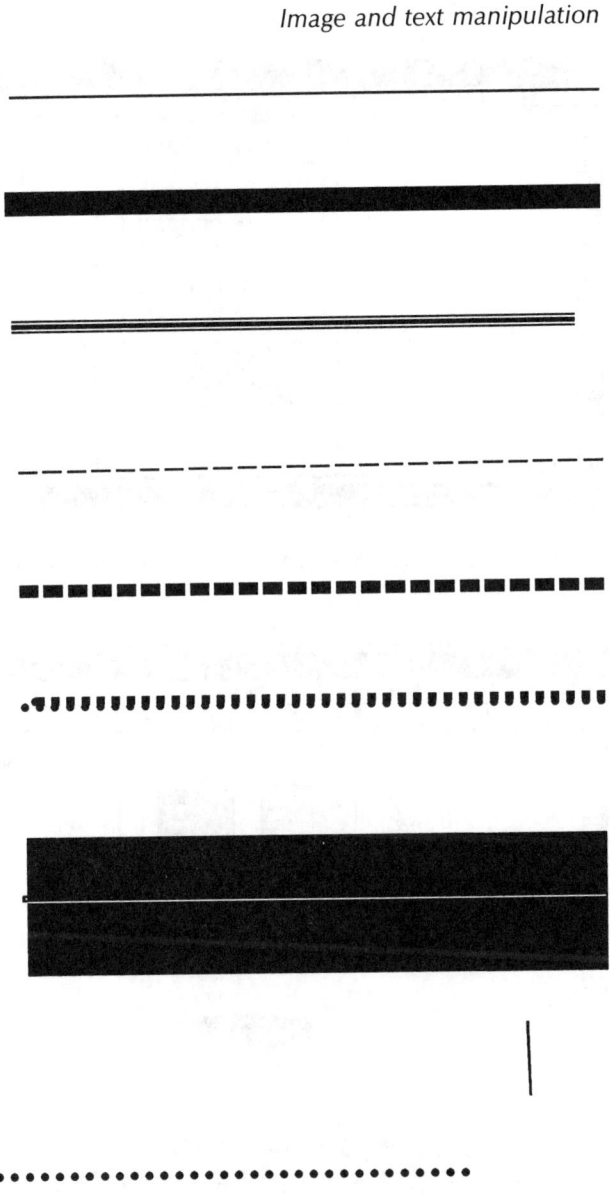

Figure 6.17 Viewing lines on a magnified page will show the relationship of line thicknesses more clearly

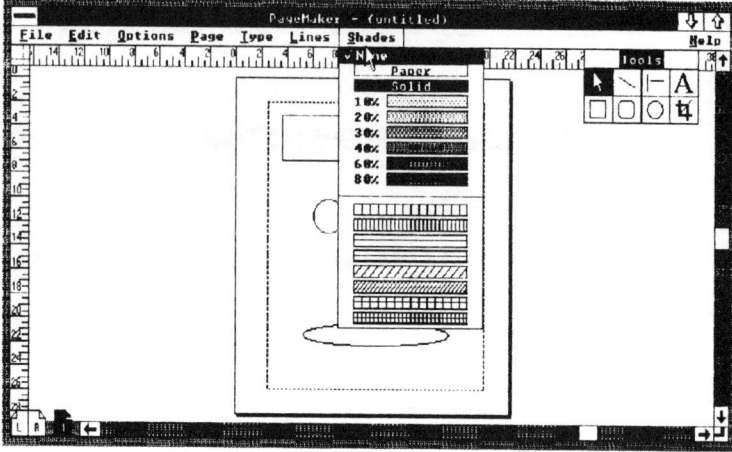

Figure 6.18 Some closed shapes and the *Shades* menu brought down to choose a filling pattern

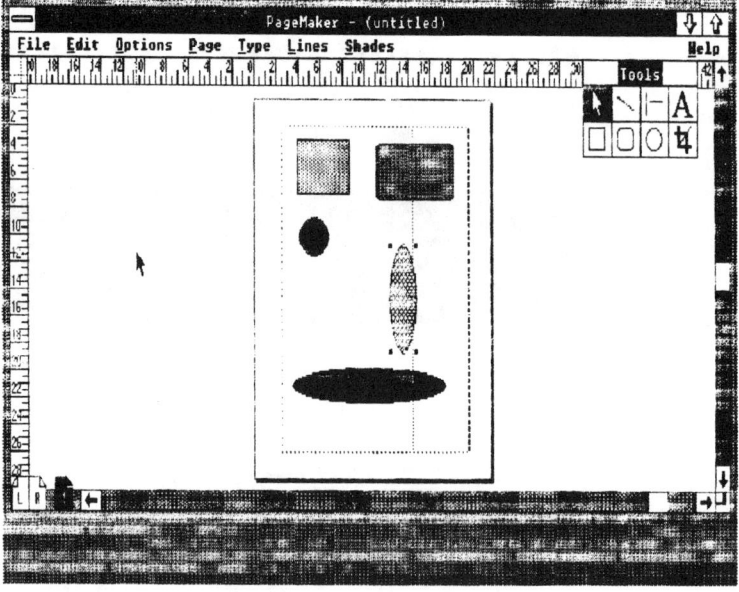

Figure 6.19 The effects as seen on screen of using some of the shading patterns

182

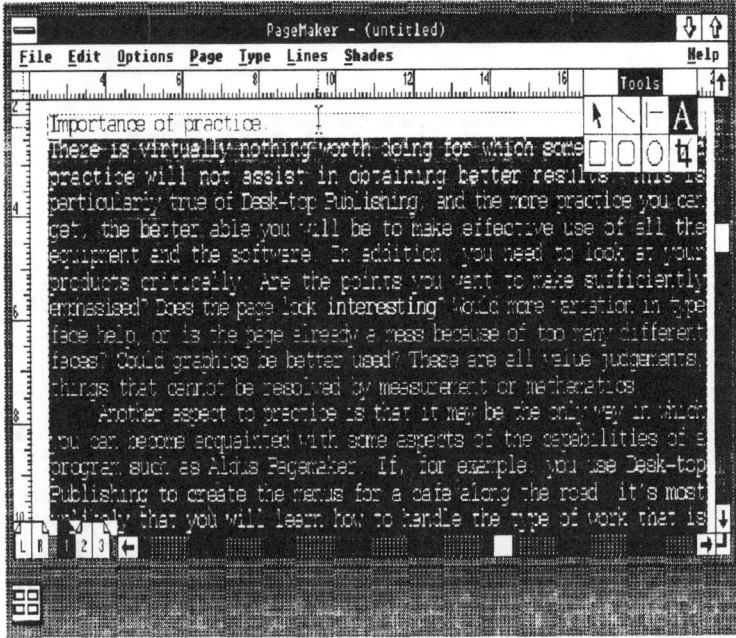

Figure 6.20   Marking text by using mouse dragging

screen line is used. Hence there is no difference in appearance between 1-point and 2-point lines on screen. In practice, one screen line is often used to display line thicknesses up to 4-point thickness.

Filling shapes

The box and circle tools of a DTP package can be used along with the line options to create enclosed shapes in various line styles. In addition, these shapes can be filled with various shadings which can be used to replace the use of colour fill on a monochrome printer (as most are). Some care needs to be taken in this respect. When the boundary of a closed shape uses a continuous line, the filling that is put in place will remain inside the shape. If, however, the surrounding line is dotted there is a risk that the filling will 'escape' and shade all of the rest of the page.

PageMaker allows box and circle shapes to be created, with the option of rounded corners for the boxes. As created normally, these shapes are not filled, and the Shades menu is used to specify the filling pattern.

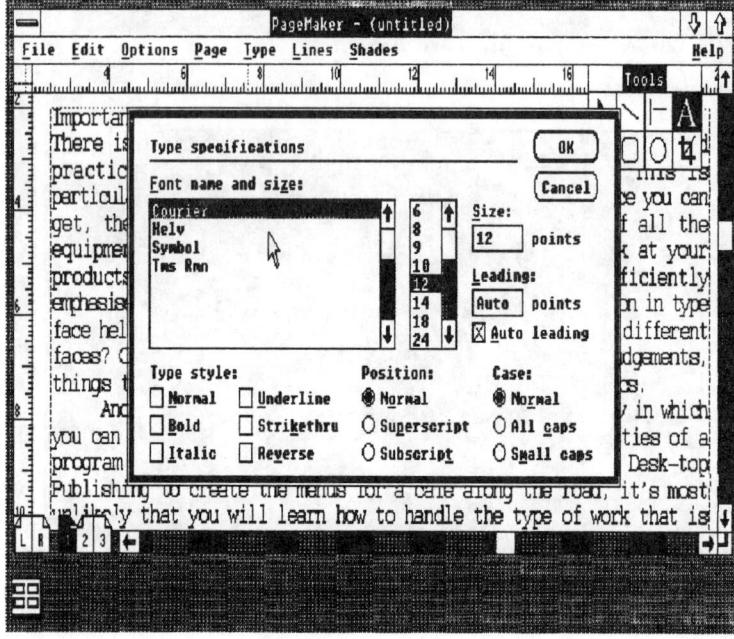

Figure 6.21 Selecting a font for the marked text. Times Roman will be selected in place of the Courier shown here

- Figure 6.18 shows some closed shapes drawn and the Shades menu brought down to pick filling patterns.
- This menu includes None, Paper and Solid. The 'None' option leaves the shapes transparent so that other shapes or text will show through. The Paper option leaves the shading white, and the Solid option makes the shading black.
- Figure 6.19 shows the effect of picking some shading patterns.
- Remember that if the boundary lines are dotted, the filling will move from the enclosed shape to fill the whole page.

Questions

5 Which of the following is NOT a re-orienting action:
   (a) transposing an image laterally

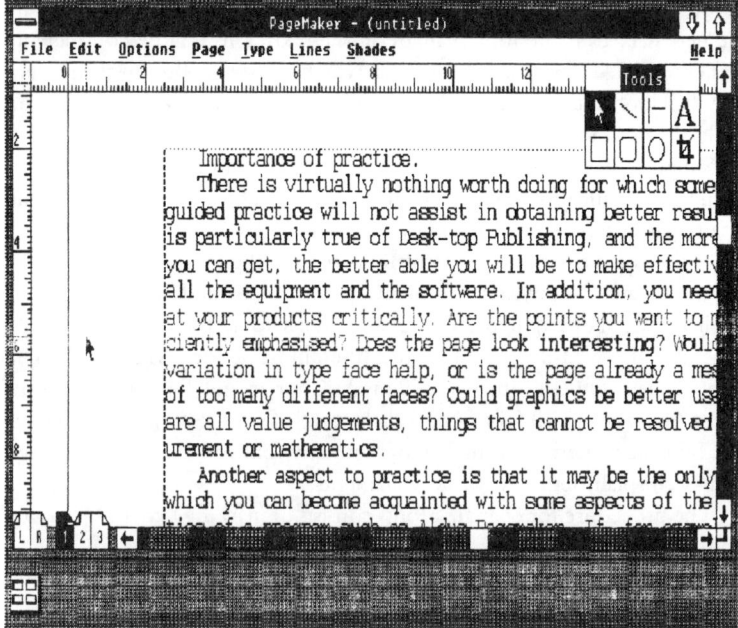

Figure 6.22 Making the changes of font and size on the marked section, and deselecting the text leaves the new fonts displayed

    (b) turning an image upside down
    (c) inverting colours
    (d) rotating the image by 90°
6 Lines in 2-point and 4-point thickness look identical on a screen. This is because:
    (a) they will print as the same thickness
    (b) this type of screen cannot show any line thinner than 4-point
    (c) there is no difference between 2-point and 4-point lines
    (d) the screen cannot show any line thicker than 2-point

Text and fonts

Text will be imported into a page, using any ruler-guides that have been set up to position the text precisely. On subsequent pages, the text will be moved so as to line up with the guides. After this has been done, particularly when the importing has been done from a word-processor that does not use style sheets that are recognized by the DTP package, it will usually be necessary to make font changes on the text. This will be considerably easier if the DTP package already has style sheets set up, but for the present we shall look at the situation of text read into a DTP package which has no style sheets ready for use.

Suppose that a batch of text has been read in, and the DTP package is using its default font – whatever that may be. The task is to change the main part of the text to Times 12-point and the headings to Times 18-point, or whatever equivalent fonts the DTP package possesses. Very often, to avoid copyright problems, fonts are named so as to suggest well-known copyrighted varieties – a Swiss font, for example, should resemble the well-known Helvetica (the old name for Switzerland). The fonts called Times Roman (or Times), Courier and Dutch are all serif fonts (there is a small foot or curl at the base of each letter); the Helvetica (or Swiss) and Letter Gothic, along with any font called Modern, will be sans-serif, plain letters with no ornaments.

The procedure for changing fonts consists of marking text and selecting fonts, and for PageMaker is done as follows:

● The text is marked by selecting the text tool (the **A**) and placing the mouse at the start of the text. The mouse button is held down and the mouse dragged over the whole of the text (down the page) until all has been marked, Figure 6.20. *Note* that this is just one of several methods of marking the whole text.
● The Type-specs option from the Type menu is selected, Figure 6.21. This allows the font name of Tms Rmn (Times Roman) to be selected, and also the size of 12-point.
● Clicking on the OK box changes the marked text to this font and size, Figure 6.22. The text has been deselected by clicking on the pointer in place of the text tool icon. Note that the word 'interesting' is in bold – this is because the original word-processed text used bold for this word and the DTP package has retained the style, since the word-processor was one whose bold and underline codes could be converted.
● The headings are now marked, and the size set to 18-point using the same methods, Figure 6.23.

Remember that the range of fonts and sizes that you can use is governed by the type of printer that you have available, and the largest range is obtained from a laser printer that uses PostScript. Another point about using manual selection of font and size is that you must be certain that the

186

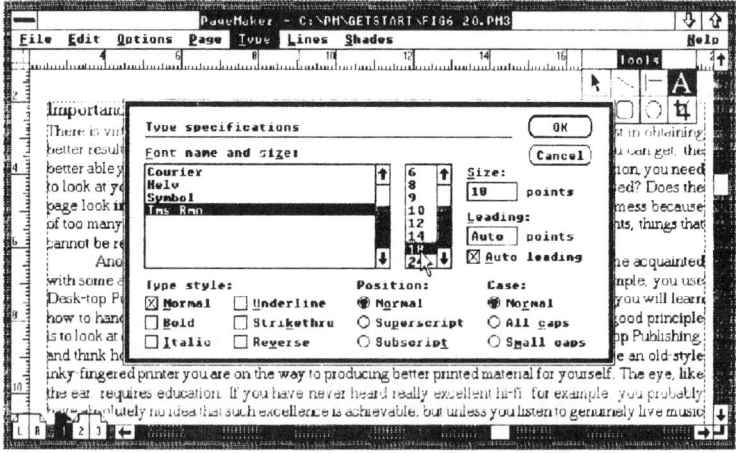

Figure 6.23 Marking the headings and selecting fonts and sizes

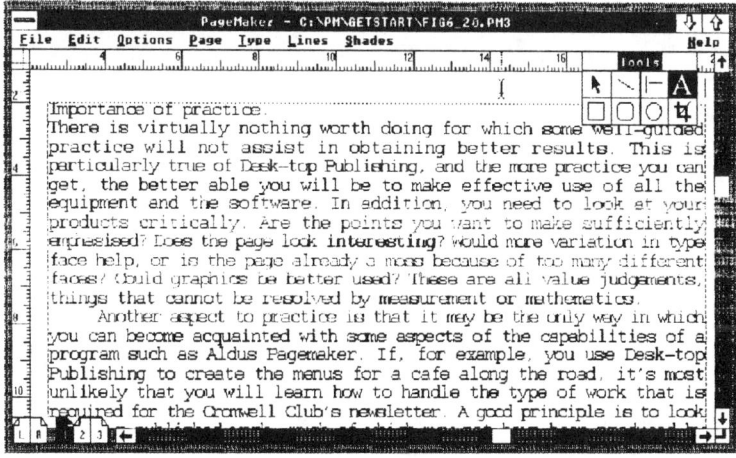

Figure 6.24 Text which has been imported in Courier 12-point

whole of the text has been marked and changed. If, for example, you mark only to the end of a page and change to a smaller size this will create a page of mainly small type but with some larger type at the end. The reason is that the smaller type occupies less space and as the type size of the marked

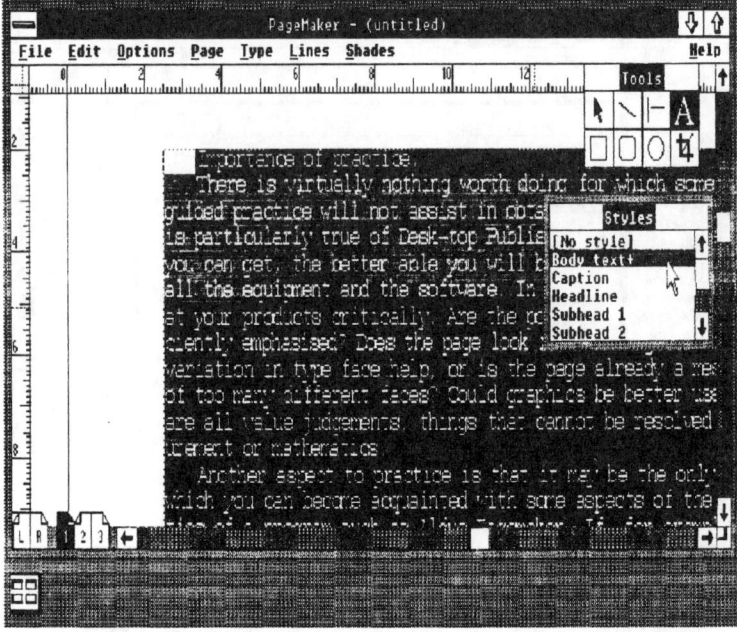

Figure 6.25   Using the Style Palette (the PageMaker Style sheet) to select body text, which in this case is Times Roman 12-point

piece of text changes, more words are placed on the page (taking lines from later pages). If these lines have not been changed they will be of the original (larger) type size.

Using style sheets

Suppose that the same text is again read in, but this time the styles will be altered by using a pre-set style sheet. The way in which style sheets are used will vary from one DTP package to another, but the methods used by PageMaker are broadly representative.

● Figure 6.24 shows text that has been imported in the Courier 12-point font and size. This is to be changed to the settings that have been created in a style sheet which has been selected earlier.
● The whole of the text is selected. In this example, the text tool has been chosen, the cursor placed at the start of the text, and the Select-All option taken from the Edit menu.

● The Style Palette is selected from the Edit menu, and when this appears, Body text is selected, Figure 6.25. This changes all of the text to the form of the main font, which is Times 12-point.

● The first heading is now marked and the Headline item from the Styles menu is selected. This changes the headline, Figure 6.26, to the font and size as defined for a headline in the style sheet.

● In this particular document, only Body text and Headline styles are to be used, but the style sheet allows for Caption (smaller size Italic) and two sub-heads also to be used. The Caption style is used for captions to illustrations.

● The other headings are now similarly marked.

Line spacing and kerning

The use of style sheets will determine the line spacings that are used and the variation of spacing between characters (kerning). The lower-cost DTP packages in general make no provision for kerning, mainly because these packages are intended for use with fonts and for publications that do not require such a degree of refinement. PageMaker, in common with other DTP programs aimed at the higher reaches of the DTP market, does make provision for kerning, either on a semi-automatic basis or by using style sheets.

Line spacing is known as leading (pronounced ledding), named after the strips of lead that were inserted between lines of lead type to maintain spacing in the days of hand-set type. In general DTP packages will set the leading automatically at a spacing equal to 120% of the type point size. For example, if a 10-point type is to be set, the leading will be set to 120% of 10 which is 12-point, so that the leading will be 12-point for 10-point text. This is known as 10/12 point setting. The automatic leading system will search each line for the largest type used, and lead accordingly. For example if the line which is mainly in 10-point contains one word or even one letter in 12-point, the leading will be arranged for 12-point, using 120% × 12 = 14-point leading. This arrangement ensures that text lines are never placed so close together as to make reading difficult because of inadequate leading.

Nevertheless, you sometimes want to change leading, often because the leading change caused by using one large letter is undesirable, or because you feel that a change in spacing will make the text easier to read – usually this means an increase in spacing. The method that is used to change the leading from its automatic setting varies from one DTP

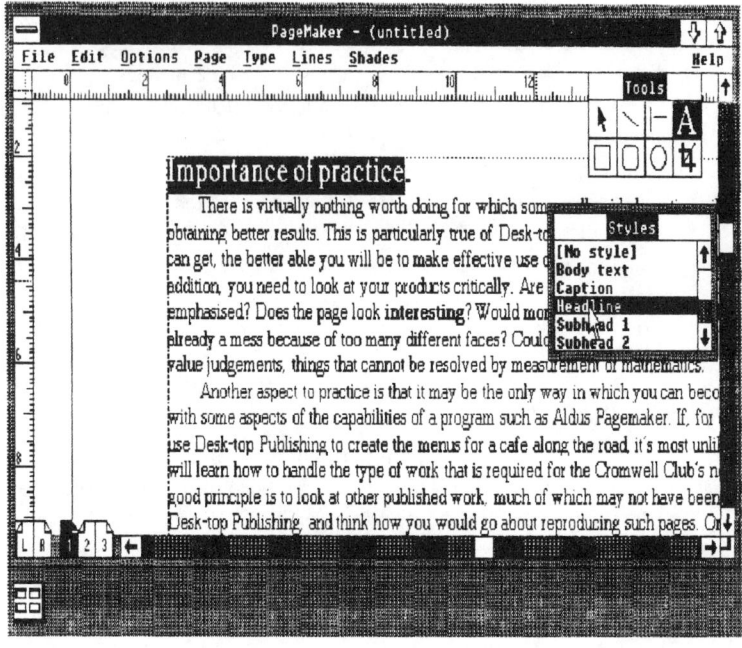

(a)

Figure 6.26(a)   Using the Styles menu to change the font and size for a headline by selecting Headline in the menu. The resulting page (b) is shown printed on the MicroLaser

package to another, but will use either a line-spacing menu or a type-style menu. PageMaker allows either menu to be used to alter leading for large pieces of text.

● Figure 6.27 shows some text (previously marked) and the spacing menu. This menu deals with word spacing, letter spacing and line spacing. It shows the default setting of 120% for the leading, using Proportional leading (the option is to gauge from the top of capital letters).

● By moving the cursor and retyping the figure, the Auto-leading can be changed to 150%.

● The spacing is now noticeably greater, Figure 6.28.

● Note that PageMaker will re-lead all of the existing text if any text is marked, but will re-lead only new text if no text has been marked.

190

Importance of practice.

There is virtually nothing worth doing for which some well-guided practice will not assist in obtaining better results. This is particularly true of Desk-top Publishing, and the more practice you can get, the better able you will be to make effective use of all the equipment and the software. In addition, you need to look at your products critically. Are the points you want to make sufficiently emphasised? Does the page look **interesting**? Would more variation in type face help, or is the page already a mess because of too many different faces? Could graphics be better used? These are all value judgements, things that cannot be resolved by measurement or mathematics.

Another aspect to practice is that it may be the only way in which you can become acquainted with some aspects of the capabilities of a program such as Aldus Pagemaker. If, for example, you use Desk-top Publishing to create the menus for a cafe along the road, it's most unlikely that you will learn how to handle the type of work that is required for the Cromwell Club's newsletter. A good principle is to look at other published work, much of which may not have been produced by Desk-top Publishing, and think how you would go about reproducing such pages. Once you learn to think like an old-style inky-fingered printer you are on the way to producing better printed material for yourself. The eye, like the ear, requires education. If you have never heard really excellent hi-fi, for example, you probably have absolutely no idea that such excellence is achievable, but unless you listen to genuinely live music (no microphones, no amplifiers, no loudspeakers) you probably won't appreciate hi-fi because you have no basis of comparison. Similarly, unless you learn to appreciate how the pages of a newspaper have been put together and how emphasis has been made, pictures used, headings and sub-headings placed, you are unlikely to be able to produce pleasing results for yourself.

Technology assists.

Good technology, as provided by the PC machine, a PostScript laser printer and a DTP program of the Aldus Pagemaker class, helps you along the way, but in the final analysis the appearance of your Desk-top Publishing efforts depends on your own eyes, and how critically you use them. In this book we are considering black and white text and images only. This is difficult enough, and the addition of colour, available only on very expensive packages, is yet another dimension. Many males are partly colour-blind, and you cannot rely on your visual senses to criticise a colour layout unless you are certain that your colour vision is perfect. Unless you can make these judgements, your work is not likely to please you, and if it doesn't please you it probably doesn't please anyone else.

The Design Brief.

When you are required to design a piece of work for publication, the basis of the work is the design brief, a short description of what is required. This might be in very general terms (make a handout on the new range of flummox-gobbers) or it might be more detailed (use double sided A5, with the existing illustration enclosed), but it will nearly always leave you with the crucial decisions on the final appearance of the published document. These are:

* The amount and content of text
* The number and size of graphics
* The size and number of pages
* The fonts and styles to be used
* The layout of the text and graphics

Even if text is supplied, some editing is likely to be needed. Authors are never well-equipped to criticise their own work, and text is often supplied from very inexperienced authors. You will

(b)

Changes of spacing for the whole of a text may not be required, and the method that PageMaker uses for altering leading only for new text if no existing text has been marked allows for different parts of the text to use different leading. If you want to make several alterations in the leading of a

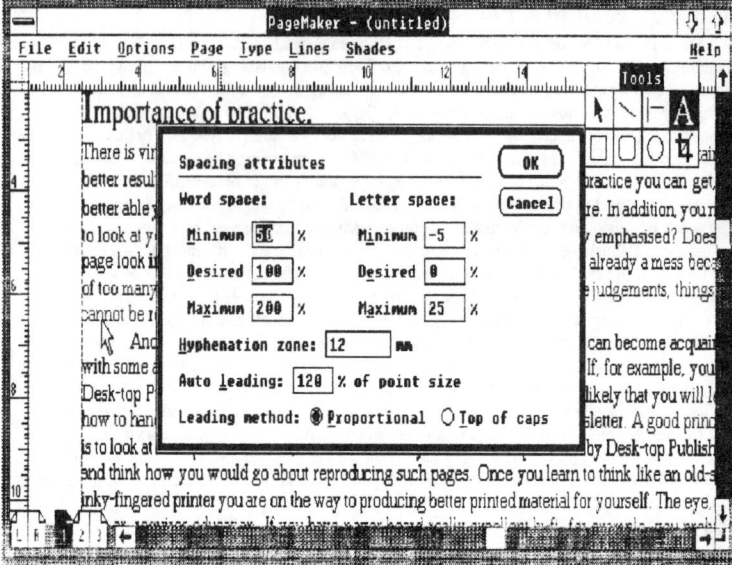

Figure 6.27   Marked text with the *Spacing* menu selected to alter the leading

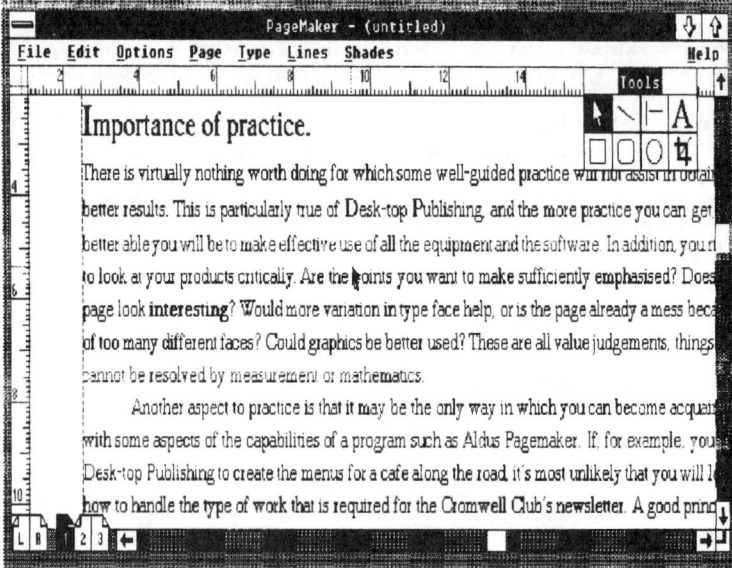

Figure 6.28   The result of altering the leading in the first paragraph

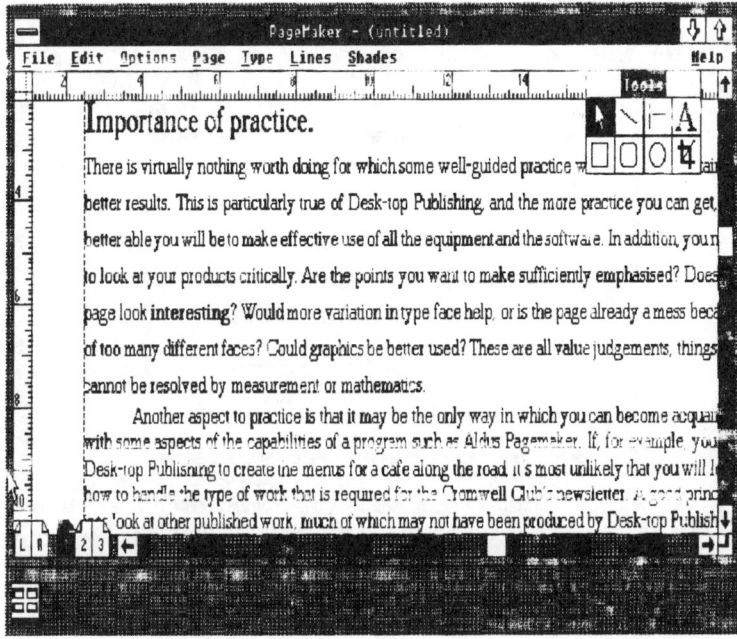

Figure 6.29   Altering the leading figure to 20-point in the first paragraph

piece of existing text, the easiest method is to turn off the automatic leading.

- The paragraph or other piece of text is marked.
- The Type style menu is selected from the Type menu.
- Automatic leading is turned off (click the mouse pointer over Auto leading).
- The figure for leading is set to another value – 20-point in the example of Figure 6.29 so as to be really noticeable.

In practice, such large changes in leading would generally be avoided. One common deviation from automatic leading is to provide extra leading under a paragraph heading. The use of larger font sizes for headings will, of course, ensure that a larger leading is used under any heading, but in some cases the larger spacing is wanted between any two paragraphs and not just when a heading is used. All DTP packages provide for this to be done, but not all provide for it to be done automatically. The PageMaker method is illustrated here.

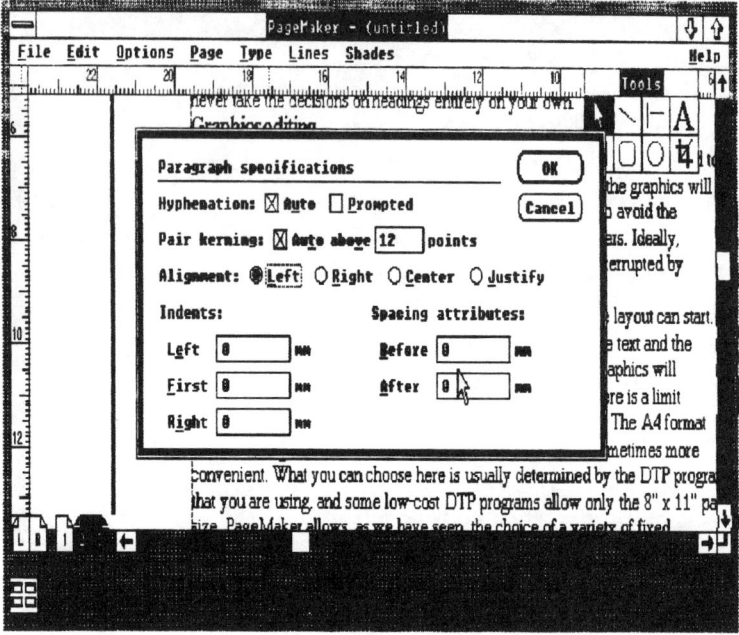

Figure 6.30   Selecting *Paragraph Specifications* so as to alter the spacing before and after a paragraph

● The Paragraph Specifications menu is selected from the Type menu, Figure 6.30.

● The Spacing attributes contain space before and space after a paragraph, and the default is zero, making the spacing equal to that determined by the leading settings.

● By typing figures into these boxes, additional spacing can be obtained, Figure 6.31. This illustration shows 2 mm extra space used before and after a paragraph.

● Care should be taken here – if the file that has been imported from the word-processor contains a carriage-return at the end of each line, each line will be treated as a paragraph and the extra space will be inserted.

The spacing of individual characters in words, and between words in lines, is treated very differently by different DTP packages. The lower-cost packages will make little or no provision for altering the spaces between words or between individual characters, either to make a fixed

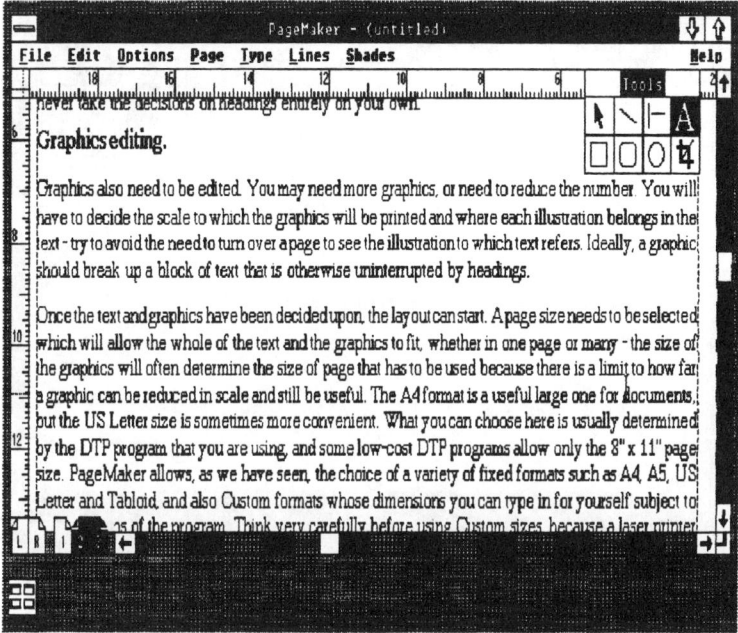

Figure 6.31   An example which uses 2 mm extra spacing before and after a paragraph

spacing setting or to provide for kerning, though most will provide type-faces which are proportionally spaced. The more expensive packages, by contrast, will provide for kerning, usually on an automatic basis, and often as a default.

Figure 6.32 shows a (strange) sentence which has been chosen on the grounds that it contains several pairs of characters whose spacing is the subject of kerning. These are Yo, We, To, Tr, Ta, Tw and Wo. The enlarged version of this, Figure 6.33, shows that the kerned version has used slightly smaller spacing between these particular letter pairs, although on casual inspection the difference is very slight. Slight as the difference is, it makes type more readable and is obvious to the trained type-setter. By making pair-kerning a default in PageMaker, there is never any need to mark paragraphs in order to switch kerning on. Kerning is not used when monospaced fonts such as Courier are applied.

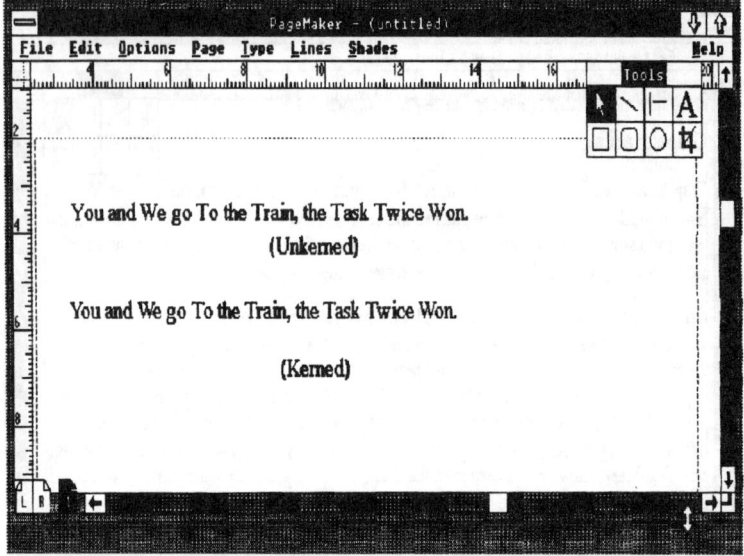

Figure 6.32   An unusual sentence, illustrating the pairs of letters which are some of those subject to kerning

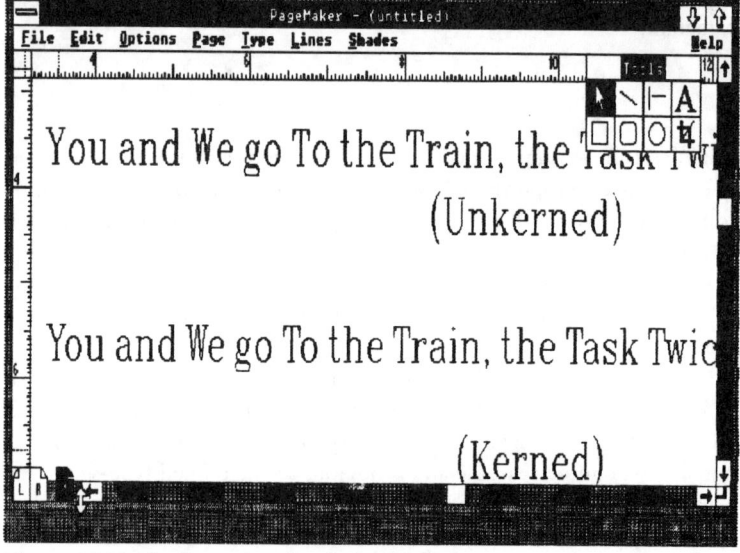

Figure 6.33   The kerned and unkerned lines seen in a magnified view

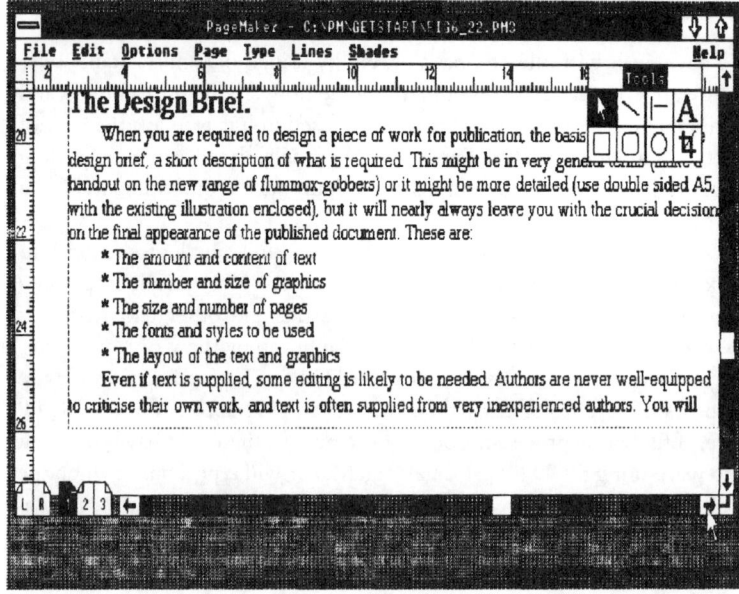

Figure 6.34   Imported text in which asterisks have been used to mark items on a list

Questions

7 Which of the following fonts is a sans-serif one:
   (a) Times Roman   (b) Helvetica
   (c) Courier   (d) Dutch
8 A style sheet ensures that:
   (a) the style of writing is correct
   (b) the text is all in one font and one size
   (c) the use of fonts and sizes is consistent
   (d) any font and size can be used
9 Kerning means:
   (a) representing all characters by small symbols
   (b) making all characters of the same spacing
   (c) making all lines of the same length
   (d) reducing the spacing between certain pairs of characters

Further emphasis

We have dealt with the emphasis of text by using bold and/or italic styles and by underlining. Two other marking methods are the use of bullets and boxing. The bullet is a large dot which is used in lists to mark the start of each separate item on a list. The box is a rectangle placed around a heading or an item for particular emphasis, or put into a questionnaire for a respondent to tick.

Word-processors of the older type do not permit a bullet to be put into a text list, but the later type of word-processors, which have incorporated many features of word-processors, possess this and other text marks. If your text contains bullets which have been put in by the word-processor, and the word-processor is one that the DTP package recognises for the purposes of importing text, then the bullets will appear on your DTP page. If the word-processor does not use bullets, these will have to be put into place using the DTP package. PageMaker will type a bullet when the Ctrl, Shift and 8 keys are pressed, and a number of other marks, such as opening and closing quotes, dashes of different sizes, registration mark, copyright mark, paragraph marker, section marker and page number marker can be put in by various other key combinations.

● Figure 6.34 shows a piece of imported text in which asterisks have been used to mark list items.
● The text tool is selected, and the text cursor is placed just to the right of the first asterisk.
● The backspace key is used to delete the asterisk.
● The bullet is typed using Ctrl–Space–8.
● Figure 6.35 shows the magnified result of some replacements using this method. The bullet, on screen, is smaller than the asterisk it replaces, but the printed version will be different.

Boxing uses the box tool of PageMaker or whatever DTP package you are using. The use of boxes must be restrained, because excessive boxing makes text difficult to read, as Figure 6.36 shows.

Error correction of text

Errors in text arise mainly when additional text has been typed rather than in text that has been imported from the word-processor. Nevertheless, imported text sometimes contains errors, often mis-typings that escape the spelling-checker of the word-processor but which make no sense,

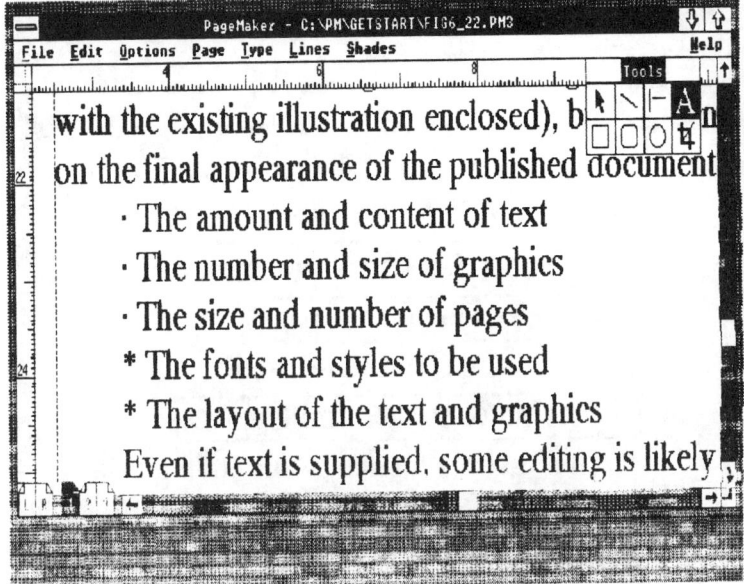

Figure 6.35 A magnified view on the screen of replacement of some of the asterisks by bullets. The bullets are much larger when printed on paper

such as using *an* instead of *and* or *inn* instead of *in*. Where a mis-typing (or sometimes a mis-spelling) creates a valid word, no spelling-checker can possibly point out an error.

Another possibility is that an entire paragraph or even more may have to be altered or removed. There can be countless reasons ranging from the subject matter now being out of date to a sudden realization that the material is libellous; whatever the reason, it will call for deletion to be done.

The simplest error correction is done while text is being typed, and it consists of back-spacing so that the offending letter (or letters) will be deleted, allowing the typing of the correct version. As has been noted earlier, this cannot be done on the scale of one complete page on the screen, because on such a scale the text is greeked. A larger magnification must be used when text is being entered directly, and this will make the correction easier to accomplish as well as making the error more obvious.

On existing text, error correction is carried out in two main ways, depending on the scale of the error.

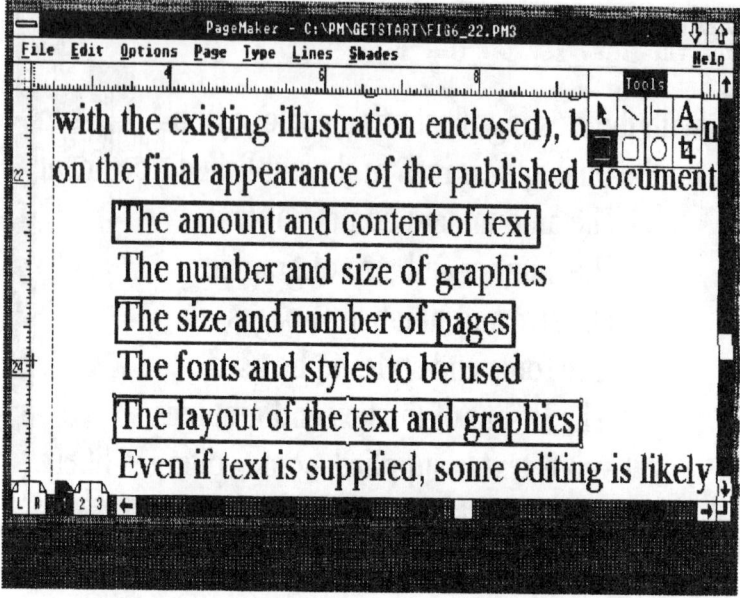

Figure 6.36   Excessive use of boxes makes text difficult to read rather than drawing attention to it

● For an error of one or two characters, the text tool is selected and the text cursor is placed just beyond the error.
● The backspace key is used to delete the character or characters and the new replacement is typed.
● For an error that amounts to a line or a paragraph or more, the section is marked and then deleted.
● New text is then typed (undesirable) or imported from the word-processor (much better) in corrected form.
● The new material is carefully checked. It may also be necessary to check how the new material agrees with the older unchanged portion of text, and with any graphics. There is little point in removing the libellous remarks about Alderman Fitzpumphouse if the photograph of him remains in place.

Cultivate the art of careful proofreading of typed material so that the rough draft from the word-processor can be as faultfree as possible. In this way, a considerable expenditure of time and effort at the DTP stage can be avoided.

Questions

10 Items on a list, or important lines, can be marked with
   (a) bullets   (b) greeking   (c) kerning   (d) serifs
11 Which of the following errors would NOT be detected by a spelling-checker:
   (a) then instead of them
   (b) bur instead of but
   (c) anf instead of and
   (d) whar instead of what

Assignment 6

Scan an image from a technical manual and print the unretouched image either from the DTP package or from a paint package. Now use a paint package with pixel editing and text facilities to:

(a) repair broken lines and irregular areas
(b) delete existing captions and substitute new ones
(c) fill in open areas with shading
(d) print the new edition.

Save the final version as a disk file to be used in future DTP work.

Recap

- Both images and text may have to be manipulated when they are imported, and ruler guides are an important way of ensuring that text and graphics are correctly placed on a page.
- Graphics images may have to be scaled so as to fit into a suitable space in the text, and cropping can be used to make the shape of the graphics image fit into a rectangular box.
- Shapes that have been drawn with the DTP package can use solid or dotted lines, and can be filled with various colours or patterns.
- Images can be moved, and in some DTP packages, re-oriented as well as having colours inverted.

Answers to questions

1 (d)
2 (b)
3 (a)
4 (b)
5 (c)
6 (b)
7 (b)
8 (c)
9 (d)
10 (a)
11 (a)

7 Page and document

Objectives

After reading this chapter you should be able to:
- explain what is meant by page parameters
- show how columns can be created on a DTP page
- explain the use of master pages and style sheets
- outline the steps in producing a simple document
- outline the processes of proofreading and marking up
- explain how a publication is previewed to check specification.

Scenario

You are entrusted with total control of the production of a promotional booklet, for which the text and graphics exist on disk files. How could you put such a document together and be sure that it contained no avoidable errors?

Page parameters

The first action in the production of a document is to attend to the layout of the page – in the case of a book or a booklet which uses printing on each side of the page this will imply designing one left-hand page and one right-hand page. The items that have to be considered in page design are called the page parameters – items which are fixed for the pages of that document, but which might be quite differently set for the pages of another document. On this basis, a parameter has been jokingly defined as a variable constant. By the time the page is being specified on the DTP package, the design of the whole document will have already been settled in the design brief (see Chapter 5).

The scheme that is used for setting up a document of several pages is the use of master pages. Master pages exist in the form of one left-hand and one right-hand master, and whatever is placed on to a master page determines what will appear on every following page, with the left-hand pages following the pattern of the left-hand master and so on. This allows for the placing of headers (and sub-headers), page number footers, ruler lines under headers and above footers, ruler guides to show where text or graphics will be placed, vertical rules at one margin and so on.

- Since the layout of the master pages determines the way that text will appear in the whole document, time must not be skimped on this part of the work.
- A mistake or a piece of poor workmanship (like a crooked ruler line) on a master page will be copied to each and every page of that type (left or right) in the document.
- It takes some experience to be able to look at a master page (which has no text) and be sure that it will look correct when text is placed into a copy of the master.

Margins are the first page setting to be made, and the design brief will have indicated whether to use symmetrical margins (making the design of left-hand and right-hand sheets easy) or asymmetrical margins, usually with a wider margin at the unbound edge. Left and right margins can be quoted in a design brief in several different ways:

- By specifying both left-hand and right-hand margins, usually in millimetres, though inch measurements are often specified, particularly if the work has originated in the USA.
- By specifying the left-margin size and the line length for a known page width.
- By specifying the line length and the page width along with the use of symmetrical margins.

Figure 7.1 shows the page setup menu for PageMaker, in which the left and right margins are specified in the form Inside and Outside. In these terms, the inside margin is the margin next to the binding, so that specifying in this form makes it much easier to work with asymmetrical pages, since the differences between left and right-hand pages are automatically catered for by the DTP program. On the budget-priced DTP packages, these differences might have to be allowed for by creating two different page types, or even by altering the page settings for each page.

If the margins are specified in a way that differs from the format used by

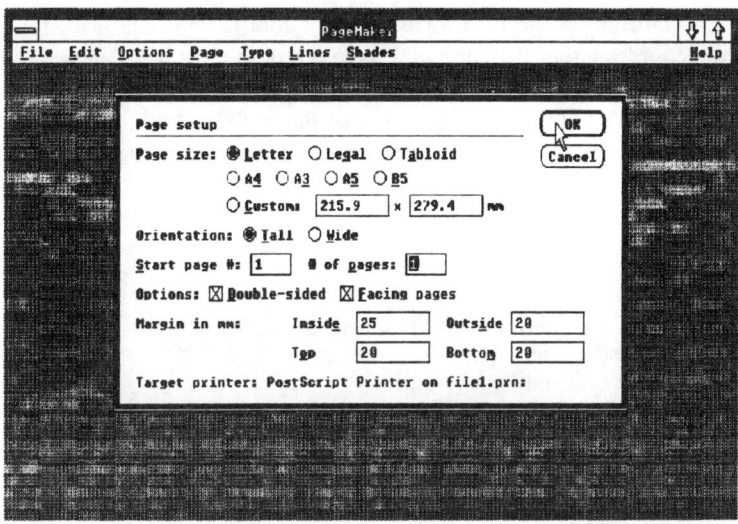

Figure 7.1 The PageMaker page setup menu, with margins specified as Inside and Outside

the DTP package, you will have to calculate the correct versions. The specification of left margin and right margin is almost universal for DTP work, so that this will be the most likely format that will be used. The conversion from other forms of margin specification is done by subtraction. For example, if the page width is given as 170 mm, left hand margin as 20 mm and line length as 130 mm, the right hand margin must be equal to the page width less the sum of left-margin and line length, which is 170 − (130 + 20), which is 170 − 150 = 20. If the page width is given as 150 mm, another common size, and the line as 125 mm symmetrical, then this leaves 150 − 125 = 25 mm for margins, 12.5 mm on each side. Always work out these calculations and write the results down before attempting to enter them into a page specification menu of the DTP program.

Top and bottom margins are virtually always quoted directly in terms of millimetres or inches, and 20 mm is a very common value for books. Where large pages are used, however, and in particular on the first page of each chapter, it is common to find larger top margins used. Some large-page formats use large top and bottom margins for no apparent reason other than to make a small book appear very large.

The margin as specified for top and bottom can include space for a header or footer, or these must be taken out of the text space, depending on the design of the master pages. Because of this, the use of a small margin on a page does not necessarily mean that the text is close to the upper or lower edge, because there might be a space between the header or footer and the text.

Questions

1 Which of the following is NOT a page parameter:
   (a) top and bottom margins
   (b) space reserved for a graphic
   (c) left and right margins
   (d) headers and footers
2 Using master pages (as defined in this book) ensures that:
   (a) fonts will always be correct
   (b) sizes of type will always be correct
   (c) page parameters will be consistent throughout
   (d) graphics will always be put in the same place on each page

In general, DTP packages provide for headers and footers in a way that is different from the methods used by the older types of word-processors. PageMaker, for example, deals with this by using the master pages. One left-hand and one right-hand master page will be created, and each contains the appropriate header and footer. For a book chapter, the header might use the book title as the header on the left-hand master page and the chapter heading as the header on the right-hand master page. The footer on either type of master page would consist of the word *page* followed by the page number. Using this scheme, only the header of the right-hand master page needs to be changed when a new chapter is being set out. An example is illustrated later.

The next part of the design brief that needs to be considered is the number of columns. Books in general will use only one column, making their design considerably easier in this respect. For newspaper work and for some advertising flyers, two, three or even more columns may be used, depending on the width of paper that has been specified. Remember that the office type of laser printer cannot handle the wider paper sizes, but the 'tiling' action of PageMaker makes it possible to create work in sections using printers whose page width is inadequate.

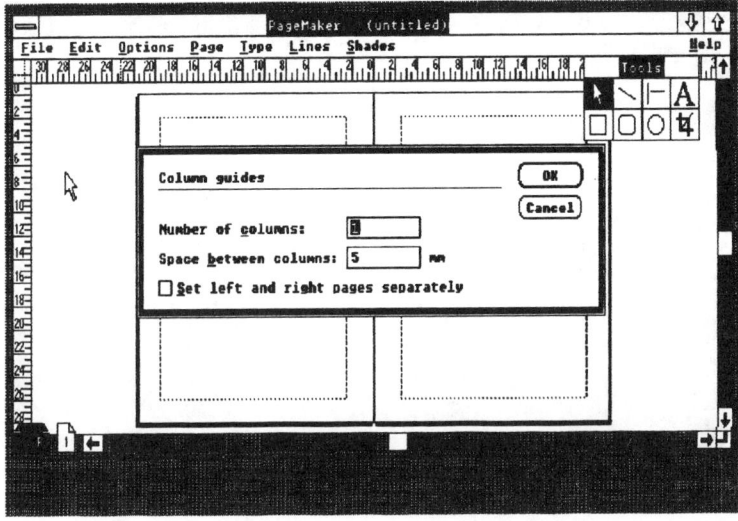

Figure 7.2   The *Column Guides* menu of PageMaker which is used to set up column requirements

Figure 7.2 shows the Column Guides menu of PageMaker as an illustration of the type of specification that is used. Even the very low-cost DTP packages provide similarly for the use of columns, requiring you to specify the number of columns on the page and also the space (the *gutter*) between the columns. Where there is provision, as shown here, for setting left and right hand pages separately, the number of columns and the gutter size can be set at different amounts on the left- and right-hand pages.

Once the column settings have been determined on the master pages, the column divisions should be visible on the screen, Figure 7.3. This example shows a two-column layout on the left-hand page and a three-column layout on the right-hand page. This has been done simply to show the form of marking that is used and does not imply that many publications will use two columns on one side and three on the other.

Any layout lines can now be placed into the master pages. These usually take the form of a ruler line drawn across the top of the page, extending to either margin, and sometimes a similar line at the bottom. Care must be taken to ensure that these lines are not crooked – PageMaker uses a special line-tool which will produce only perfectly horizontal or vertical lines.

A header can be typed above the top line, and a footer below. In general

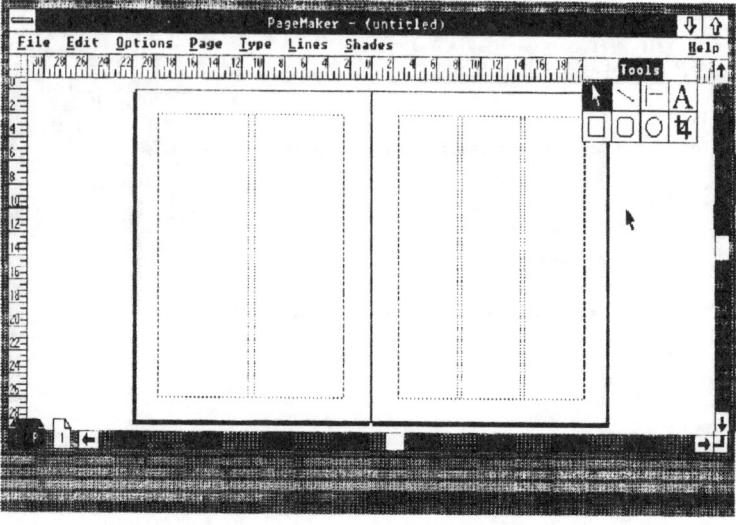

Figure 7.3   The column divisions are seen on the screen, but these lines are not printed. You can, however, use these lines as a guide for a vertical rule if this is required

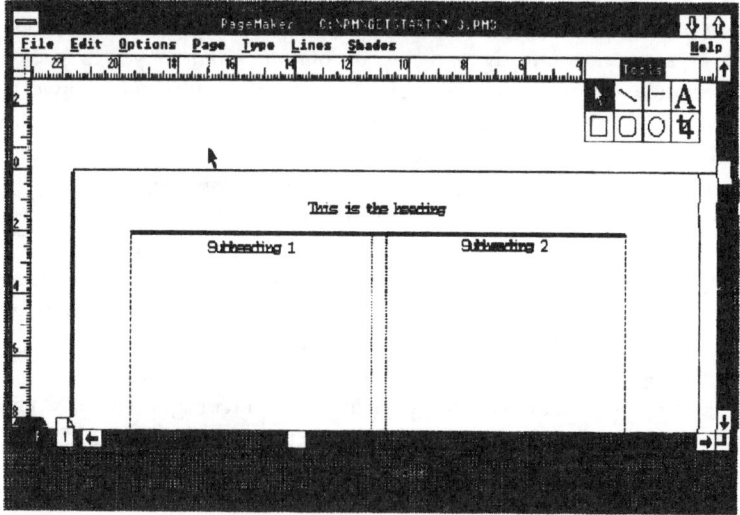

Figure 7.4   Using sub-headers which can be placed at the top of a column

the footer will carry a page number and usually some fixed text, such as the word *Page* and possibly a chapter number. Such text can be put into the footer position on the master pages, along with the character that is used to provide the page number automatically – on PageMaker this is Ctrl–Shift–3. The page number is shown as zero in the master pages. The Page Setup menu allows the starting page number, default 1, to be altered. This would be necessary when the master pages were altered for a new chapter of a book, for example.

For some purposes, sub-headers may be used. These might be placed at the top of each column in the example illustrated in Figure 7.4, or they might be used below the main header of a one-column page to carry supplementary information. For example the main header might carry the chapter name and number and the sub-header the name of the main topic for that particular set of pages. This type of use would call for frequent changes of the wording in the master pages and is not common.

Activity

Prepare master pages for a document which uses three columns on A4 landscape paper, with an 8 mm gutter. Run text into the columns, fully justified and with automatic hyphenation on, to show how the columns will be occupied.

Producing the document

Once the master pages have been made ready they should be saved as a file – they can be saved even before work is complete, as a way of ensuring that an interruption does not result in the loss of a considerable amount of work. Budget DTP packages very often make no use of master pages as such, and some allow very few pages to be created at a time, holding text in reserve so that pages are created and printed one or two at a time. PageMaker, in common with other high-cost packages, allows the number of pages to be fixed before text is added, with a maximum of 128. This allows for a short book, and is more than enough for a book chapter. In general, since the master pages would have to be changed for each chapter, the allocation is generous enough for virtually all printing requirements.

The production of a document usually starts with loading in the text, using the methods that have been described earlier. If sub-headings have

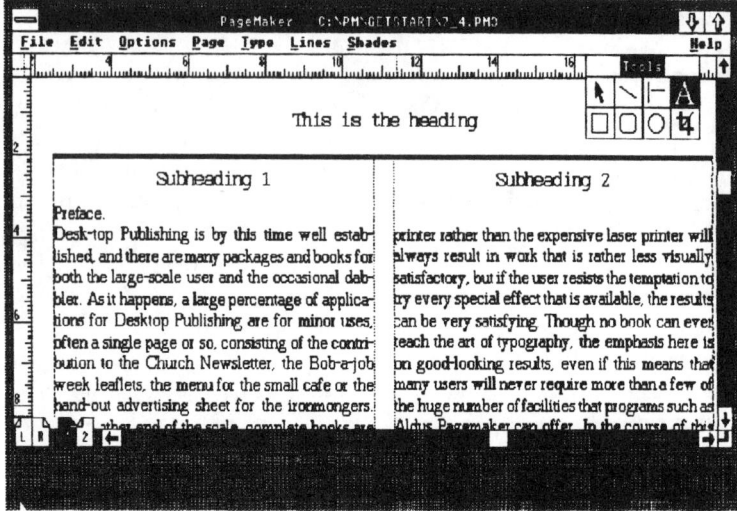

Figure 7.5   Selecting and dragging text to line up with another page. This becomes much easier if ruler guides have been drawn

been placed in the text area some care will be needed to prevent the text from over writing them. The first page is easy to cope with – the starting point for the text can be placed below a sub-heading. On subsequent pages, the text must be selected bodily (click the mouse anywhere on the text) and moved (dragging the mouse) so as to line up with the other page – Figure 7.5 shows an example.

This also emphasizes that headers and footers are best kept away from the text area, because to do otherwise invites a lot of work when the text is being placed. This might not be too arduous if the publication consisted of only a couple of pages, but for any long work, the more that can be handled automatically the better. The ruler lines that PageMaker displays, along with ruler guides placed into the master pages, are a considerable assistance to placing text, but it is much easier to be able to rely on automatic placement.

Automatic placement is certainly desirable for graphics, and it is usually easier to load in graphics after the text has been loaded. With the text in place, it is usually possible to see a 'natural' position for inserting a graphic; if you start with the graphic in place there is no guarantee that the text which ends up flowing round it will be the text that makes reference to

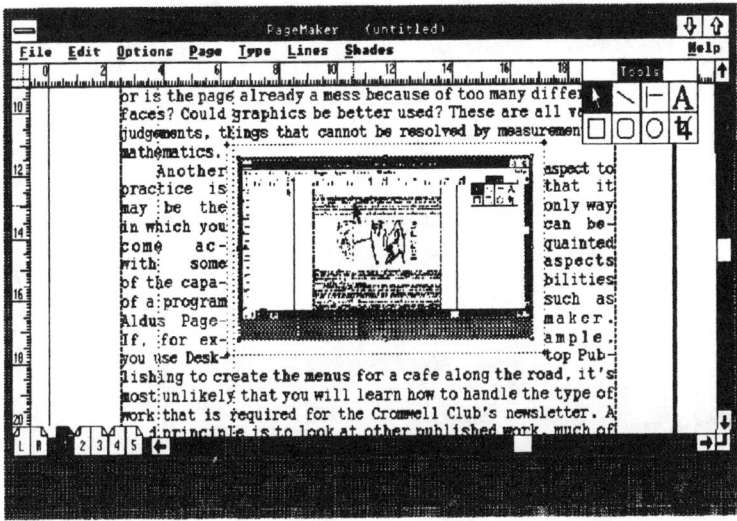

Figure 7.6   A screen view of a page in which a graphic has been inserted

the graphic. When this is done, the graphics should be inserted in page order, since each graphic that is inserted will cause text to be moved onwards to later pages.

Taking an example, Figure 7.6 shows the screen view of text on a page for which the master has been defined as described earlier. A graphic has now to be added – the example used will not have any particular relevance; it is simply one of the screen-shots used in the illustrations for this book. The type of flow that has been specified here – flowing around the graphic – is not really suitable, because it causes words to be hyphenated and broken each side of the graphic. It is usually better to specify no text around the sides of the graphic, and allow the flow to be above and below only, Figure 7.7.

If the graphic is simply loaded into the page, however, it will need some adjustment before it fits into the correct position. Each graphic has a surrounding space which for PageMaker is set at 4 mm and which must be allowed for. Placing the graphic top edge, for example, at the line under a paragraph end does not necessarily ensure that the graphic will be neatly placed between one paragraph and the next. Unless enough room is left for the surrounding space, the graphic will split the last line of the paragraph, and it is equally easy to split the first line of the following paragraph.

211

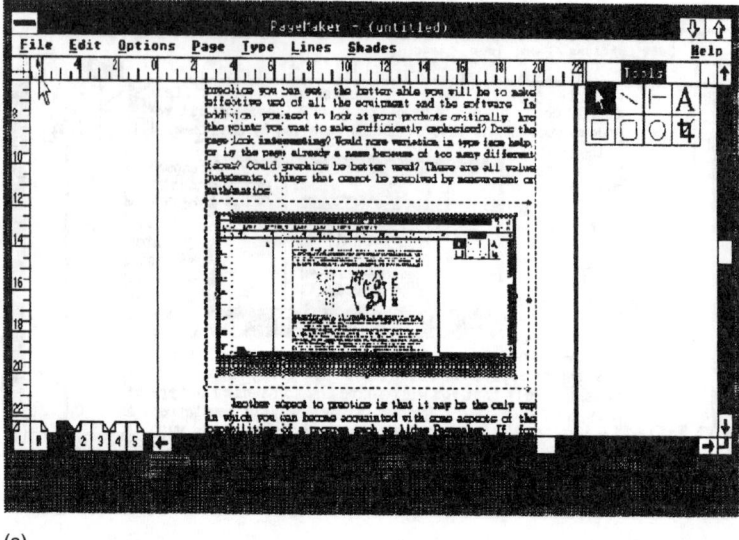

(a)

Figure 7.7 If the flow of text (a) is allowed only above and below the graphic, not round the side, the results are usually more readable in narrow columns. The page as printed (b) shows how the text is spaced round the graphic

Another method of dealing with graphics is the use of graphics placeholders. A placeholder can be a simple frame or suitable graphics shape which can be trimmed to size and inserted into a page. A rectangle drawn by the graphics tools of the DTP package can be used as a placeholder, allowing the layout of text and graphics to be inspected before the correct illustrations are imported. This technique is particularly useful when a master page is being made up that will be used for many documents of a standardized form, such as an estate agent's description sheet. PageMaker provides for such pages to be saved as Templates, so that only minor changes of text, some text import and rearrangement and replacement of graphics will be needed.

Text placeholders can be used similarly, using pieces of text whose content (such as NAME/ADDRESS) indicates what should be used for replacement. An ancient convention among some printers is to make text placeholders using Latin text, so that the placeholder can be instantly recognized as such and cannot be mistaken for the text that will eventually be used. Not many books are written in Latin these days.

212

Importance of practice.

There is virtually nothing worth doing for which some well-guided practice will not assist in obtaining better results. This is particularly true of Desk-top Publishing, and the more practice you can get, the better able you will be to make effective use of all the equipment and the software. In addition, you need to look at your products critically. Are the points you want to make sufficiently emphasised? Does the page look **interesting**? Would more variation in type face help, or is the page already a mess because of too many different faces? Could graphics be better used? These are all value judgements, things that cannot be resolved by measurement or mathematics.

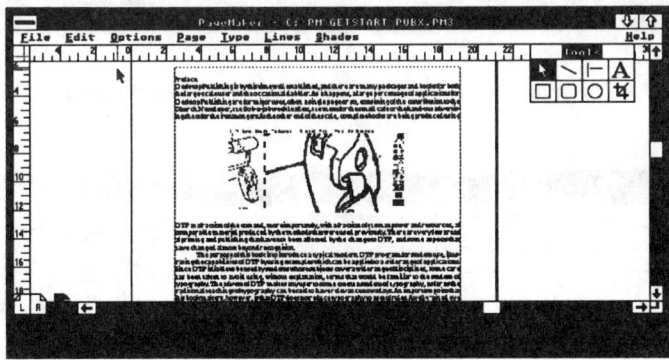

Another aspect to practice is that it may be the only way in which you can become acquainted with some aspects of the capabilities of a program such as Aldus Pagemaker. If, for example, you use Desk-top Publishing to create the menus for a cafe along the road, it's most unlikely that you will learn how to handle the type of work that is required for the Cromwell Club's newsletter. A good principle is to look at

(b)

Figure 7.8 shows a typical template layout for text only, such as a report. This has been designed for A4 paper (297 mm × 210 mm) with 20 mm margins left and right, 25 mm top margin and 30 mm bottom margin. A line has been drawn at 20 mm from the top of the page, using the 75%

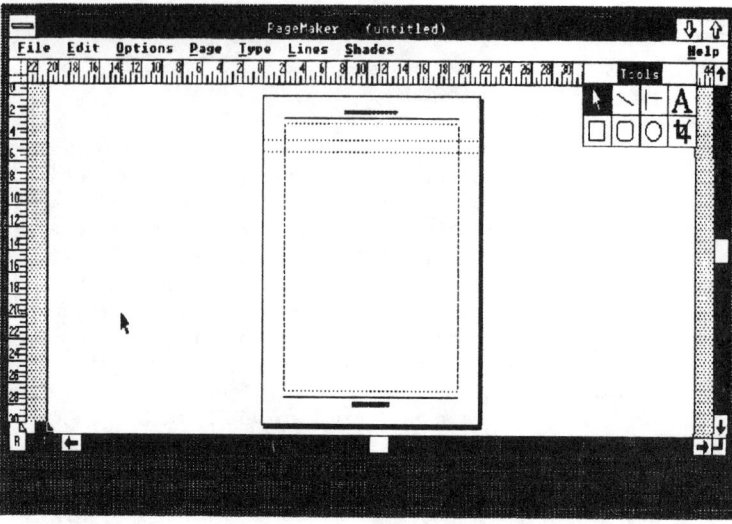

Figure 7.8 A typical text-only template layout for A4, with ruler guides

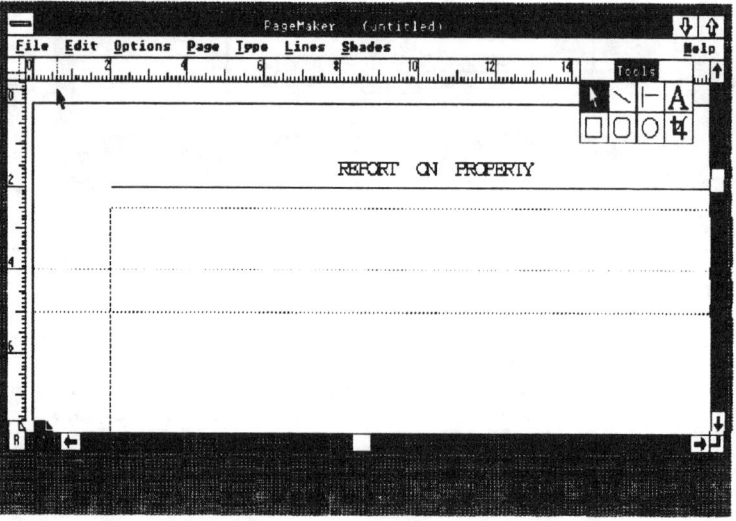

Figure 7.9 A magnified view of the top of the page showing the use of the ruler guides in placing the title line

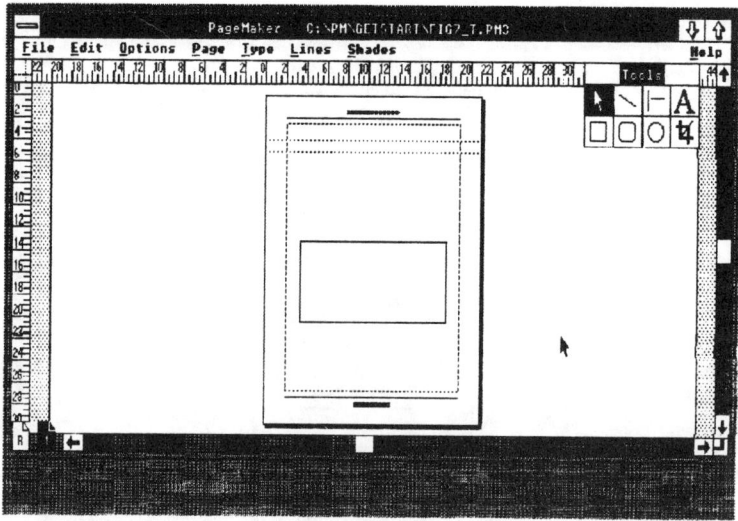

Figure 7.10 Creating a graphics placeholder using the rectangle drawing tool

scale view and the side ruler lines to ensure accuracy. Another line has been drawn at 25 mm from the bottom of the page (5 mm under the end of the text). The heading wording has been placed on the line above the rule and the page number has been placed below the bottom rule. Two horizontal ruler guides have been put into position at 40 mm and 50 mm respectively from the top of the page. Figure 7.9 shows a magnified view of the top of the page, showing how the ruler guides can be used to position a title line at the start of the main text.

If a graphics placeholder is needed in a document of this type, it can be drawn in using the rectangle drawing tool, as illustrated in Figure 7.10. Remember that you have full control over the size and position of the rectangle as you draw it, and also subsequently when it is selected. You can adjust the final position by using the side or top/bottom handles once the size of the rectangle is correctly established. This rectangle can be shaded to make its position more obvious, and if it is marked before the text is imported, the text will flow round the rectangle in whatever way you have selected – Figure 7.11 shows a full-page view, for example, in which the size of blank space on each side of the rectangle has been set so as

215

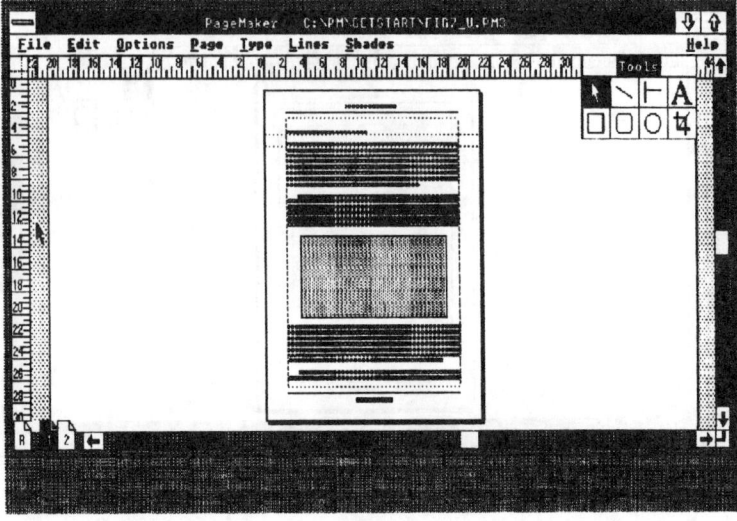

Figure 7.11   A full-page view of the previous example. The blank space is arranged so as to prevent text from appearing on either side

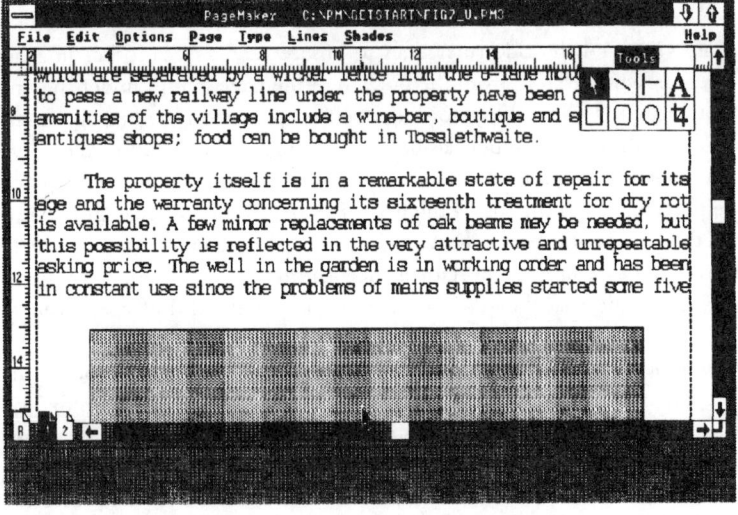

(a)

Figure 7.12   A magnified view (a) of the page around the placeholder. After shifting the text, the printed page appears as in (b)

This most desirable property is positioned in the main thoroughfare of the charming village of West Shovelpot some two miles as the crow meanders from the bustling market town of Tosslethwaite. The aspect of the frontage is southerly, looking on to delightful well kept gardens which are separated by a wicker fence from the 8-lane motorway. Plans to pass a new railway line under the property have been dropped. The amenities of the village include a wine-bar, boutique and some fourteen antiques shops; food can be bought in Tosslethwaite.

The property itself is in a remarkable state of repair for its age and the warranty concerning its sixteenth treatment for dry rot is available. A few minor

replacements of oak beams may be needed, but this possibility is reflected in the very attractive and un-repeatable asking price. The well in the garden is in working order and has been in constant use since the problems of mains supplies started some five years ago. The level of the well is suc

(b)

not to allow any text to either side. Figure 7.12 is a magnified view of the text around the graphics insert placeholder.

● PageMaker 'threads' text, meaning that the text is kept together in order. Even if some new text is inserted, the older text will still remain in its threaded form so that if it is, for example, exported, it will not contain the insertion. Text can be unthreaded by cutting it and pasting it back (even if it is pasted back into the same place).

● PageMaker tries to guard against mistakes in two ways, the Undo command and the Restore Last-Saved Version command. The Undo will reverse the effect of the last command which was executed, and can save a piece of work from being scrambled. If a whole document is beyond rescue, using the last-saved version will restore the version which was most recently saved to the disk.

Questions

3 If a page number is used in the footer of a master page:
  (a) the number is incremented and printed automatically on each page
  (b) the number is shown on screen and must be typed into each page
  (c) the same number will be printed automatically on each page
  (d) the pages are numbered on screen, not on paper
4 A typical header would be used for:
  (a) a summary of the page contents
  (b) a book or chapter title
  (c) a set of notes on the text
  (d) space for additional text
5 A placeholder is:
  (a) a piece of empty page waiting for text
  (b) a space for graphics or Latin text for text
  (c) a shaded area which cannot be used
  (d) a complete dummy document

Proofreading and marking up

No matter how much care is taken in the production of a document, it must be carefully proofread at several stages in its production. At one time, certainly up to the 1970s, this proofing would consist of three parts, editorial checking, galley proofs and page proofs. The editorial checking consisted of working on the author's original manuscript, checking for mistakes of spelling, typing and meaning and also marking in instructions to the printer about how the text should be set. This latter part involved marking the font and size for main text and headings, any changes of style (bold, italic, subscript, superscript) and special setting (as for mathematical equations). The text was then set into type, requiring a compositor to type all the material again from the edited copy. This in itself was a process which tended to insert errors even if the original manuscript was in double-spaced typewritten form, but in those days, as now, there were always some who rejected any attempt to make their work readable and who would have used quill pens if they had been able to master the art of making them.

The result of the work of the compositor was a set of galley proofs, the text laid out in one-column form on long narrow strips of paper. These would be printed, with one copy retained by the printer, one by the editor and one sent to the author. The author would then check the galleys, using the agreed set of correction marks. At this stage, corrections were regarded as being relatively easy to make, and some authors grossly abused this by making considerable changes to the text. This led to the almost universal adoption in publishers' agreements for the author to bear the cost of changes that extended to more than 10% of the original. Putting this into perspective, we now regard 1% of changes as constituting rather a lot of work on a set of proofs.

The galleys that were returned by the author were further checked by the editor or sub-editor, who had the responsibility of finding the mistakes that the author had overlooked. This was extremely important, because an author seldom sees his/her own mistakes – you will find when you try to check your own work that you tend to see what you thought you typed rather than what is on the page. The editor then used the author's galleys as a guide to marking up another set, since few authors ever marked up in the approved way.

Another set of corrected galleys would then be produced (and sometimes sent back with more corrections because new mistakes had been typed in) and used for page layout by pasting-up. A set of page outline sheets was used for this, with the page size marked in dotted lines, and the sub-editor would cut the galley copy into strips and paste them onto the pages. It was at this point that any illustrations and captions would be added – the captions would have been included on the galleys, and illustrations would have been produced separately and cropped or reproduced to the size required. The paste-up therefore required a good sense of layout because it required the sub-editor to place the text, illustrations and captions correctly first time – there was no real provision for adjustment unless the paste was fluid enough to allow the paper to be moved slightly for a short time. Mistakes had to be corrected by taking another galley and re-pasting.

After pasting-up, the proofs would be sent back to the printers so that the type could be set along with the blocks for illustrations into the form of pages. Once this was done, another set of proofs, the page proofs could be produced, and these also were sent to the sub-editor and to the author. By this stage, the text ought to have been correct, but it was not uncommon to find that some new errors had been introduced, and some authors still insisted on making changes to their work. Changes made at this stage were very expensive, of the order of £1 or more per line, and such changes were strongly discouraged.

When the page proofs were finally corrected, the printing of the work could start. By this time the covers would have been designed and would have gone through similar stages of proofing. The printed copy would be sent for binding, an expensive operation, usually in batches determined by the estimated demand. If some 5,000 copies were printed but only 1,000 bound, the sale of that first thousand would cover the costs of the remainder. If sales flopped, the bound copies represented the main loss, and the unbound text could be scrapped with slightly less anguish.

Modern proofreading

Proofreading for authors is little changed nowadays apart from the elimination of the galley pages, though these are sometimes still used even though the typesetting methods have entirely changed. Proofreading for DTP users is a very different art which must, however, still be based on the methods of the past. The main reason is that proofreading from a screen is unreliable for several reasons:

● The reader is often the author of the text, who cannot be relied on to see his/her own mistakes.
● It is not always possible to see the text clearly on the screen, particularly when the DTP package is in use – you can see either the page view with text greeked, or a magnified view with some of the text beyond the edges of the screen.
● It is very difficult to attend to mistakes in the text and the layout of the text at the same time.

Because of these factors, proofing text from the DTP screen is strongly discouraged except in cases where time is the overriding factor, as it often is in daily newspaper production. For all other applications, the preferred method is:

● Text production in a word-processor.
● Graphics production with a graphics package, with or without a scanner.
● Use of the DTP package for text assembly rather than for text checking.

All proofing should be carried out on hard copy (on paper) rather than on the screen. This does not imply that screen checking should not be carried out, simply that it must not be the only checking that is used. If a glaring error is seen on the screen (and only a glaring error would be seen on the screen) it should be corrected when it is seen.

Activity

Take a piece of text produced from a word-processor which is known to contain several errors. Print this text and proofread it, marking it up suitably using BS symbols. Mark up also the fonts and sizes for printing, make the corrections on the disk file and import the text into a DTP document.

The proofing of text should start when the text is complete and has been saved on a disk. The text should be imported into the word-processor and the spell-checker used to search for mis-spellings and mis-typings so that all of the errors that can be found in this way are eliminated. Remember that spell-checkers are often idiosyncratic and can be slow to use, but they do at least remove the worst of the errors. A spell-checker is particularly useful when the typing of the text has been enthusiastic rather than precise; its use for detecting mis-typing is considerably more helpful than its application to find mis-spelling even in these days of school-induced illiteracy.

There are, however, some typing and spelling errors that the spelling checker program cannot find, such as *then* typed in place of *than*, or *rover* in place of *river*. If the result of a mis-typing or mis-spelling is a valid word, it is not likely to be caught by any form of program. The final check must therefore be made on paper, preferably printed with double-spaced lines to make the text more readable and to leave space for corrections.

The draft text from the word-processor should be scrutinized carefully, particularly if you originated the text yourself. It is always better if the work is proofed by someone other than the author, but for some DTP applications this is not easy to arrange. Using double-spaced lines allows you to place a ruler on the page below the line that is being proofed, and the proofing should be done with reference to the original text, using a marked copy of the original. If the document was originated on screen, there will, of course, be no other text, but very often the word-processed copy has been made from a written or typed version, particularly when DTP is being used to publish a magazine, an advertising flyer or similar material.

Instruction	Textual Mark	Marginal Mark
Insert in text the matter indicated in the margin ⅄		New matter followed by ⅄
Delete	/ through character(s) or ⊢━━━━┥ through word(s) to be deleted	♪
Set in or change to capital letters	≡≡≡ under character(s) to be set or changed	≡
Set in or change to bold type	∿∿∿ under character(s) to be set or changed	∿
Run on (no new paragraph)	⊂⊃	⊂⊃
Close up. Delete space between characters or words	linking ⌢ characters	⌢

Reproduced by permission of BSI

Figure 7.13 Examples of BS proof markings

This stage must not be glossed over, because this is the most important proofing step. Any mistakes that pass this point will cost more to eradicate later, and may not be seen until too late. Any doubts must be resolved at this stage – mistakes in syntax, mistakes of fact, possible libels, all must be rooted out at this stage if they have survived thus far. Corrections are made using the BS set of proofing marks, some examples of which are reproduced in Figure 7.13. For the complete set of symbols see BS 5261:Part 2:1976. Printers and editors do not necessarily adhere rigidly to these marks – for example, it is still very common for the word *stet* to be used to indicate that underlined text should be kept unaltered, and to use the **#** sign to mean inserting a space. In addition, editors often use 'private' or 'house' marks which are outside the BS set.

The marked draft is then used for making corrections to the text. The text is again fed into the word-processor and the corrections as marked in the draft are made on screen. The text format is rechecked and the new version saved on disk, preferably as a new file, so that all versions in the development of a file are held. If there is any remaining doubt about the text, another draft copy should be printed and checked again. The aim is to ensure that the text is at this stage as perfect as human frailty can allow.

Questions

6 Galley-proofs are:
  (a) pages of type which are ready to be printed
  (b) printed sheets which show text and graphics
  (c) a way of inviting an author to provide more text
  (d) long strips of type that will be cut into pages
7 A proofreader marks ⌐⌐ at the side of a page to draw attention to a fault in a line. This means:
  (a) two words need to be transferred elsewhere
  (b) two letters have been transposed in a word
  (c) a graphics image is to be transformed into something else
  (d) text and graphics positions need to be interchanged
8 Text proofreading should be done at the word-processing stage because:
  (a) the text exists as a disk file
  (b) the text is easier to check on the screen
  (c) there are no graphics to cause confusion
  (d) the text can more easily be spellchecked, printed and proofread

---

Graphics preparation

The graphics for the document should also be checked. An important point here is that graphics as seen on screen are often considerably distorted as compared to the paper version, so that it is particularly important to work on paper copies. The screen version can be useful in magnified form to show errors that may be difficult to see on paper but which ought in any case to be eliminated, but the paper version is the one that will be seen in the document.

There is no standard scheme for proofing graphics, and the usual system is to make notes and, if necessary, sketches, on the margins of the paper. When the graphics are (unusually) of the vector type originating from a CAD program, for example, they will need to be replaced in the same program for amendment. Graphics that have been obtained by scanning or by the use of a paint type of graphics package will normally use file types that are reasonably well standardized, such as the TIF or PCX type, and these can be edited in a variety of packages. Another proof copy should be printed after such editing, particularly if bit–editing has been used.

Activity

Load from a file a graphics image which is known to be of poor quality and make a print-out (using DTP or a graphics editor program). Mark the faults and then edit the image using a suitable graphics package. Make a new print to see how well the editing has been done.

Collecting up

The DTP stage starts when the text and the graphics are available in corrected form on disk files. Care must be taken to ensure that only the corrected files are used – it is better to keep older versions on separate disks. Even at this stage a considerable amount of effort can be saved if the publication can use templates of master pages from an earlier work, since these will have been checked before. The more times anything is checked (without adding new errors) the better it is, so that the maintenance of old templates and master pages is a very important part of document prod-uction.

The DTP work then collects the text and the graphics into pages, following the procedures that have been described in the earlier parts of this book. The maximum use should be made of style sheets, templates and existing masters, particularly when all typographical work has to follow a house style. Before any text or graphics file is imported, the layout of the master pages should be checked carefully to ensure that the specification is being met. There is little point in making a perfect job of a publication on A4 paper if the specification called for 8″ × 11″ to be used. You should ensure at this stage that any ruler guides that will help in the

224

positioning of text are put into place and are in the specified place. The master pages should be printed out to ensure that they meet the specifications.

Unlike old-style typography, the DTP user has the advantage of enormous flexibility. If the page looks wrong with the arrangement of text and graphics you have created, then it is comparatively simple to rearrange everything. Remember, however, that rearrangement takes time, because all of the text and graphics that lies beyond the point where changes are made will also be rearranged. This is a good argument for working in fairly small sets of pages at a time. Though programs such as PageMaker will permit the production of up to 128 pages in a single document, you should try to avoid the use of such large numbers. Always start any rearrangement at the first page of the document, or at the earliest point where changes are needed.

Previewing the publication

Once the screen layout of the pages of the document appears to be satisfactory, the pages can be printed. A laser printer or an inkjet type must be used, because the dot-matrix is ruled out on the dual grounds of quality and time required. Modern inkjet printers are in some ways superior to laser printers where large areas of black need to be printed, because laser printers tend to give disappointing results on large black areas which often show lighter shades in the middle. The inkjet will be slower in action than the laser printer, but its silence and low cost make it a very attractive proposition. The only drawback is that the modern form of inkjet printer is not necessarily available for every DTP package because no suitable printer driver software is available, and there are no PostScript inkjet printers (though there is software that allows inkjet printers to operate from PostScript files).

When the pages have been printed, they should be subjected to a rigorous inspection to check that the specifications are being met. At this stage, it is still comparatively easy to make corrections, and since all of the major errors should have been detected at earlier stages, this inspection should be for minor points of specification – though no opportunity should be missed to check also for other mistakes.

If the client whose specification is being used can also see the pages at this point, many potential disagreements can be avoided. A print specification may seem perfectly clear, but an inexperienced client in particular may not know how the specification will be interpreted (how are margins measured, how much is allowed for binding, what line spacings are used?) and may feel that the pages, even though perfectly to specification, are not what was visualized when the specification was drawn up.

It should not be the task of the DTP user to educate the client, but someone has to do it, and it greatly helps for future relationships if the layout of the pages is discussed with the client, pointing out how well the specification has been met. If this means some changes then, for the sake of good relations, these should be considered at least. The main point is that an inexperienced client can soon become an experienced client, making future work considerably easier.

Questions

9 There are no standards for proofing graphics because:
   (a) graphics never needed to be proofed before now
   (b) graphics were always treated separately before now
   (c) graphics were never used in publications before now
   (d) artists never made mistakes on paper
10 The main advantage that DTP offers, as compared to conventional publishing methods, is:
   (a) it can use a greater range of fonts and sizes
   (b) it can work with both text and graphics
   (c) it is much more flexible, allowing changes up to the time of printing
   (d) all of the work is held on disks

Assignment 7

You are provided with both graphics and text files which have been checked. Lay out an A4 page, using margins of:

Left 20 mm Right 20 mm Top 15 mm Bottom 20 mm

The page should use two columns with a 1 mm vertical rule between columns and a 4 mm gutter gap either side of the rule. Use a 2 mm rule along the bottom of the page extending to each margin.
Make a heading in a sans-serif face centred in the top margin, using 18-point type.
Put the page number, centred, in the bottom margin, using body font/size.

The body text must use a serif face 12-point on 14-point leading, fully justified.

Sub-headings must use a sans-serif face, bold, 14-point on 18-point leading, with a 1 mm rule under each.

One framed graphic is to be placed at the top of the first column, using full column width. The second framed graphic is to be placed between columns, using a space of 70 mm × 70 mm, with the text flowed around the graphic on each side.

Each graphic should be provided with a left-justified caption in a serif italic face of 10 points size.

Recap

● The page parameters are the settings of margins, word, line and paragraph spacings, indents, etc. that are used in each page of a document.

● DTP documents can be produced in single or multiple column form. In general, columnar form is best suited to a set of small items when a wide page is used.

● A typical document is likely to use both text and graphics, both of which should be imported from disk files. Ruler guides can be used to assist placing text and graphics. Where documents follow a standardized form, placeholders can be used to make a template which can be stored as a disk file. Graphics placeholders can be rectangles, text placeholders are often pieces of Latin text.

● Proofreading is essential to ensure that text is error free and that graphics are of good quality and match the text. Text should be thoroughly proofread at the word-processor stage, because word-processors allow the use of spellchecking to remove the more serious mistakes; the text must also be thoroughly checked on paper. Graphics images must also be printed out and inspected closely, preferably in conjunction with the text that refers to them. When the master pages are prepared, they should be checked for conformity with the print specification. The printed pages also need to be checked again to ensure that the DTP stages have been correctly carried out.

Answers to the questions

1 (b)
2 (c)
3 (a)
4 (b)
5 (b)
6 (d)
7 (b)
8 (d)
9 (b)
10 (c)

8 Printing

Objectives

After reading this chapter you should be able to:
- explain the working principles of the laser printer
- explain the working principles of the offset-litho printer
- describe how to load paper and print with the laser printer
- describe how a laser printer can be used to produce a rough draft and how multiple copies can be obtained
- show how a print run on the laser printer can be cancelled
- show how an offset-litho machine is set up for use
- explain how an offset-litho master plate is produced.

Scenario

The pages of a promotional booklet are proofed and ready to print. You must now use the laser printer to make the master set that will form the plates for the offset-litho, and start the printing run on the offset-litho machine. How is all this to be done?

Principles of the Xerox copier

Laser printers work on a principle called Xerography (Trade Mark of the Xerox Corporation) which was discovered in the 1960s. The similarities between the laser printer and the Xerox photocopier are so great that it is easier to understand laser printing if the principles of the Xerox copier are understood first. In addition, since the Xerox copier is used almost as much in DTP work as the laser printer, a knowledge of the copier machine is equally useful.

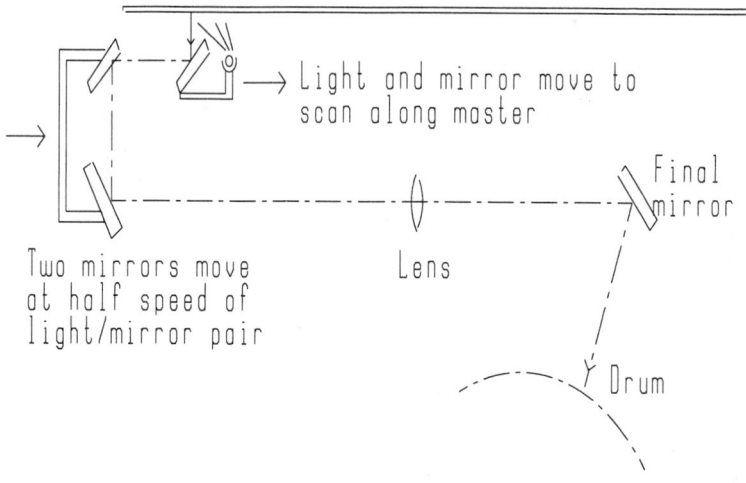

Figure 8.1   The working principle of the Xerox copier scanning mechanism, which is the basis of the photocopier

The Xerox copier uses a drum of material which is electrically charged (by an electrical discharge or *corona* through air which as a by-product produces ozone). Any electrically charged object will attract small particles to it, and the purpose of charging the drum is to make it possible for finely-powdered ink (called toner) to adhere to the drum. The material of the drum, in addition to being a material which can be electrically charged, is also photoconductive, meaning that it becomes an electrical conductor when it is struck by light. When the drum becomes conductive, the electrical charge will leak away so that the drum can no longer attract particles. The principle of the copier is to make the drum conductive in selected parts.

The overall charge is removed when the material is rendered conductive by being struck by a light beam. As the drum rotates, a light beam is scanned across the page which is to be copied, and the reflected light from the page is scanned by moving the light assembly, along with mirrors and lenses, across the page to be copied, Figure 8.1. The use of lenses ensures that the reflected light casts a focused image of the page on the drum as it rotates.

Once this scanning process is complete, the drum will contain on its surface an electrical voltage 'image' corresponding exactly to the pattern of ink on the material that is being copied, typically 100 volts for white areas, 900 volts for dark areas, and intermediate voltages for half-tone regions. Finely powdered resin, the 'toner' will now be coated over the drum and will stick to it only where the electric charge is large – at each black dot of the original page. The coating process is done by using another roller, the developing cylinder, which is in contact with the toner powder, a form of dry ink.

The toner is a light dry powder which is a non-conductor and also magnetic (some machines use a separate magnetic developer powder), and the developing cylinder is magnetized to ensure that it will be coated with toner as it revolves in contact with the toner from the cartridge. A scraper blade ensures that the coating is even. As the developing cylinder rolls close to the main drum, toner will be attracted across where the drum is electrically charged – relying on the electrical attraction being stronger than the magnetic attraction. Note that two forms of attraction, electro-static and magnetic, are being used here.

Rolling paper over the drum will now pass the toner to the paper, using another corona discharge to attract the toner particles to the paper by placing a positive charge on to the paper. After the toner has been trans-ferred, the charge on the paper has to be neutralized to prevent the paper from remaining wrapped round the drum, and this is done by the static-eliminator blade. This leaves the toner only very faintly adhering to the paper, and it needs to be fixed permanently into place. This is done by passing the paper between hot rollers which melt the toner into the paper, giving the glossy appearance that is the mark of a good photocopier. The drum is then cleared of any residual toner by a sweeping blade, recharged and made ready for the next page. Figure 8.2 shows the principles in a diagram.

The main consumables of this process are the toner and the drum. The toner for most modern copiers is contained in a replaceable cartridge, avoiding the need to decant this very fine powder from one container to another. The resin is comparatively harmless, but all fine powders are a risk both to the lungs and in terms of explosion danger. The drum is usually coated with selenium, which is not a material that should be handled if you can avoid it, and which will give off very toxic gases if it is ignited (selenium is a close relative of sulphur, and is flammable). **Never** open a photocopier which is operating. Some copiers use the less objec-tionable zinc oxide form of coating, and a few, such as the TI Microlaser featured in this chapter are now using organic photoconductors (OPC)

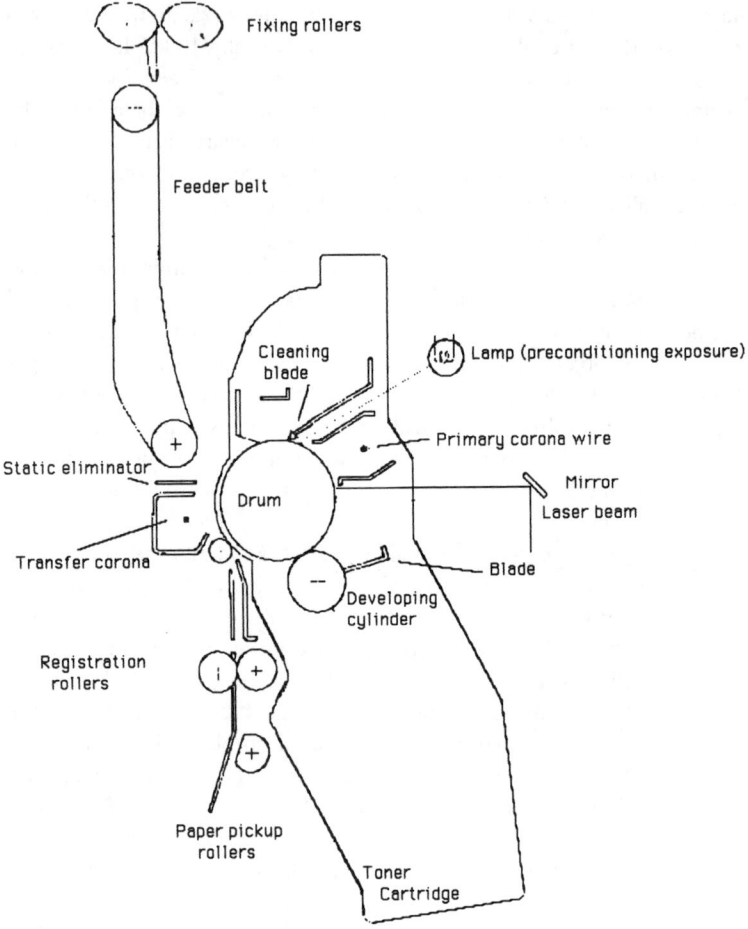

Figure 8.2   The principles of the laser printer which apart from the method of scanning the image are identical to those of the copier

which are of low toxicity and which do not have to be returned to the manufacturers after replacement. Drum replacement will, on average, be needed after each 80,000 copies, and less major maintenance after every 20,000 copies. Some models use a developer powder (a magnetic powder) in addition to toner, and the developer will have to be replenished at some time when the toner is also exhausted.

Questions

1 A laser printer or Xerox copier:
   (a) uses liquid ink
   (b) is based on electric attraction
   (c) uses photographic paper
   (d) uses toxic gases for processing
2 The developing cylinder of a laser printer or Xerox copier:
   (a) transfers the dry toner to the paper
   (b) carries out photographic development
   (c) makes a negative image
   (d) is renewed for every copy

Laser printers

The laser type of printer, which also includes variants such as LED-bar printers and LCD-mask printers, is now the predominant type of printer used with small computers for high-quality output, and is almost universally used for DTP work. As noted earlier, these printers base their technology on Xerographic copiers, and are fast and silent in action. The laser types are page-printers, meaning that it is necessary to store a complete page of information in the memory of the printer in order to print the page. This is because a page cannot be printed until the drum is fully 'printed' with charges. In addition, the mechanism depends on the paper being moved continually against a drum, rather than in one-line steps. When elaborate fonts are used, this can require a large amount of memory – laser printers require at least 2 Mb of memory to function satisfactorily for DTP work.

In addition to memory, the laser printer also contains the components of a computer, with a main processor of its own. This processor is used to convert the pattern of bits in the memory into instructions for guiding the laser beam and turning the beam on or off so that the drum can be discharged in the correct places. This is how the laser printers can work with such a wide range of fonts and sizes and also with graphics.

There are some types of printers which are classed as laser printers but which do not use a laser. These are LED-bar or LCD-mask types which use the same principles of light beams affecting a charged drum, without the use of a laser beam. These types are not page printers, and can work line by line, requiring very little memory. They were originally intended as replacements for daisywheel and dot-matrix printers for word-processing applications rather than as a competitor for the DTP type of laser printer, but several have now been developed into suitable machines for DTP use, and some of them now make use of PostScript.

The quoted speed of most laser printers, 6 pages per minute upwards, refers to repeated copies of a single page and does not refer to normal printing, which can be considerably slower. This is because a substantial amount of the time that is needed for printing consists of building up the instructions in the memory for forming the charge pattern on the drum; if this pattern remains fixed, page printing can be as fast as the speed of the drum permits. When each page is different, and in particular if graphics images are used on each page, the time needed to form the pattern makes the printing rate very much slower. All quoted printing speeds for printers of any kind tend to be highly optimistic. The T.I. Microlaser which was used during the preparation of this book is one of the fastest of a group of twelve printers tested by *Personal Computer* magazine. These tests indicate a time of 79 seconds to print a one-off graphics sample and 101 seconds for a page of one-off text. When repetitive work was done, the speeds were 6 pages per minute for text and 0.76 per minute for graphics. Note that this is time to print – the time to load memory and set up to print a page is considerably longer.

The laser printer is basically a Xerox copier in which the drum is scanned by a laser beam rather than by a light-beam which has been reflected from a master document. The laser beam, being a beam of concentrated light, also has the effect of making the material of the drum conductive when the beam strikes at full brilliance. The beam intensity and direction is controlled by a pattern of signals held in the memory of the printer, and enough memory must be present to store information for a complete page. This requires about 0.5 Mb as a minimum for text work, and 2 Mb or more if elaborate high-resolution graphics patterns have to be printed. The remainder of the action is identical to that of the electrostatic copier – the only difference between the machines is the method of discharging the drum with light signals to form the charge pattern. This implies that the same type of toner and photosensitive drum is used for each type of machine.

Choice of printer

Most of the lower-cost laser printers use as their standard the Hewlett-Packard Laserjet, and emulate the codes used by that printer (which is itself not expensive). This type of printer is excellent for word-processing and graphics, and virtually all word-processing and graphics software will provide printer driver software for the H-P printer. Most DTP packages will also provide for the use of this printer.

The more expensive option is the use of a printer that is fitted with the PostScript command language and with enough memory to allow Post-Script to be used. This automatically pushes up the price of the printer to considerably higher than the level of the H-P type of machine, though these prices have been dropping steadily since the first laser printers were introduced, and are still falling at the time of writing. The advantage of using PostScript is that it allows for graphics to be scaled without loss of resolution, and it also allows a large variety of fonts to be used in soft form. Several makes of printer (notably H-P and Texas) allow PostScript to be added in cartridge form so that the low-cost printer can later be upgraded to full PostScript capability. This is a useful path at a time when the price of the PostScript addition has been falling rapidly.

A soft font is one that is loaded into the DTP package as a file, as distinct to the use of a plug-in cartridge to the printer, and the considerable advantage of a PostScript soft font is that it also can be scaled. The amount of scaling that can be used in practice depends on the amount of memory that is available at the printer, and when work is scaled, text and graphics will remain in registration – something that is very difficult to achieve when bit-mapped fonts are used. The other important advantage of using PostScript for a laser printer is that PostScript is also used by professional typesetting machines, so that the laser printer can be used to produce draft copies of material that can be used to provide PostScript files that Lino-tronic or similar typesetting machines can also use for very high quality output. As a comparison, laser printers are generally capable of 300 dots per inch, and this can be doubled by altering the electronics inside the printer. A typesetter, by contrast works with 1200 – 2400 dots per inch, allowing good half-tone reproduction which is not achieved with the lower resolution of the laser printer.

The agreed essential specification for a laser printer suited to DTP work is:

- high printing speed, particularly for graphics work
- a paper feed capable of dealing with a large number of sheets, prefer-ably 250 or more
- first-class print quality, particularly for large fonts
- PostScript capabilities, or easy upgrading to PostScript

Activity

Compare laser-printed documents with the same material printed by a dot-matrix printer and (if possible) an ink-jet printer. Find the purchase costs of the machines that have been used, and also their running cost per sheet of copy. Compare these figures.

Maintenance of the laser printer

The working heart of the laser printers is known as the *engine* and there are only a few basic engines (such as the Canon) used in all of the laser printers that are currently manufactured. This makes it all the more surprising that there is not more interchangeability between makes for such items as font cartridges, toner cartridges, replacement drums and so on. If you are buying a laser printer for the first time, it pays to enquire about the costs of these consumable items, because these costs are much more important than the cost of the printer itself.

Paper is the most consumed item, and laser printers use, as might be expected, the photocopier grade of paper whose cost is at least twice that of ordinary paper of the same density. The reason for the additional cost is that because of the way that the toner is deposited on to the paper, the paper must consist of fibres which are all aligned along the longer axis, making it behave more uniformly when subject to electric charges (and discharges). It also allows the paper to feed through the machine with less tendency to curl. In addition, since the toner is fixed to the paper by fairly intense heating, the paper must not darken or curl when it is heated. These requirements make the paper more expensive to produce, though some shopping around can reveal better prices than can be obtained from large suppliers.

● Whatever is claimed by manufacturers, the use of very heavy (more than 70 grams per square metre) and expensively finished paper is not justified.
● Such paper will often feed badly, forming ridges, and will allow ink to smear badly.
● Lighter and more absorbent papers usually produce better results – try cheap grades first.

One point to remember is that laser printers, like the rotary copiers of olden days, use a mechanical paper feeder system which is not always perfectly efficient. A page may be missed, two pages grabbed at once, or a page turned sideways as it enters the machine, all resulting in problems. This makes the paper consumption of the laser printer considerably more than that of the dot-matrix machine which uses pin-fed paper with its trouble-free grip of the paper.

The other major costs are replacement of toner and of the print drum. Toner is a fine powder which must not be allowed to spill into the atmosphere, and the print drum is constructed using a photosensitive material which must not be handled. In addition, if the element selenium is used for the print drum there is a hazard due to the poisonous nature of selenium (and the selenium dioxide which is generated if it overheats). Some manufacturers have made the replacement of both toner and drum particularly easy for the user, for other machines the task is far from easy and better done by a maintenance mechanic. Maintenance does not simply cover the replacement of the toner and drum, it also concerns cleaning. Because of the way that electric charges attract all small particles, laser printers tend to become clogged up with fine dust, composed of stray toner and house dust in almost equal measure. Dust is, as always, an enemy of mechanical parts, so that cleaning and lubrication schedules are of considerable importance. Lubrication almost always uses silicone oils – mineral oils are totally forbidden on the plastics which are almost universally used for bearings on light machinery.

● Users are often advised to start a new run with a fresh toner supply. Though it is inadvisable to start a run when the toner is almost finished, replenishing toner is not advisable before a major piece of work.
● When toner has been replenished, the first set of pages will usually be over-inked and badly smudged.
● Following toner replenishment, always make some test copies onto absorbent paper until you are sure that the toner is flowing correctly.

Questions

3 Laser printers intended for DTP work:
  (a) must use the LED-bar type of principle
  (b) must use the LCD-mask type of principle
  (c) need to contain a large amount of memory
  (d) can use any variety of paper
4 The laser printer:
  (a) needs no maintenance

    (b) requires only the correct grade of paper
    (c) is very cheap to run
    (d) requires toner and drum replacement at intervals
5 Which of the following is *not* a hazard peculiar to laser printers:
    (a) danger to eyesight
    (b) toxic ozone gas
    (c) danger to lungs from fine dust
    (d) poisonous ink ribbons

Installing a laser printer

Laser printers are often placed on any convenient surface, but the recommended site requirements are:

● A main supply whose voltage does not vary by more then 10% from its nominal voltage.

● A temperature variation of not more than 10°C to 32.5°C and humidity variation of not more than 20% to 80%.

● No nearby water taps, humidifier, refrigerator or the outlet of an air-conditioner.

● No exposure to open flames, dust, ammonia fumes or direct sunlight.

● Good ventilation must be provided.

● The surface on which the printer is placed must be level and strong enough to support the printer. There must also be sufficient space around the printer to reach the controls and the paper stacks.

● If the printer has just been unpacked it must be given at least one hour to warm up and dissipate moisture before use.

Note in particular the point about avoiding direct sunlight, because laser printers are often placed near windows in order to provide ventilation. Sunlight is a problem because of its ionizing effects as well as the more obvious risk of strong reflections reaching the internal drum of the printer. Note that when a photosensitive drum is being replaced sunlight *must* be excluded. Exposing a drum to direct sunlight can make the drum totally useless.

Using the laser printer

The following notes relate to the use of a Texas Instruments MicroLaser PostScript laser printer used along with PageMaker, but the methods are

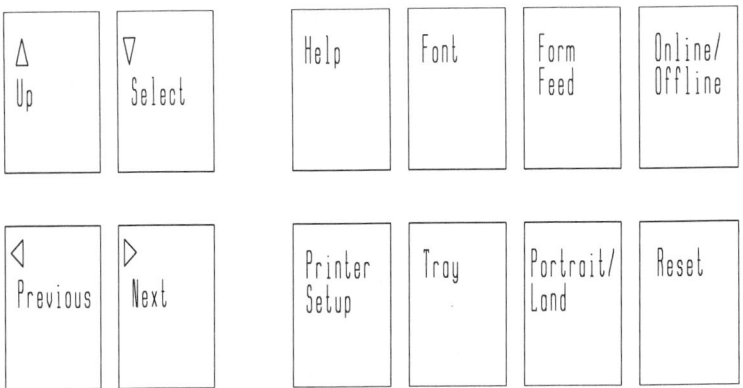

Figure 8.3 The printer panel controls of the MicroLaser, typical of many small laser printers

applicable to any laser printer that can be used for high-quality DTP work. The TI MicroLaser fulfils all the requirements of the specification listed earlier, and has the considerable advantage that its paper-tray is built into the machine rather than clipped on. This makes the whole machine very compact for desktop use. PostScript can be added to the basic printer by way of a cartridge which is about the size of a credit card, and a Laserjet emulation can be provided in the same way.

The laser printer should have been set up on a horizontal surface in accordance with the maker's instructions, and the presence of toner/developer checked. The paper tray should be loaded with a suitable paper, paying attention to which way round the paper must be loaded. Most photocopy/laser grade papers specify which side is the printing side and the printer manual will state which way round (printing side up or down) the paper has to be laid on the tray.

● The printer should be connected to the computer, and the computer switched on.
● Wait until the printer is ready. Most printers will display a *Self-Test* message while warming up, and will show a message such as: *On-line PS Idle* when ready for use.
● If a *Paper Jam* message shows, this is usually caused by failure to remove a sheet that was left in the printer; but the message can be delivered if the type of paper is not suitable.
● The printer front panel controls, Figure 8.3, may need to be altered,

239

depending on the type of work, though this is generally not needed for PostScript printers.

● Some of these controls display a menu and items have to be selected by using Up, Down, Previous, Next and Select buttons.

Once the printer is ready, the DTP program can be run, and a publication loaded in. The DTP program should be set so as to connect to a PostScript printer (if it has been using any other printer) and the usual printer Setup run (to determine such factors as portrait or landscape etc.). Note that the printer may also permit the options of portrait or landscape independently of the DTP program.

● The Print command of the DTP programs will then start the printing sequence of actions.

● This does not immediately result in printing – several minutes can elapse between starting a print action and actually making the print.

● This time is due to the amount of data being transferred from the computer to the printer, and the extensive work that has to be done inside the printer, particularly for a graphics image.

● During this time, the printer will display messages to show that processing is going on, and the print run can be aborted, either by the DTP program (in the first part of the time) or at the printer itself by pressing the Online/Offline button or by using the Reset button of the printer.

● The actual production of the print is heralded by a sudden increase in noise from the printer, following which the page will be produced.

● If multiple copies have been requested from the DTP program, the copies will be produced very rapidly once the first stage of filling memory has been completed.

● Some DTP programs provide for draft copies which will be produced in a much shorter time, but at lower resolution.

During the printing session, various problems can arise, though these ought not to be exaggerated – most print runs proceed smoothly. Problems are usually notified on the small report screen of the printer itself and can include:

● Paper jamming – this will require the printer to be opened to remove the paper. CAUTION: Several parts of the opened printer may be very hot – observe any directions in the printer manual about allowing the printer to cool. If jamming is frequent, change the type of paper.

- Black vertical lines on paper are caused by a dirty corona wire – the printer should be serviced.
- Poor print quality is due either to a worn-out print drum, bad developer (if a separate developer is used) or unsuitable paper.
- Smeared or dirty printing is due to spilled toner, overfilled toner cartridge, dirty cleaning pads, marks on the photosensitive drum or unsuitable paper (too glossy, for example).
- Paper feed faults (no sheets delivered, several sheets delivered at a time, blank sheets delivered) are almost all due either to unsuitable paper or to incorrect paper handling (sheets should be fanned out before loading, loaded correctly into tray, kept dry and warm).
- Most errors other than poor print quality are advised by way of the printer's own screen display, and appropriate action should be taken with reference to the manual.

Activity

Set up the laser printer for producing a document of more than one page. Print a draft copy and note the time required. Print a high quality copy and note this time. Try also printing the same number of pages in high quality, but making multiple copies of one page, and note this time also. Which comes nearest to the quoted speed of printing (usually quoted in pages per minute)?

Ink-jet printers

Printing of a quality second only to that from a laser printer, and in some respects superior, is attained by the modern form of ink-jet printer. The original type of ink-jet printers used a single jet of ink, and attempted to guide the jet by using electric forces on tiny metal plates. These early ink-jet printers were not successful, the ink could not be guided accurately enough so that the resolution was poor even in comparison with a 9-pin dot-matrix printer. In addition, these early ink-jet printers needed frequent cleaning because the spray of ink bounced from the paper to cover rollers and other moving parts, eventually dripping to the bottom of the casing.

All of this changed with the arrival of the two makes of modern ink-jet printers, the Canon Bubble-jet and the Hewlett-Packard Deskjet. Both of these printers operate by squirting tiny jets of ink at paper from a set of miniature syringes arranged in a matrix pattern. These jets can be placed close enough to allow the ink-jet printer to attain the same 300 dots-per-inch standard of resolution as the laser printer. These printers, however, are useful only if the DTP package includes printer drivers specifically for the ink-jet types.

The outstanding names for such printers are Hewlett-Packard, Canon and Epson in order of ascending price, but all ink-jet printers offer excellent print quality and reliability at comparatively low prices. If you need graphics printing with large areas of pure black, you might find an ink-jet superior to a laser in this respect because it is easy to blast a sheet of paper with ink, less easy to arrange the charge on a drum so that repulsion does not occur on a large area of the same charge. The laser printer uses electric forces to control the toner, and the basic principle is that like charges repel and unlike attract. The charge on the drum causes an opposite charge to be induced on the toner and attracts the toner, but when a large area of toner is on the drum all of the toner will have the same sign of charge, and this causes repulsion. The effect is that some of the toner drops off in the areas of dense black, making these areas paler when they are printed.

The paper quality for ink-jets is less critical than for a laser printer, but the cost of consumables is still high (though not so high as for the laser printer) because the whole set of nozzles is usually renewed along with the ink reservoir; the whole assembly is made in cartridge form. The ink-jet types are line printers and are remarkably silent, some are even quieter than laser types (many of which have a noisy cooling fan). Some suppliers offer ink reservoir replenishment or do-it-yourself replenishing kits.

One point to note is that Hewlett-Packard make a colour ink-jet printer, the Paintjet; one of the very few printers for small computers that can produce colour output at a reasonable price. The drawback is the lack of support from software because in order to work, the Paintjet must have driver software installed in the package that uses the printer.

Litho offset principles

Once pages have been produced from the DTP package, and have been approved, they must be copied by some suitable mass-production method. For a very small run, possibly appropriate to a newsletter for a rural church, the pages can simply be mass produced from the laser printer, setting the printer to make multiple copies of each page. If this would tie up the time of the computer to an unacceptable extent, the pages can be photocopied, once again setting the copier for the number required of each page. Most photocopiers will work on both sides of a page, though not all will accept paper that is still hot, and a few give noticeably inferior copies on the second side. Even when numbers approach 100 copies, this can still be the most economical method of production.

For larger runs, the method that is needed for good quality reproduction, and which is essential for headed paper and business cards, is offset litho. The principle is a very old one, that ink made with an oil base will not adhere to water-wet surfaces. The name of lithography comes from the Greek word for a stone, because early lithography operated using a flat stone surface. If a mirror-image copy is made in ink on a stone, and the stone is then moistened, then when you run an inked roller over the stone the ink is deposited only on the parts which have already been coated in ink. A piece of paper laid on the stone can then be pressed down by another roller, and when the paper is stripped off it will retain a perfect impression of the master copy. This assumes, of course, that the stone is perfectly flat, and that the ink is free from lumps.

The use of stone has been consigned to the stone age, although stone lithography is still a medium for artists, and modern lithography is of the offset variety. This means simply that the text which is to be used as the master copy is *not* prepared on the material which is used for lithography. Modern small offset machines, such as the Rotaprint or the A.B. Dick, use either metal or plastic masters, and these are prepared from your pages of text using a photocopier. Laser printers can prepare such masters directly on to the master sheet, using the plastic or paper form of master. Once a master is made, it can be used on a small lithographic rotary or flat-bed press at very low cost. The cost is so low that the method is used in educational work (sometimes, alas, to make unauthorized copies from textbooks in contravention of copyright), and the cost of the masters is also low.

Offset litho can be viable for as few as 10 copies, and is economical for large numbers. It gives much clearer copies than the older type of ink duplicator and the master is much less fragile than a wax stencil, and has a longer working life. The small-business user of desktop publishing can seek out a printer who will make litho copies of designs for headed paper, business cards, advertising literature and brochures.

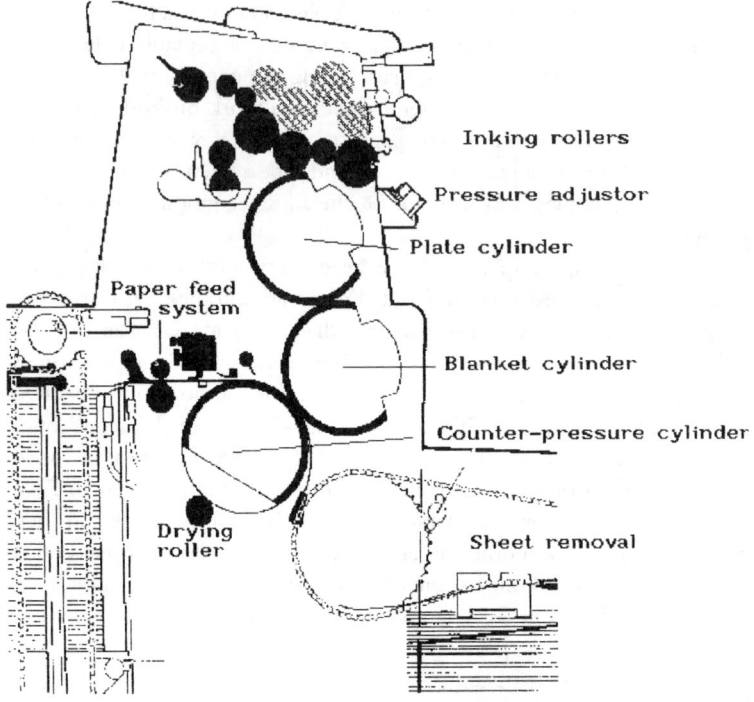

Figure 8.4   The principles of the Rotaprint R30/95 offset litho machine

The offset machine

The master plate is made of metal or paper, and its ink image is rolled on to a resilient surface, usually a plate of synthetic rubber (known as a blanket) laid on a cylinder. This in turn transfers the ink to the paper by being rolled and pressed against each sheet of paper. The machine must deliver enough ink to the master to keep the copies well inked, and enough water (usually modified by a wetting-agent solution that is supplied by the makers of the offset machine) to dampen the parts of the plate which are not inked.

The master, whatever type is used, carries an image that is inked in a greasy material and, when the machine is running, both ink and the water solution will be delivered in metered quantities. The relative amounts are critical, because a shortage of solution will allow drying out, and permit

244

more of the master to be ink-coated. Too much solution, on the other hand, will make the ink adhesion poor, yielding thin and poorly printed copies.

Figure 8.4 shows a side view of the Rotaprint R30/95, a large machine which is suitable for rates of up to 6000 copies per hour. The small rollers are all part of the inking mechanism, and are necessarily elaborate to ensure an even ink coating on the master plate. Two of these rollers oscillate from side to side during operation in order to improve the uniformity of inking. The water solution is also transferred on these same rollers of which one, the plate roller, is placed into contact with the plate cylinder when printing is taking place.

As the plate cylinder, which carries the master, rotates, it picks up ink and solution, and as the master rotates an ink image is transferred to the blanket cylinder. This cylinder carries the rubber 'blanket' for the offset image. Note that because the image is transferred to this intermediate roller, the original image can be the correct (readable) way round, making the intermediate image reversed and the final (paper) image the correct way round. As the blanket cylinder rotates it also presses against the paper which is fed between the blanket cylinder and the counter-pressure cylinder. A drying roller under the counter-pressure cylinder ensures that this cylinder does not become wet, since such moisture would transfer to the underside of the paper and make inking uncertain.

The main problem that attends all offset machines is obtaining the correct consistency of ink for the work that is being done, and ensuring uniformity of inking. For many purposes the type of work is almost unchanging, reproduction of text and images on A4 paper, so that the ink consistency, once found, can easily be maintained. The evenness of inking is dealt with by incorporating adjustments that allow for the inking to be controlled through (typically) 25 ducts, each individually adjustable, across the width of the paper.

The quality of printing from an offset machine is so much better than that from wax stencils that these machines have almost completely replaced the older types. Considerable care is needed, however, in keeping rollers clean and keeping inking ducts in correct adjustment. Most offset machines can print in colour, passing the paper through again for each different ink colour that is to be used. This demands very high standards of paper feed and location, and offset machines often use mechanisms such as suction feed, in which each sheet of paper is picked up on a suction pipe and placed very precisely before being caught by the rollers.

Questions

6 Modern ink-jet printers:
   (a) use a single jet which is guided by electric forces
   (b) use a matrix of individual jets
   (c) use ordinary ink
   (d) use special paper
7 The principle of lithography is:
   (a) that dark areas of the image are coated with a water-repelling greasy substance
   (b) that dark areas of the image are coated with a watery layer which repels ink
   (c) that the whole of the master plate is coated with ink
   (d) that the whole of the master plate is coated with water
8 The word 'offset' as applied to lithography means:
   (a) ink is picked up from a tray on to rollers
   (b) the cost of the master is offset by lower printing costs
   (c) the inked pattern is transferred to an intermediate cylinder, the blanket
   (d) colour documents have to be printed three times with different inks

Using the offset machine

The larger types of offset-litho machines are intended to be used by skilled operators only, and most DTP users will be running the office type of off-set litho machine which is smaller and easier to use. For large-scale production at high speeds, however, the larger machines must be used, and operated in accordance with their manuals. In particular, the procedures for loading in a master and for cleaning after use are considerably more involved than for the simpler office machines. Before starting a session, the machine, whatever its type, should be inked up and loaded with enough paper for the job in hand.

Typically, the master is held upside down and hooked on to the head-plate clip. The machine is then slowly turned round by hand (with the ink rollers pulled back and no pressure applied to the other rollers) until the master has been fed in without wrinkling, and can be attached to the tail-clip. A previously-used metal plate may have to be wiped with a solution to remove its preserving solution; a paper plate needs to be moistened with a different solution. Since plates will soon dry out, the machine should be started as soon as possible and the ink level moved to its

246

normal running position. The number of copies is set, and the machine will run until the required number has been completed.

Cleaning will normally be carried out after a days use, and must be done thoroughly because of the nature of the ink. All the rollers need to be cleaned and the ink duct and water fount emptied and cleaned. This must be done meticulously, because even distribution of ink depends critically on a large number of small passages being kept clear, and if ink is allowed to harden inside these passages it can be difficult to remove. In general, the smaller machines are easier to work on. Very great care must be taken when working on the larger machines, because the cylinders are usually very heavy, and no attempt should be made to remove them single-handed.

Colour work

Where colour printing is required, the usual method is to make three sets of masters, one for each primary printing colour. This requires the three sets of images to be very precisely registered with each other, and if DTP is used to prepare the masters considerable care has to be used in the preparation and printing of the masters. The usual procedure is to make a print run of more copies than will be needed using the first of the primary colours. The machine is then thoroughly cleaned, and loaded with the second primary colour of ink. The second master is put into place, and a print made on to a blank sheet to check for even inking. Once this has been achieved, one print is made on a sheet which has already been used for the first colour, and this is critically examined to ensure that the images are correctly registered, with no fringes of colour showing in white areas. The master may need to be adjusted and this process of making a print repeated until registration is perfect. Following another print run, the ink is changed again, and the whole procedure repeated until the last print run can be made, yielding the full colour copies.

Questions

9 The blanket of the offset litho machine is made from
   (a) copper or steel
   (b) wood or plastic
   (c) natural or synthetic rubber
   (d) wool or cotton

10 After each print run on an offset-litho machine:
  (a) the blanket can be left as it is
  (b) the rollers must be cleaned and the ink-ducts emptied
  (c) the water needs to be replaced
  (d) lubrication is needed

Assignment 8

Under supervision, carry out the replacement of toner (or toner cartridge) in a laser printer. Observe safe methods, using a face-mask and gloves. Carry out a drum replacement, also observing safety regulations. Carry out the cleaning actions on an offset-litho printer, paying particular attention to the blanket cylinder, master cylinder and pressure cylinder, ink-ducts and ink-trays.

Recap

● The laser printer operates on the principles of the Xerox copier, using a light-sensitive drum whose surface is coated with electric charge. The pattern of charge on the drum is altered by the laser beam, which in turn is controlled by the built-in computer in the printer, working on the data for a single page at a time.

● Laser printers of the normal 'office' type are loaded with paper, which must be of the copier grade, using a paper-feeder tray. When the machine has warmed up, it can be driven by the DTP program to produce copies either in draft mode or in high-quality mode. The DTP program can also control the printing of multiple copies, and provides for cancelling the print run.

● For a larger print run, the laser printer is used to prepare masters for an offset-litho printer. This type of machine works on the principle that ink can adhere only to greasy parts of a sheet when the other parts have been moistened with water. The inky pattern of the master is rolled on to a rubber 'blanket' cylinder (the 'offset' action), and this blanket in turn is used to print the paper. Master plates can be made by direct typing, by using the laser printer, or by using a Xerox copier.

Answers to questions

 1 (b)
 2 (a)
 3 (c)
 4 (d)
 5 (d)
 6 (b)
 7 (a)
 8 (c)
 9 (c)
10 (b)

Appendix A: Common terms and abbreviations used in DTP

Alignment The matching of two lines or points so as to be at the same distance from an edge or another point. Use of ruler guides, lines of print, edges of graphics and other items that must be positioned correctly with respect to existing features of a document.

ASCII Acronym of American Standard Code for Information Interchange. The standard code uses 7 bits of a byte for 128 letters (upper-case and lower-case), digits 0 to 9 and punctuation marks. Most computers and printers can in addition use the eighth bit to provide another 128 characters, including accented characters, currency symbols (such as £), and box-graphics shapes, but these 128 characters are not standardized on machines other than the PC type.

Aspect ratio The ratio of width to height for a screen. Most VDUs use the TV standard of 4:3, and this is reflected in the number of pixels used in vertical and horizontal directions.

Backing store (Auxiliary store) An older name for the disk system of a computer. The working store is the memory, but this loses its contents when the power is turned off. Magnetic storage on tape or disk is retained after power is turned off and backs up the data in the memory.

Backup An additional copy of a file made on another medium (floppy or tape); used particularly to guard against loss of data on a hard disk. All work should be backed up to the extent of at least one copy.

Bar chart A form of graph display in which numbers are represented as the lengths of vertical or horizontal bars.

Baseline   A line (which may be invisible) on which a line of characters rests. The descenders of the characters will extend below the baseline.

Bit   A *Bi*nary Digi*t*, one single unit of data, expressed in number-code as 0 (off) or 1 (on). All computer storage systems use this type of coding because it corresponds to the most reliable use of electrical signals as off or on.

Bit-map   An image that consists of dots, with each dot represented by one bit in the memory of the computer. A large bit-map image with high resolution requires a large number of bits – at 300 dots per inch an A4 page consists of 8 million bits (about 1 Mb of memory), hence the requirement for a large memory in a laser printer.

Body text   The main text of a document as distinct from headings, captions, sub-headings etc. Most or all of the body text will be in one type font and size, such as Times Roman 10 or 12-point.

Bold   A heavily printed version of a font which stands out in the text, used to draw attention to a word or phrase.

Bullet   A large dot used to attract attention and normally used to mark each item of a list.

Byte   A set of eight bits. Memory for a computer is normally organized into bytes, since one byte corresponds to the storage space for one character in ASCII code, even if 7-bit ASCII code is being used.

CAD   Computer-Aided Design. A program which allows the computer to be used for producing technical drawings to any scale, using vector line methods.

CD-ROM   Digital information put on to a CD disk, which can be read by a suitable drive (see Matmos for Hitachi CD-ROM drives). Some 600 Mb can be placed on a single disk. This is particularly useful as a way of distributing clip-art.

CGA   Colour Graphics Adapter. The first type of IBM graphics video board designed for the PC. A computer with a CGA board is not well suited to DTP work because of the low resolution of this system.

251

Clipboard A portion of the memory of the computer which is used to hold information (text or graphics) temporarily, used in Cut, Copy and Paste actions.

Copy To make an invisible copy of a piece of (usually) text which can then be pasted (see Paste) visibly into another part of the document or into another document. See also Clipboard.

Cursor A marker used on the screen to show where the next key typed will cause an effect. The shape of the cursor is often used to indicate the kind of action that can be expected (insert or overtype, draw line, move text, etc.).

Cut To store a piece of (usually) text into memory and remove the visible text from the screen. The Cut material can be pasted (see Paste) into another part of the document or into another document. See also Clipboard.

Default An option or value which is automatically supplied if no other choice is made. Most menus in programs supply defaults which are used if nothing else is specified.

Descenders The parts of a character which are below the baseline. Characters such as y, g, p, q contain descenders.

Digitizer tablet A flat plate on which X-Y co-ordinate data can be created and sent to the computer. A drawing placed on such a plate can be stored in the computer by placing a stylus on each point of the drawing, if suitable software is present.

Disk A thin plastic disc coated on both sides with magnetic material so that the computer's digital signals can be stored. Disks are classed as hard or floppy (qv).

Display face A typeface that is large and particularly eye-catching, de-signed for headlines.

Dot-matrix The use of a rectangular pattern of dots to create shapes, particularly for screen display and in dot-matrix printers. Dot-matrix representation is also used in laser printers, in scanners, digitizing pads and other hardware devices.

Appendix A: Common terms and abbreviations used in DTP

Downloadable font   A disk file of font information that can be sent from a computer to a suitable printer, avoiding the use of cartridges and allowing a great variety of fonts to be used if memory permits.

Draft   A rough printout made at low resolution and used for checking purposes. Dot-matrix printers can produce copy either in draft form (quick but of poor quality) or in LQ (letter-quality) form (slower but of typewriter quality).

Driver   A program for a specific piece of hardware (printer, screen, mouse, etc.) which links the hardware into the operating system so that it can be used correctly.

DTP   Desktop publishing. The use of a computer to compose text and graphics into book or newspaper pages, which can then be printed by a laser or ink-jet printer, or used directly by a typesetting machine.

Edit   To inspect text and graphics material so that changes can be made if required.

EEMS   Enhanced Expanded Memory Standard. A system for using additional memory for PC machines which allows considerably more use of the additional memory than the earlier EMS.

EGA   Enhanced Graphics Adapter. The improved form of colour graphics video board introduced by IBM to replace CGA. This offers better resolution than CGA, but is inferior to VGA or Hercules boards.

Embedded code   Number codes which are present in the normal ASCII codes of text. These codes do not cause any visible character to appear on the printed copy or on screen, but can turn on or off effects such as bold print or italics and put in spacings such as indents and tabs. Different word-processors are likely to use different embedded codes, making it necessary to use **filters** when text is imported into a DTP program (which will use its own embedded codes).

EMS   Expanded Memory System. A specification of add-on memory boards for the PC, now superceded by EEMS or LIM-4. Old EMS boards are still being sold, but are of very little applicability to the memory requirements of DTP work.

Execute   To carry out an action, such as the instructions of a program.

File   A complete set of data items which can be stored on a disk or printed. Each program or part of a program is held as a separate file, and each document of text and each graphics image can be held also as a separate file.

Fill   To place colour or pattern into a closed area.

Floppy disk   A magnetic disk which is enclosed in a casing that can be inserted into or removed from a disk drive which is part of the computer. Floppy disks are used for distributing programs and for backup, but a hard disk is preferable for day-to-day computing use.

Font   A typeface design in one size, weight and style.

Footer   A piece of text that is repeated at the foot of each page in a document, often consisting of the page number.

GEM   Graphics Environment Manager. A Digital Research program which acts as front end, allowing some window, icon and mouse operation. Used on older versions of Ventura Publisher.

Hanging indent   A left or negative indent, meaning that text is placed to the left of the normal left-margin position.

Hard disk   A disk, usually a set of disks, which are held in an airtight casing and fixed inside a drive unit that is built into the computer. Because of their construction, hard disks allow much more information to be stored than is possible on floppy disks, and the rate of reading and writing is also much greater.

Header   A piece of text which is placed at the top of each page of a document, usually within the top margin space. Headers are used to show a book name or a chapter heading on each page.

Hercules   A type of graphics adapter board which offers high-resolution monochrome graphics, excellent for DTP use. Later Hercules boards have featured colour as well as monochrome displays with very high resolution.

Incompatible   Mismatched, applied to computer systems, disks or programs which can be used on one machine but not on others. All machines of the PC type are reasonably compatible with each other, but not with the Acorn, Apple Macintosh, Atari ST or Amiga machines. Disks made by the other machines are not usually readable by the PC machine.

Indent   Positioning of text relative to the left margin. An indent is usually to the right of the left-margin position, but see Hanging indent.

Ink-jet printer   A form of dot-matrix printer which uses a set of fine jets. The jets can be closely spaced, allowing resolutions of 300 dots per inch to be achieved, and giving excellent print quality at low cost.

Input device   Any hardware device such as the keyboard, mouse, scanner or digitizing table which provides signals into the computer.

Insert mode   A word-processing or DTP mode in which typed letters are inserted into existing text which is moved to make room. See also overtype mode. Insert mode is often a default because it can never cause existing type to be replaced accidentally.

Inter-line spacing   The space or *leading* between the lines in a paragraph. Different spacing may be applied between paragraphs.

Italic   A typeface style in which the letters are thin and sloped to the right. This is used for emphasis or in captions.

Justification   Alignment of text. The name can be used to mean alignment of text so that each line has the same length. Some users prefer to call this right-justification, using the term *left-justification* for text with a ragged right hand edge. Full or right justification is done by altering the spaces between words.

Kerning   Adjusting spacing between characters to give a pleasing appearance. Applied in DTP mainly to pair-kerning, meaning the reduction in spacing between certain parts of characters such as **To**. Kerning is particularly needed when large sizes of type are being used.

Keyboard   Any input system that uses a set of keys which are pressed to form a character-signal. The usual English alphabetical keyboard is called the QWERTY type from the layout of the first six letters on the top line – the corresponding French keyboard is the AZERTY. See also *keypad*.

Keypad   A small keyboard for numbers only, usually set to the right of a main keyboard.

Landscape   Paper positioning (orientation) with the long dimension of the sheet horizontal, making the width greater than the height.

Laser printer   A printer which uses the principles of the office photo-copier. A laser beam is controlled by a built-in computer system to form character patterns on a drum of sensitive material. Resolutions of 300 to 600 dots per inch can be achieved. Well known types include the AppleLaser and the Hewlett-Packard Laserjet.

LCS   Liquid Crystal Shutter, also known as Liquid Crystal Mask. A method of exposing a photosensitive drum to a light image, used in printers which are in other respects similar to laser printers. The advantage of LCS is that lines rather than pages are printed, so that huge memory is not needed.

LED   Light Emitting Diode. Devices used as signal lights on keyboards and computers, also used in scanners and in another form of laser printer which also prints one line at a time rather than in pages.

LIM   Lotus-Intel-Microsoft. A standard for expanded memory agreed by three companies with a substantial interest in memory expansion. The LIM 4.0 board is recommended for expanding the memory of PC machines so as to allow the use of large DTP programs. See also EMS, EEMS.

Machine-readable   Data in the form of a recorded disk which can be used by a computer program such as a DTP or word-processor program. Machine-readable data is much easier to work with, as it needs no further conversion.

256

Master page   A page (or pair of pages) which carry information that will be used on each page of a document. Typically, a master page will define margins, indents, paragraph spacings, page numbering, use of columns, headers and footers. Another aid to consistency is the use of style sheets, qv.

Monospaced   Referring to type which uses the same spacing between all pairs of letters, irrespective of the size of the letters. All typewriters use monospaced type, so that this type of font, such as Courier, is often used to simulate typewriting. Monospaced fonts are necessary for tabular work, to ensure that columns of letters or numbers remain in line.

MSDOS   Microsoft Disk Operating System. The standard operating system for PC machines, still running in parallel with the later OS/2, and used by the vast majority of PC owners.

Original   The text, artwork or sketch which has been produced by the author, artist or designer and which needs to be put into a form (machine-readable form) which can be used by the computer. In some cases, the original may be created in machine-readable form, eliminating the need to convert.

Orphan   The first line of a new paragraph which is left on the bottom of a page rather than with the remainder of the paragraph. See also Widow.

Orientation   Angular positioning relative to some fixed line, applied mainly to paper (landscape or portrait) or screen images.

Output device   Any hardware device which handles output from a computer system. Typical output devices are the screen and the printer, both of which convert the computer signals into readable form.

Overtype mode   A typing mode in which newly typed characters replace existing characters, see also Insert mode.

Package   A set of computer programs which is used to carry out a complicated task such as word-processing or DTP.

Page   One side of a sheet of paper or the visible area of a screen. Paper page sizes follow internationally agreed metric standards (such as the A or B set), though computers are often set up for US sizes such as Letter or Legal.

Pagination   Division of text and graphics into units of page size. The pagination will alter when character sizes are changed and the text or graphics is inserted or removed. A page number is usually applied in the course of pagination.

Paste   To fix a piece of text or a graphics image into a space on a page or into several pages. See also Cut, Copy.

PCL   Printer Control Language, the main alternative to PostScript, used in the Hewlett-Packard Laserjet machines and in many low-cost printers which emulate the H-P standards.

Pitch   The spacing between characters on a line. For monospaced fonts, the pitch can be measured as the number of characters per inch; for proportional fonts an average value of characters per inch is quoted.

Pixel   Acronym of Picture Element, meaning the smallest units (dots) from which a picture can be built up, usually referring to the screen. Each pixel must be addressable, meaning that the computer keeps a reference number (an address number) for each pixel so as to allow the pixel to be changed (change of colour or shading).

Plotter   An output hardware device which is used in conjunction with drawing software to produce geometrical drawings using coloured pens controlled by the computer. Programs such as CAD programs which use plotter generally work with vector-graphics (qv).

Point   A unit equal to 1/72 inch, used in measuring type sizes.

Portrait   An orientation of a page or image with the longer dimension vertical so that the depth is greater than the width, see also Landscape.

Printer   A hardware output device which prints text and graphics from a file under the control of the computer.

Printer-plotter   Any printer which can print both text and graphics. All computer printers, with the exception of the old daisywheel type, are of this form.

Appendix A: Common terms and abbreviations used in DTP

Program   A set of instructions in number-code form which cause the computer to perform a task such as editing a document or printing a document. A simple word-processor might use a single program, but it is more usual to require a set of programs called a package (qv).

Proportional font   A font in which the width required for each character is proportional to the size of the character, so that the *m* takes more space than the *i*.

RAM   Random Access Memory. All memory is random access, but the name is used to mean read-write memory as distinct from read-only.

ROM   Read Only Memory. The form of memory that is not erased when the machine is switched off, so that its programs remain ready for use when the machine is switched on. These programs are used to control the disk system so that the remainder of the Disk Operating System (DOS) can be loaded into memory

Sans-serif   See *Serif.*

Scale   A scale means the relationship between one quantity and another, often applied to dimensions. To scale an image means to alter its dimensions so as to make an enlarged or a reduced copy.

Scanner   A hardware input device which can read text or graphics images and convert them into machine-readable digital form. Simple scanners can be used to read line drawings, more complex scanners can create a digital form of a photograph. Additional software called OCR (optical character recognition) allows a scanner to produce a file of ASCII codes from a piece of text, eliminating the need to copy the text by typing.

Search and replace   A word-processor or DTP action in which text can be searched for a word or phrase and another word or phrase substituted. This can be done over the whole text (globally) or over a designated part (locally) of marked text.

Serif   Small tails at the end of characters which are traditionally included with the intention of making the text easier to read. Sans-serif text omits these tails, and several modern typefaces are of this kind.

259

SIMM Single In-line Memory Module (SIPP also used). A module which allows a large number of memory chips to be inserted in one operation, using a standard carrier card.

Soft font A font which is fed to a printer from the computer rather than being built into the printer as a ROM.

Software The program files which make a computer system useful. The relationship of software to hardware can be compared to the relationship of cassettes to tape-players.

Spelling checker A program which can be run in conjunction with a word-processor, which examines each word in a document and compares it with words in a dictionary file.

Status line A line of data placed on the screen, usually at the top or bottom, to carry information on the work. Typical status information is the filename of a document, page number, line number and column number for the cursor position, typestyle in use, etc.

Stet A Latin word meaning 'let it stand', used in proofing to indicate that an alteration should NOT be carried out. The BS equivalent is the tick at the side of the page, with the word/phrase underlined with dots.

String A set of characters, a word or phrase, as distinct from a graphics image.

Style sheet A device used in word-processors and DTP programs to ensure that different documents use the same styles, and that style is also consistent within a large document. This is done by recording the fonts and styles used for the body text, headings and sub-headings and captions and selecting these names from the style sheet rather than having to specify the complete set of options each time a change is made. See also master page.

Text All non-graphical material, consisting of letters and digits, spaces and punctuation marks. Also known as alphanumeric data.

Text wrap The automatic carrying over of a word to a new line while it is being typed, if there is not sufficient space on the existing line. All word-processors use text-wrap to avoid the need to enter a carriage return at the end of each line. Automatic text wrap makes it possible for the machine to alter line lengths easily as, for example, when character size is changed.

In DTP work, the terms *text wrap* and *text flow* are used to describe how text is laid around the boundary of a graphics image.

Typeface   A style of type, identified by name. Typeface names used in DTP are often not identical to those used in printing, for copyright reasons, but will suggest the names used in printing.

Type style   A variation on a typeface, such as bold, italic, etc.

Typographical   Relating to the layout and design of type.

Vector graphics   Images which do not consist of dots (bit images) but of instructions such as 'draw a line from point 22,36 to point 25,39'. Images which use vector graphics can be expanded or shrunk with no loss of resolution, and the printed resolution of a vector graphics image depends on the printer resolution, not on the resolution of the original drawing device. Vector graphics are produced by Computer Drawing packages (CAD programs) and by business-oriented graphics packages.

VDU   Visual Display Unit, another name for a monitor display.

VGA   Video Graphics Array. The most recent IBM graphics adapter for high resolution and colour. A VGA adapter makes a machine eminently suitable for DTP work.

Widow   The last line of a paragraph which has been carried over to a new page instead of remaining with the rest of the paragraph.

Window   A framed portion of a VDU screen which can be used independently of other parts of the screen. Windows can be re-sized, moved and created or deleted, allowing more information to be seen on the screen.

Windows-3   A program from MicroSoft which allows full WIMP operation of modern (386 and 486) computers; it also allows several programs to be active in the machine at one time, running in separate screen windows.

WYSIWYG   What You See Is What You Get – the unattainable ideal for DTP work in which the screen shows *exactly* what will be printed. The range of sizes of type and the shape of the screen combine to make this almost impossible to achieve except at great cost.

Appendix B: PostScript laser printers

The list shows representative models, claimed speed, interface, maximum sheet-feeder capacity and maximum paper size in mm.

Note – all of the major manufacturers of printers update their range frequently, so that models shown in this list will not necessarily be available at a later date. The list is intended as a guide to manufacturers and the current variety of the smaller printers available.

Apple Laserwriter II NT/NTX   8 ppm   serial   200 sheets   212 × 350

Brother HL8 PS/QS   8 ppm   serial/parallel   250 sheets   216 × 356

Canon LPB   8 ppm   serial/parallel   400 sheets   216 × 356

Fujitsu RX7 100PS   5 ppm   serial/parallel   300 sheets   216 × 356

Gestetner P-800   8 ppm   serial/parallel   500 sheets   A4

Kyocera P-2000   10 ppm   serial/parallel   250 sheets   330 × 210

Mannesmann Tally MT 910DP   10 ppm   parallel   500 sheets   216 × 355

Star LP8 II   8 ppm   parallel   200   sheets   454 × 492

Texas MicroLaser   8 ppm   parallel   250 sheets   216 × 355

Appendix C: Suppliers of hardware and software

Digitask Business Systems Ltd.,
Unit 2, Gatwick Metro Centre,
Balcombe Road, Horley,
Surrey RH6 9GA
Tel: (0293) 776688
Fax: (0293) 786902

Huge stocks of computers and all associated DTP hardware, including chips, disk drives, add-on cards etc. for upgrading systems.

Hypertec (Europe) Ltd.,
Bank House,
40 High St.,
Pewsey, Wilts, SN9 5AQ
Tel: (0672) 63936
Fax: (0672) 63709
Contact: Stephen Marmoy

Specialize in add-on cards for memory and speed, including a range of 286 cards for popular XT machines, including the Amstrad range. The range of memory boards provides expanded or extended memory up to 8Mb, allowing machines to tackle DTP work more easily.

Matmos Ltd.
Unit 11,
The Enterprise Park,
Lewes Road,
Lindfield,

W. Sussex RH16 2LX
Tel: 04447 2091/3830
Fax: 04447 4258
Contact: Graham Duncan

An unrivalled source of low-cost add-on units including disk drives, monitors, keyboards, power supplies, printers and other hardware, now also dealing in complete computers. For current best-buys, look for advertisements in *Personal Computer World* magazine.

Mektronic Ltd.
Linden House,
116 Rectory Lane,
Prestwich,
Manchester M25 5DB
Tel: (061) 798 0803
Fax: (061) 773 6335
Email: (061) 773 7739 (300, 12/75,1200,2400 8 bit No parity)
Contact: Brian Benster

Hardware and software, including several DTP systems along with diagnostic and Toolkit software. An advisory service is run, and there is also a bulletin board for customers.

PW Computer Supplies,
Dawlish Drive,
Pinner,
Middx. HA5 5LN
Tel: (081) 868 9548 or (081) 866 2258
Fax: (081) 868 2167

Supply paper, laser and ink-jet printer consumables, printers, software and all DTP items.

Texas Instruments Ltd.,
Alpha House,
London Road,

Bracknell,
Berks. RG12 2TH
Tel: 0344 489441
Fax: 0344 860206

An excellent compact and well-designed range of laser printers, with or without PostScript. An unusual feature is the built-in paper tray for 250 sheets, allowing the printer to take up less space on a desk than its competitors.

Appendix D: Public domain software library

The PDSL exists to supply disks of programs that are virtually free for inspection, and the only cost to the user is the cost of copying the disks. PDSL can supply on a range of disk formats, and in some cases are virtually the only source of software for some exotic machines. All of the programs are either public domain or shareware. Documentation for each program is included as a disk file, usually with the DOC extension.

A public domain program is one for which the author has surrendered all copyright, allowing the program to be copied freely by anyone who wants to use it (the way schools used to copy textbooks when photocopying came out of an unlimited budget and books came out of a carefully rationed budget). Many public domain programs are short utilities, and you would normally buy them on a disk that contained 20–50 such items. Other PD programs are distinctly longer, and though some of them do not have the polish of a commercial program they must have represented hundreds of hours of effort. The writers are often professional programmers working at a hobby topic and glad to share the results of their efforts.

Shareware is a rather different concept. The author of a shareware package is hoping to sell directly to the user, cutting out the huge overheads that are involved in having a program manufactured and distributed commercially. In the early days of shareware, the programs were full working versions, and the poor response by way of payment was a severe blow to authors, particularly in the UK, where users were always less willing to pay for programs than in the USA where the idea started. It has become more common now for shareware programs to be limited to some extent, perhaps running on only a single video card, or unable to use a printer or to create disk files. The user can run the program to a sufficient extent to see if it is likely to be useful, and will have lost very little if it is not. Registering with the author can be done directly (it is easy to phone an author in the USA and quote a credit card number) or by way of the

PDSL if this can be arranged. The current catalogue contains many programs of particular interest to DTP users, including clip-art, graphics conversion and editing programs, printer utilities, vector-line drawing programs, support for Ventura Publisher users, etc.

Registration can often be done at various levels, with the minimum level entitling you to a copy of the program with all limitations removed. The documentation will be, as for PD items, as a DOC or READ.ME file on the disk. At a higher fee, a full manual is provided and the user is entitled to upgrades at nominal cost.

The address for PDSL is:

Winscombe House,
Beacon Road,
Crowborough,
E. Sussex, TN6 1UL
Tel: (0892) 663298
Fax: (0892) 667473

At the time of writing, membership subscriptions were £21 per annum for private membership, £69 per annum for corporate membership, and disks were copied for prices of £3.75 each (members) or £5.00 (non-members) with discounts for quantities. There is a surcharge, currently 90p for 3.5″ 720K disks.

Appendix E: Installing Aldus PageMaker

To make effective use of PageMaker, you need to have the program correctly prepared for use with your machine, the process called installation. PageMaker is written so as to take advantage of a running system called Microsoft Windows, which allows mouse and windows operation of the computer, obviating the need to type commands. If your computer already uses a full version of Windows (preferably V.3.0 or later) then PageMaker can be installed very quickly, because practically all of the work will already have been done when Windows was installed. If your computer is not installed with Microsoft Windows, PageMaker contains its own scaled-down version of Windows, and this requires installation.

Typically, installation, whether for PageMaker running with its own version of Windows or for other comparable programs, consists of supplying information on the following topics, usually by selecting from menus:

- the type of screen card and monitor (for example, VGA Mono)
- the type of printer(s) (for example, T.I. Laser)
- the size and type of any added memory (for example, EEMS 3 Mb)
- the type of mouse, or lack of mouse (for example MSMOUSE)
- the choice of type fonts appropriate for the printer(s) that you intend to use (for example, ROMAN, COURIER)

Installation will create a directory named **PM** on your hard disk and place a set of files into this directory – the selection of files will depend on the options you have chosen in the installation menu. For example, if you have opted to use only a simple 9-pin dot-matrix printer, the installation process will provide only the very few fonts that can be printed reasonably well with such a printer. If, by contrast, you have opted for a laser printer with PostScript capabilities, the range of fonts will be very much greater. Because only a selection from the large number of files on the original disks will be used, the size of PageMaker once it is installed on the hard

269

disk is much less than might be expected. A typical set of installed files amounts to about 2.6 Mb.

Once the files are installed, PageMaker is ready for use, but other preliminaries are needed before pages of a document can be printed. One important setting-up action is matching printer(s) to connections. Printers are connected to computers by way of **ports** which can be parallel or serial, matching the printers. The parallel ports, which can be used for practically every important type of printer, are labelled as LPT1, LPT2 and LPT3; assuming that the computer provides more than one such port. If only one parallel printer port is provided, as is usual, it is labelled as LPT1. The serial ports are labelled as COM1, COM2, COM3 and it is once again quite common to have only one serial port, COM1.

Setting up connections for PageMaker means that each printer which has been installed, and any added subsequently, should be assigned to a port. For example, if your main printer is a H-P Laserjet you will probably have it connected to the parallel printer port. By using a Connections menu of the Control Panel of PageMaker (part of the Windows system) you can assign this printer to LPT1, ensuring that printing will take place when this printer is selected. If you have another printer, for example a 24-pin Star, it can be assigned either:

● to another parallel port LPT2 if one exists
● to a serial port COM1 or COM2 if you have a serial interface on the printers and a serial port on the computer that is free for use
● to no port at all, so that the printer could not be used unless the Connection menu is used first
● to a file, so that any print directed to this printer will in fact result in a disk file of codes that can be fed to the printer later, even from another computer which can use the disk file. This other computer need not be equipped with Windows or PageMaker. This is the means by which it is possible to turn out work on a laser printer even if you do not possess one, since a disk containing files can be sent to an agency for printing.

Once these connections have been made, the printer(s) can be used. There are also provisions for other actions, such as varying the time after which a printer will be reported as not responding to signals (if, for example, you have forgotten to switch it on, or it has run out of paper). Of the options, connecting to a file so as to make a file of printed material is the most difficult and is beyond the scope of this book. It requires editing a file called WIN.INI, and details can be found in the book *Microsoft*

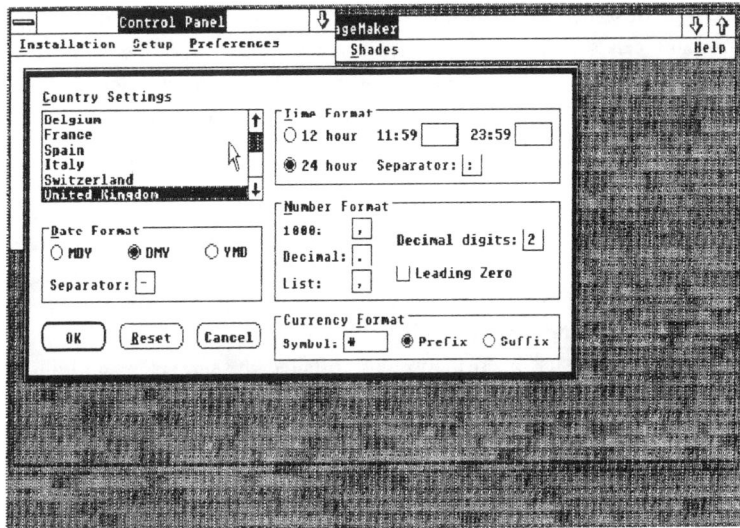

Figure E.1   The Country Options of the Control Panel, which is part of the Windows system used by PageMaker

Windows, published by Dabs Press Ltd. Normally, as a user of DTP these selections should have been made for you, but it is useful to know what has had to be done before a program of this type can be successfully used.

Once the all-important connections have been made, there are some Preferences in the Control Panel which are useful. If you are using a colour screen, you might like to specify what colours will be used for different parts of the text, menus, borders, cursors and other parts of the display. Another important set of preferences is for Country, allowing you to choose not only the country but the time format (12 hour or 24 hour clock), date format (Month–Day–Year, Day–Month–Year or Year–Month–Day), number format (use of commas and points) and currency (sign and whether before or following numbers). Figure E1 shows this set of options in Aldus PageMaker. In fact, this set is part of the Windows system rather than a part of PageMaker itself.

Note that using less extensive programs of a simpler nature does not absolve you from the need to install whatever program is used. All DTP programs need to be able to take complete command of the screen and the printer, and whatever means they use, they must rely on installation to indicate what will be connected. In some cases, particularly PageMaker,

271

the type of screen that is being used can be sensed automatically, but no program can sense what type of printer is attached to the computer. Programs which do not make use of established systems (such as Windows, DESQview, or Gem) for using mouse, icon and window will need to make use of their own method of control.

If installation of the program has been incorrect or incomplete, you might not be aware of the problem until later. If, for example, the wrong printer has been installed, the effects will not be noticed until you need to print a document. On DTP programs which require the type of screen (such as CGA, EGA, VGA or Hercules) to be installed, incorrect installation will maker the program unusable or difficult to use almost immediately. If a mouse has been incorrectly installed the screen image will be normal but the mouse will have no effect on the cursor.

Index